*Surveillance in the
Time of Insecurity*

CRITICAL ISSUES IN CRIME AND SOCIETY
Raymond J. Michalowski, Series Editor

Critical Issues in Crime and Society is oriented toward critical analysis of contemporary problems in crime and justice. The series is open to a broad range of topics including specific types of crime, wrongful behavior by economically or politically powerful actors, controversies over justice system practices, and issues related to the intersection of identity, crime, and justice. It is committed to offering thoughtful works that will be accessible to scholars and professional criminologists, general readers, and students.

For a list of titles in the series, see the last page of the book.

Surveillance in the Time of Insecurity

Torin Monahan

Rutgers University Press
New Brunswick, New Jersey, and London

LIBRARY OF CONGRESS CATALOGING-IN-PUBLICATION DATA

Monahan, Torin.
    Surveillance in the time of insecurity / Torin Monahan.
      p. cm. — (Critical issues in crime and society)
    Includes bibliographical references and index.
    ISBN 978-0-8135-4764-0 (hardcover : alk. paper) —
    ISBN 978-0-8135-4765-7 (pbk. : alk. paper)
    1. National security—United States. 2. Internal security—United States.
  3. Electronic surveillance—United States. 4. Technology—Social aspects. I. Title.
    HV6432.M647 2010
    363.325'1630973—dc22

                                   2009031021

A British Cataloging-in-Publication record for this book is available
from the British Library.

Visit our Web site: http://rutgerspress.rutgers.edu

Manufactured in the United States of America

CONTENTS

PART ONE   SECURITY CULTURES

PART TWO   SURVEILLANCE INFRASTRUCTURES

Figures and Tables

Acknowledgments

IF SURVEILLANCE HAS MULTIPLE DIMENSIONS, including those of "care" and "control," I can safely say that this book has benefited from the most caring forms of surveillance by others. The international Surveillance Studies Network and the editorial board of the journal *Surveillance & Society* deserve special mention for generously welcoming me into their community, challenging me to develop my scholarship, and allowing me to collaboratively shape the direction of the growing field of surveillance studies. I am especially indebted to Kirstie Ball, Kevin Haggerty, Hille Koskela, David Lyon, David Phillips, David Murakami Wood, Dean Wilson, and Nils Zurawski.

Other scholars have gone out of their way to mentor me. John Gilliom, Gary Marx, and Michael Musheno have been invaluable in this regard, each reading significant amounts of my writing and pushing me to improve. Many others have graciously provided comments on my work and offered much-needed advice and support along the way, including David Altheide, Lynn Chancer, Simon Cole, Martin French, Oscar Gandy, Randy Hanson, Leon Hempel, Tad Hirsch, Aaron Kupchik, Pat Lauderdale, Shoshana Magnet, Cecilia Menjívar, Hector Postigo, Priscilla Regan, James Rule, Minas Samatas, Bill Staples, Rodolfo Torres, Michael Welch, Tyler Wall, and Jennifer Whitson.

Much labor goes into the production of a book, and oftentimes it is hidden in the final product. With the intention of rendering some of that labor visible, I am glad to acknowledge research assistance from Jennifer Murray and Michael Coyle, who both braved Arizona's cruel sun to conduct some of the interviews for my projects. I must also recognize the many research informants who gave their time and shared their experiences with us. Laura Dugas expertly transcribed all the interviews. Finally, the series editor, Ray Michalowski, and the editorial team at Rutgers University Press, especially Adi Hovav, have made the production of this book a pleasure.

The research for this project was supported, in part, by the National Science Foundation under Grant No. SES-0423672. Additionally, I thank the following journals for permitting the use of previously published chapters or chapter sections: *Criminal Justice Matters*, *Cultural Studies <=>Critical*

Methodologies, Media, Culture, & Society, Social Justice, Social Semiotics, The Communication Review, Theoretical Criminology, and *Urban Affairs Review.* An abbreviated version of chapter 2 was originally published in the book *Reading 24: TV Against the Clock,* edited by Steven Peacock and published by I. B. Tauris.

As always, I have extreme gratitude for my family and friends, who fully encourage the work that I do. In particular, this book has grown—as have I—from the many critical insights and unflagging support of my life partner, Jill Fisher. I look forward to returning the favor for many years to come.

Surveillance in the
Time of Insecurity

Introduction

CONSTRUCTING INSECURITY

WHAT DOES INSECURITY MEAN TODAY? Vulnerability to terrorist attacks might spring to mind as an initial response. Whether the targets are the World Trade Center in New York City, the Pentagon in Washington, D.C., public buses in London, or subways in Tokyo and Madrid, high-profile terrorist attacks command the public's attention. Next, environmental disasters demand notice. From hurricanes to floods to earthquakes, the fragility of ecosystems and our vulnerability to systemic environmental imbalances, such as global warming, have become critical concerns. Next, especially at present, housing and financial crises resonate as key areas of widespread insecurity, undermining the economic stability of entire countries and compelling extravagant government bailout packages for financial industries. On the level of individuals and communities, people are certainly confronting related insecurities in the form of house foreclosures, unemployment, and unaffordable health care, especially in the United States.[1] Finally, crime represents a constant source of insecurity, galvanizing a host of responses, including zero-tolerance laws, private security forces, gated communities, and technological surveillance. Each of these is a likely response to the question of what insecurity means today, and many others could be added to this list. What is more difficult to perceive, though, are the mechanisms by which insecurities are shaped and acted upon.

This book investigates the social construction of insecurity. It takes as its focus the processes, mythologies, and technologies that solidify insecurity as lived cultural experience. Media programming and political discourses play an integral role in the construction of everyday insecurities. In addition, many technological systems of surveillance and fortification integrate with our institutions and built environments to control our lives and communicate to us that we are not safe. While insecurity is not a new phenomenon, the context of the "war on terror" expands external threats to universal proportions, such that *national security* tends to eclipse widespread *human insecurity*, such as poverty, in the public imaginary.

Saying that insecurities are socially constructed does not mean that they are not real. The attacks of September 11, 2001, and the catastrophe of Hurricane Katrina in 2005, for instance, each highlight the vulnerability of American populations to serious dangers. Whereas these examples received widespread attention because they operated—symbolically and politically—as issues of national vulnerability and media spectacle, less visible are the multiple human insecurities that confront people every day: homelessness, imprisonment, domestic violence, chemical exposure, automobile accidents, and so on. The process by which some insecurities are perceived as dire and others inconsequential, some as the domain of the state and others the responsibility of individuals, is one of social construction. The social construction of meaning, values, and categories of thought occurs through engagement with others and the built environment and through interpretation of stories and symbols.

Just as insecurity is constructed, so it constructs us. Specifically, discourses of insecurity posit a certain type of ideal citizen who can flexibly respond and adapt to the vicissitudes and uncertainties of modern life without relying on the state. This *insecurity subject* anticipates risks and minimizes them through consumption, regulates exposure to potentially threatening Others through systems of fortification, believes that economic inequalities are natural and social exclusion justified, voluntarily sacrifices privacy and civil liberties on the altar of national security, and fully supports punitive state policies, whether against immigrants, criminals, terrorists, or the poor. As an ideal type, the insecurity subject becomes the reference point against which individuals, and increasingly institutions and automated systems, evaluate behavior and make decisions.

The ecosystem within which the insecurity subject flourishes is neoliberalism. Neoliberalism is generally understood as an orientation toward governance that emphasizes the privatization of public institutions and the deregulation of industry. Beyond that, however, neoliberalism is a market rationality that colonizes most spheres of public life and transforms their functions to prioritize economic gain over all other measures of quality or success. From education, to health care, to transportation, to public safety, neoliberal policies and practices have come to dominate public institutions over the past few decades. This shift in governance predictably pushes responsibility onto individuals for what used to be the purview of the state, effectively depoliticizing social problems and normalizing social inequalities.[2] For example, if access to health care is seen as something that can be chosen and purchased on the open market, rather than something that is a right, then this absolves the state of responsibility for providing health care and legitimates conditions of unequal access.[3] Moreover, there is a disciplinary dimension to neoliberalism, whereby those who fail—or are unable—to comply with the now-pervasive market logics are excluded or criminalized.[4] Therefore, existing social services, such as welfare programs, adopt policing functions to spy on, punish, and exclude those who are already presumed guilty because they are poor.[5] Conditions of economic insecurity, or the inability to meet one's needs through consumption, are suspect in this brave new neoliberal world.

A destructive feedback loop has emerged between responses to national and social security threats, which are two broad—but certainly overlapping—forms of insecurity. On one hand, the state is charged with mitigating perceived "external" threats to collective well-being, such as terrorism or natural disaster. In the era of Homeland Security, the state responds by centralizing power structures, under the executive branch, for instance, while simultaneously outsourcing responsibility for the success of these national security tasks either to state and local governments or to private industries and contractors. On the other hand, individuals and communities increasingly bear the brunt of addressing "internal" threats to well-being and providing for social security, ranging from health care, to housing, to food for those in need. In combination, these two movements give rise to a political climate and an insecurity culture that magnifies a sense of vulnerability to external threats, which in turn prioritizes national security over social security, thereby further eroding social security nets. For instance, if people feel economically vulnerable, they may be more inclined to view undocumented laborers as threats to their well-being and therefore support the creation of vast, and costly, security infrastructures to police the nation's borders and regulate the mobility of undocumented immigrants. In this climate, devoting resources to national security becomes politically expedient and necessary, whereas funding social security programs may be construed as misguided and wasteful. But without sustained state attention to social security needs, perceived threats to national security are unlikely to dissipate.

Although this narrative prioritizes the structural dimensions of contemporary insecurities, psychological manifestations of insecurity clearly matter on individual and societal levels. After all, perceptions and experiences of risk both respond to and reproduce the social field—they organize collective understandings of the world, its dangers, and preferred responses to them.[6] The media, it must be acknowledged, play a crucial role in shaping insecurities in the social imaginary. As David Altheide explains, "fear is socially constructed, packaged, and presented through the mass media by politicians and decision makers to protect us by offering more control over our lives and culture. Fear entertains us and helps others control us."[7] More than that, though, fear and perceptions of insecurity colonize life worlds and spread virally, spawning paranoia, and motivating hypervigilance and self-regulation.[8] On the level of lived experience, the social construction of fear is much more than just an instrumental exercise of power over people. Through it, people mold their identities and situate themselves in relation to others, whether through acts and discourses of solidarity or exclusion.[9] Thus, psychological experiences of insecurity serve as social structures in their own right, subtly constraining that which is considered possible and desirable.[10] For these reasons, it is necessary to investigate the cultural processes by which insecurities are cultivated and sustained, as well as the material mechanisms by which they are codified and institutionalized.

To this end, this book examines the interplay of contemporary security cultures and surveillance infrastructures. The term *security cultures* refers to prevailing understandings of threats and appropriate responses to them. *Surveillance infrastructures* are the many technological systems used to mitigate risks and regulate populations. With attention to the political, cultural, and economic context of modern insecurities, especially in the United States, this book seeks answers to the following questions: What are the cultural means by which insecurities are constructed? What are the technical mechanisms by which insecurities are reinforced and sustained? Why are certain forms of insecurity privileged in popular discourse while others are ignored? How does a collective sense of insecurity cohere and circulate, and to what effect? Any inquiry into the construction of insecurity is perforce an inquiry into representations and power relations. In order for certain representations or narratives of insecurity to obtain hegemonic status, they must be reproduced constantly in the face of challenges and counternarratives.[11] For instance, these alternative discourses might take the form of challenges by civil society organizations, such as Amnesty International or the American Civil Liberties Union, to government-sponsored domestic spying programs or torture of terrorist suspects. Thus, on a meta-level, this book interrogates the assemblage of cultural meanings, political ideologies, and technological infrastructures that hold "national insecurity" together as a dominant social fact.

The remainder of this chapter will develop these two theoretical frames—security cultures and surveillance infrastructures—and provide a brief overview of the book.

SECURITY CULTURES

At least three articulations of security, each with different temporal and ideological origins, constitute the present political climate. First, *nation-state security* emerged in the seventeenth century (with the Treaty of Westphalia in 1648 and the development of international law) as a means of securing sovereign territory against external enemies through diplomacy, military actions, and border control; second, *population security* grew out of late nineteenth-century social welfare efforts to collectivize risk, typified by public health and welfare programs; third, *civil defense* became the principal response to threats of nuclear annihilation after World War II, as can be seen in efforts to protect public infrastructure (such as highways and electrical grids) and manage potential threats with preparedness strategies (such as evacuation procedures).[12]

These security phases are not distinct; instead they iterate and fuse with each other, such that all three are clearly discernable in their present amalgamation. Nation-state security (or national security) is quite visible in today's military operations and surveillance programs, for instance. The attacks of 9/11 neither caused current security configurations nor instigated a radical break with security operations of the past. Rather, responses to 9/11 betray an *intensification* of security practices that were already under way prior to the attacks.[13] Similarly, population security regimes of the past can now be witnessed in government schemes to stockpile anthrax or avian flu vaccines. And although civil defense originated with the Cold War, it still largely characterizes the present strategy for dealing with threats. Now, however, it has shifted somewhat to emphasize "critical infrastructure protection" and "all-hazards management."[14] In the United States, the coordination of these functions falls under the Department of Homeland Security (DHS), which centralizes authority over many federal agencies but simultaneously decentralizes a great deal of responsibility for ensuring public safety, passing it on to citizens, businesses, and communities.[15]

While strong continuities exist between the protective measures taken during the height of the Cold War and today's "war on terror," several key differences indicate a notable shift in security logics. Whereas the emphasis for the United States during the Cold War was on containment of communism and prevention of nuclear war through mutually assured destruction, the strategy now is upon military expansionism and preemptive war, seen in Iraq, as a method of proactive risk management.[16] As President George W. Bush asserted: "Deterrence, the promise of massive retaliation against nations, means nothing against shadowy terrorist networks with no nation or citizens to defend. Containment is not possible when unbalanced dictators with weapons of mass destruction can deliver those weapons on missiles or secretly provide them to terrorist allies."[17] Unlike the Soviet Union, whose threat to the United States during the Cold War was symmetrical, terrorism presents an asymmetrical threat, the likes of which lend justification to preemptive action.

The nature of security operations in the United States and abroad has also mutated toward privatization and the suspension of law. In keeping with neoliberal ideology, security contractors have been granted unprecedented responsibilities for fighting wars, rebuilding infrastructures, and coordinating civil defense. As of 2007, it was estimated that more than 180,000 U.S.-hired contractors were serving in Iraq, including non-American contractors.[18] Contracts for security industries now surpass those of any other time in U.S. history.[19] Thus, as many scholars have been slow to grasp, the Iraq war may have very little to do with ensuring safety at home or instituting democracy in the Middle East; this security operation, much like other instantiations of neoliberalism, may be fundamentally about the transfer of public funds to

private corporations.[20] Finally, the suspension of law marks a particularly brutal return of disciplinary power, enabling extraordinary rendition of suspected
"enemy combatants" to countries that condone torture, legal-discursive
moves to circumvent the Geneva Conventions, elimination of habeas corpus
for terrorism suspects, and illegal spying on U.S. citizens by the National
Security Agency, Federal Bureau of Investigation, and Department of Defense.[21]
Especially under the Bush administration, population security and civil
defense took on an aggressive tone toward active intervention, ostensibly on
behalf of national security. There is some evidence that this is shifting under
the Obama administration, but institutional practices are tenacious, so it is
unclear at this point how—or to what extent—this general orientation will
change.[22]

Meanwhile, terrorist threats have come to epitomize modern insecurity.
Instead of presenting discernable risks that can be calculated, predicted, and
controlled, terrorism is an effective tactic precisely because it appears irrational
and unpredictable. It produces maximum affective shock and fear on a subjective and personal level, while simultaneously generating images and stories that
can circulate widely, infecting others with their contagion. Whereas the "risk
society" concept, as originally formulated by Ulrich Beck, focused on technological systems whose risks exceed the capacity of the institutions charged with
managing them (such as the nuclear, chemical, and biotechnology industries),
terrorism—especially suicide-based attacks—defies institutions on an altogether different plane.[23] Terrorism is an assault on institutions and governments through human and technological means, through the fusing of people
with weapons, through the killing or maiming of innocent civilians, and
through the creation of fearful citizens and reactionary governments.

At least for the United States, the terrorist attacks of 9/11 engendered a
certain configuration of a security state, operating *symbolically* around the
"war on terror"; *institutionally* through the creation of the Department of
Homeland Security to consolidate and reorient government agencies toward
security operations; *legally* around "states of exception," most notably for preemptive war, domestic surveillance, and the torture of terrorist suspects; and
practically through the establishment of elaborate surveillance rituals for citizens (for example, airport screening) and the outsourcing of lucrative security
contracts to private industries. In these ways, the "war on terror" has become
the central layer through which all conceivable national security threats are
filtered and weighed for importance, which can be seen readily with the spe-
cious conflation of terrorism with illegal immigration, identity theft, and even
public protest.[24]

The framing of insecurity around terrorism tends to occlude, among
other things, the role of structural conditions in producing inequality and violence. Economic globalization, especially, has catalyzed a greater degree of

job insecurity and inequality among people within countries, even as the inequality among countries appears to be diminishing.[25] One interpretation of this is that multinational corporations and the affluent tend to be profiting handsomely from economic globalization, whereas the majority of people have become vulnerable. Similarly, while travel across borders has increased dramatically, some people commute for business or pleasure with relative ease while others flee ethnic violence and poverty only to find fortified borders and hostile immigration policies blocking their paths.[26] These trends are, of course, interlinked. In current incarnations of economic globalization, deterritorialized capital, which can be seen with the outsourcing of jobs and offshoring of factories, combines with neoliberal policies in other countries, which provide a fertile ground for corporate profit even while the standard of living and job security of most people in so-called developing *and* developed countries is actually diminishing.[27] In response to human insecurity brought about by deterritorialized capital and expropriated national resources, mobility of the subaltern—whether as immigrants or refugees—becomes a survival tactic that is typically viewed as threatening to the integrity of nation states.

New modalities of nationalist xenophobia arise from the cauldron of globalization precisely because of perceived economic and national insecurity on the part of majorities. Minorities, whether within a given country or elsewhere, become ready scapegoats for the nation-state's failure to preserve economic prosperity and democratic rule. As Arjun Appadurai explains:

> Given the systemic compromise of national economic sovereignty that is built into the logic of globalization, and given the increasing strain this puts on states to behave as trustees of the interests of a territorially defined and confined "people," minorities are the major site for displacing the anxieties of many states about their own minority or marginality (real or imagined) in a world of a few megastates, of unruly economic flows and compromised sovereignties. Minorities, in a word, are metaphors and reminders of the betrayal of the classical national project.[28]

This may help explain the rise in violence in the post–Cold War period, especially in the form of ethnic cleansing.[29] If economic insecurities brought about by globalization can be blamed on minority populations, however they are defined, then deeper structural problems can be ignored and sublimated in a quest for some kind of national purity.

The various "security cultures" of the United States are inflected by the somewhat contradictory rationalities of globalization, neoliberalism, and racism. Dominant constructions of insecurity vacillate between a recognition of unavoidable ambiguity and irreducible difference, on one hand, and a desire for certainty and fixed identities, on the other. Thus, lines are intentionally blurred between civilians and soldiers, public and private, legal and illegal, and peace and war.[30] If the "war on terror" is an absolute state and if terrorists make no distinction between civilians and soldiers, then neither should citizens make such distinctions, so politicians and the media advise. As the *Washington Post* proclaimed the day after 9/11, "We are all soldiers now."[31] At the same time, rigid boundaries and fixed identities are sought in other domains or for other political purposes. The borders between the United States and Mexico and Canada are being militarized and heavily fortified; legislation requiring proof of citizenship for access to social services is being passed in many states; social-spatial segregation is reaching an all-time high within cities, whether for places of residence, schooling, consumption, or employment; surveillance systems are implemented at airports and elsewhere to filter out "dangerous" populations from "prioritized" ones; and, the political rhetoric of public figures like President George W. Bush erects clear, if dubious, binaries between those either "for" or "against" the United States in the "war on terror."

Security cultures, therefore, emerge from the selective blurring or fixing of spaces and identities in political discourses and media representations. One underlying logic is that borders should be porous for capital and preferred travelers, but sealed for people who are perceived as threatening or in need. Another logic is that we should all become insecurity subjects who take responsibility for addressing insecurities through consumption. In most cases, the structural dimensions of human insecurity, such as economic globalization and neoliberal policies, are either absent or normalized in mainstream representations of the risks and dangers associated with the modern world.[32] As the next section will discuss, contemporary security cultures are also reproduced by the surveillance technologies meant to minimize insecurity.

SURVEILLANCE INFRASTRUCTURES

Surveillance has become a powerful, if dubious, symbol of national security. However, as with all technologies, surveillance functions in a polyvalent way to mediate and regulate interactions among people, organizations, and the built world. To the extent that information and communication technologies (ICTs) have the capacity to capture and store data for retrieval and analysis, whether at a later date or on the fly, they possess a modality for surveillance. Broadly defined, surveillance systems are those that afford control of people through the identification, tracking, monitoring, or analysis of individuals, data, or systems. The control element is crucial for determining whether surveillance is occurring because otherwise *all* interactions with ICTs would constitute a surveillant relationship. Surveillance is, by definition, about power. That being said, people are subject to surveillance throughout their everyday lives and are often completely unaware of it. Moreover, one need not wait until some exercise of control is felt in order to predict what systems have surveillance potential and under what conditions surveillance might be asserted. Surveillance systems, seen as such, proliferate throughout society: in urban infrastructures, transportation systems, cell phones, identification documents, computer programs, frequent shopper cards, medical and consumer products, and much more. Whether mobilized by the government, industry, employers, or peers, surveillance systems modulate experiences of the world.

This view of surveillance presumes that technologies shape social practices in non-neutral ways. Much like legislation, technological systems provide a set of rules, or scripts, encouraging certain uses or interactions and discouraging others.[33] For example, video cameras lend themselves to the remote observation of others; highways lend themselves to vehicular transportation; walls and gates lend themselves to the regulation of belonging. The scripts of technological systems partially determine social practices by exerting agential force upon people and contexts. Moreover, technological systems introduce a series of dependencies—such as those upon electricity, data networks, or security systems—that require institutional commitments for the continued operation of the systems. Because technologies frame what is possible and practical, for people and organizations, they can be said to be "political," even though decisions about them are seldom made through democratic processes. This neither denies the agency of people nor depends upon a simplistic belief in technological determinism. Instead, it sets the stage for a critical reading of surveillance in society, including an analysis of its role in instituting and maintaining social inequalities and insecurities.

Broadly speaking, there are two mechanisms by which surveillance can establish or sustain social inequalities. The first is what scholars in the field of surveillance studies refer to as *social sorting*.[34] As Emile Durkheim noted a century ago, modern societies depend upon differentiation among people, especially in regard to function or specialization. Contemporary surveillance technologies are tools of societal differentiation. They serve simultaneously to diagnose someone's "proper" place in society and to pressure people not to deviate from their assigned categories. Although social sorting with surveillance can be seen with regard to any perceived or actual difference among people (such as race, class, gender, sexual orientation, or age), capitalist measures of status and place predominate. These can include preferential treatment of the relatively affluent in domains of commodity consumption, with discounts based on past purchases; transportation, with dedicated toll roads and lanes for those who can pay; communication, with higher bandwidth and priority data routing for elite subscribers; energy access, with budget plans for "low-risk" groups, compared with pay-as-you-go plans with added surcharges for "high-risk" groups; housing, with screening for "desirability" by home owners' associations and lenders; and so on. What is new about these trends are the fine-grained levels of differentiation and the automation of social sorting made possible by ubiquitous ICTs.[35] Unlike social sorting practices of the past, which were obviously discriminatory, such as the use of passbooks in apartheid South Africa,[36] the technological mediation of social sorting masks discrimination because people tend to think of technological systems as neutral rather than inherently biased.

The second mechanism by which surveillance reinforces inequalities is through differential exposure to surveillance systems based on one's social address. Unlike the social sorting examples given above, where people are often treated differently by the same technological systems, many systems of surveillance are disproportionately applied to marginalized populations. Examples could include systems for tracking and controlling the purchases of welfare recipients, routine drug testing for workers in low-paying service jobs, intrusive screening of students in inner-city public schools, or the remote monitoring of employees by managers with global positioning systems, key-stroke-tracking software, or radio-frequency identification tags. This general form of surveillance, which could be called *marginalizing surveillance*, demonstrates an explicit power relationship of enhanced control of populations considered to be risky, dangerous, or untrustworthy. In the process, marginalizing surveillance affixes those characteristics to the objects of surveillance, thereby reifying identities of suspicion and legitimizing the ongoing selective deployment of surveillance. For instance, if one scrutinizes welfare recipients to determine if they are "cheating the system" in some way (for example, by not reporting some cash income), one will likely find instances to support this suspicion. This can, in turn, legitimize the further surveillance of those populations without any consideration, necessarily, of the next-to-impossible rules imposed upon welfare recipients to begin with.[37] Both social sorting and marginalizing surveillance illustrate that the profusion of surveillance technologies throughout societies in no way indicates the democratization of surveillance. Surveillance both grows out of and gives rise to power relations and specific institutional configurations, which are predicated more and more upon the mitigation of financial or legal risk to government and corporate entities.

Surveillance intersects with security in interesting ways. Often, surveillance is depicted as a tool for safeguarding security, ranging from biometric systems at airports to nannycams in homes. Discourses about surveillance and security typically present false trade-offs, frequently between security and privacy. This framing implies that surveillance works as promised, that people can make rational choices about adopting surveillance or exposing themselves to it, and that surveillance will not create new insecurities or problematic situations.[38] Most of the time, people are given little or no choice but to submit to surveillance, whether for purposes of national security, market research, theft prevention, or employee monitoring. Additionally, because surveillance is often not efficacious for *preventing* terrorism or crime, only for identifying perpetrators after the fact, the presence of such systems may evoke a false sense of security at great financial cost.[39] Finally, just because surveillance may not necessarily work as intended does not mean that it does not work to produce social relations and spaces. The increase of voyeuristic monitoring of women by men, for example, whether in official video surveillance control rooms or with cell phone cameras on the street, is one unanticipated result of surveillance that can subject women to new forms of harassment and make social spaces more hostile than they were previously. In spite of these and other caveats, the relationship of surveillance to security is usually discussed as abstracted from social context, thereby obstructing any analysis of the political economy or the complexity and multiplicity of modern insecurities.

Placed in context, specifically in a neoliberal context, surveillance can be interpreted instead as contributing to individual and collective fears and dictating specific market-oriented responses to them. Scholars have found, for instance, that the presence of surveillance cameras can generate experiences of fear in people who presume there must be a discernable threat to which the cameras are responding.[40] Security companies have both generated and fed off public fears to grow into a $215-billion industry,[41] catering to government agencies, businesses, and individuals alike with their high-tech security "solutions."[42] Surveillance melds with other forms of fortification as well, such as walls, to regulate inclusion and exclusion as a form of risk management. The empirical validity of such risks is apparently irrelevant. For example, statistically speaking, schools continue to be some of the safest places for children, much safer than the home, the street, or other settings, yet the demand for surveillance systems and police in schools has reached an all-time high.[43] The convergence of surveillance and neoliberalism supports the production of insecurity subjects, of people who perceive the inherent dangerousness of others and take actions to minimize exposure to them, even when the danger is spurious. Social exclusions and inequalities become mere collateral damage in the battle for the semblance of personal safety, not political problems for which society shares collective responsibility.

BOOK FRAMING

This book is divided into two main sections: *security cultures* and *surveillance infrastructures*. The first section draws upon political discourses and media representations as primary sources for analyzing popular constructions of insecurity. Examples include official government rationalizations for torturing terrorism suspects, the mobilization of "preparedness" as a response to threats of terrorist attacks and natural disasters, the counterterrorism-themed television show *24*, new public-private partnerships for security provision, the media-fueled moral panic about identity theft, and Christian fundamentalist literature about the apocalypse. The second section draws upon ethnographic research on surveillance systems in public places to analyze the controlling effects of surveillance. Examples include video surveillance in low-income public housing and affluent gated communities, roadway surveillance systems for regulating transportation and coordinating city evacuation, and activist interventions for challenging the proliferation of public surveillance. In sum, this book argues that social inequalities are being normalized by dominant constructions of and responses to insecurity. Any deep understanding of insecurity must take into account the cultural meanings, practices, and technologies that constitute it.

PART ONE

 Security Cultures

CHAPTER 1

Securing the Homeland

MODERN SECURITY REGIMES are defined by extremes. Practices of spying, torture, indefinite detention, and preemptive war have represented favored responses by the United States to threats of terrorism. But insecurity as a unifying concept has expanded virally since 9/11, spreading into domains of public health and disaster management, among others. Interestingly, whether for the mitigation of potential terrorist threats, flu pandemics, or hurricanes, executive power and individual responsibility prevail as dominant framing mechanisms for responses. In addition, responses to insecurity are increasingly technologized and militarized, whether in forms of technological surveillance, command-and-control organizational structures, or pervasive cultures of secrecy. These are not simply discrete actions played out on the level of nation-state policy. Instead, the field for social practice and conceptions of appropriate governance are transforming rapidly in this climate of constant threats. It is appropriate and necessary, therefore, to assess the implications of security regimes upon public institutions, modes of governance, and forms of life.

This chapter begins this project by analyzing the discourses surrounding torture and disaster preparedness in the United States. Both torture and disaster preparedness might be thought of as forms of surveillance that mesh with security cultures. As interrogation, the rationale for torture is to extract information through the constant monitoring of prisoners while inflicting physical pain or psychological distress. Disaster preparedness, on the other hand, invites scrutiny of the self and others to minimize threats through the adoption of different control strategies: locating weaknesses, developing plans, spying on others, and purchasing products to ensure safety. While much more than "surveillance" is occurring with torture and disaster preparedness, monitoring and control are key to both modes of engagement.

LOGICS OF TORTURE

In the United States's protracted "war on terror," fear of devastating, indiscriminate attack upon civilian populations has been mobilized by politicians and the media to justify extreme military actions and security operations.

Often, these practices rely upon the suspension of law both within and beyond the country's borders. Law can be suspended in many ways. Individuals can be declared extralegal "enemy combatants" or moved to locations beyond law's reach. Or, laws can simply be declared inapplicable to the present circumstances, as was proposed for parts of the Bill of Rights in legal documents prepared by the Bush administration. Whatever the means of suspending law, these practices enable a false semblance of social order predicated upon universal rights, which can exist in principle while obliterated in practice.

Since the United States set out on the "war on terror," stories about the routine torture of suspected enemies have seeped through the veils of secrecy intended to keep these practices hidden from the public. Whether the torture is conducted by U.S. military personnel, Central Intelligence Agency interrogators, private sector contractors, or allies in other countries, there is now little dispute over the fact of its occurrence. The Abu Ghraib prison in Iraq stands as the most infamous of these cases, where, in 2004, digital photographs of tortured and humiliated prisoners circulated, sparked public outrage, and led to military investigations. Punishment of low-level military personnel followed, but no high-level commanders were held accountable. Since Abu Ghraib, similar stories of tortured civilian prisoners have emerged, especially in the Guantánamo Bay detention camp in Cuba, which has become an international symbol of U.S. violations of human rights. Other stories make less news, such as the brutal treatment and killing of prisoners in Bagram, Afghanistan. At this prison site, in addition to sexually abusing prisoners, intimidating them with dogs, depriving them of sleep, and keeping them shackled in stress positions, "Further evidence of systematic abusive tactics is the use of the 'common peroneal strike,' referring to a blow to the side of the leg just above the knee that can cause severe damage. The taxi driver, Dilawar [a prisoner in the Bagram Theater Internment Facility], died after 'blunt force injuries to the lower extremities' stopped his heart, according to the autopsy report."[1]

Other disturbing incarnations of such extralegal zones are seen in the (almost invisible) practices of extraordinary rendition, or transfer of "enemy combatants" to prisons in countries where they are tortured in so-called black sites.[2] These are "concentration camps" in the deepest sense of the word: they strip away rights, knowledge, and humanity, reducing people to a state of "bare life," whereupon language, consciousness, and civilization cease to exist.[3] These instances should not be altogether surprising given the more-or-less visible legal and military strategies leading up to such practices.

The discourses surrounding the treatment of enemies in the "war on terror" reveal a great deal about contemporary cultures of control. The questions facing policy makers and security personnel include the messy particulars of sordid exceptions: What kinds of torture techniques are permissible, when, where, and applied to whom? Under what circumstances can we assassinate enemies, even if they are not in combat zones? Under what conditions can we detain individuals, perhaps indefinitely, without due process? These are some dominant questions in what Pierre Bourdieu would call the "universe of discourse."[4] Such questions beg a set of meta-questions, however, that lie outside public debate: What does it mean that these are seen as the questions of today? What do they say about our values, the state of democracy, or our system of governance? What do they indicate about how we perceive and valuate others? How do they serve to rationalize historical and ongoing complicity in terrorist practices by nation-states? Unfortunately, root questions of this sort remain on the periphery of the universe of discourse when policy makers instead concern themselves with rationalizations such as those for torture.

The contours of the policy problems concerning the treatment of enemies in the "war on terror" are well defined in policy reports like *Protecting Liberty in an Age of Terror*.[5] The content for this policy report was cultivated through "closed-door" conversations with notable advisors under the aegis of Harvard University's "Long-Term Legal Strategy Project for Preserving Security and Democratic Freedoms in the War on Terror." The forum that gave rise to the report included seventeen U.S. advisors, such as Robert McNamara, Michael Chertoff, and Rand Beers, along with half a dozen "observers" from the United Kingdom. This report is completely unlike secret documents such as the now infamous "torture memos" constructed by Jay Bybee and John Yoo to legally justify executive powers to detain and interrogate subjects without due process or adherence to the Geneva Conventions. Because the Harvard report aims to preserve democratic practice, the conclusions it reaches about acceptable interrogation techniques are all the more revealing and disturbing.

The goal of *Protecting Liberty in an Age of Terror* is to establish clear guidelines for executive powers and their oversight. To this end, it advocates for various methods of accountability, transparency, and "accurate reassessments," by which it means that sunset provisions and periodic evaluations should be instituted because "[b]road new executive powers should not be allowed to survive any longer than the extraordinary danger that justifies them."[6] Most of the recommendations of the report seem to be reasonable, serious, and well thought out. Examples include: "Without exception, the United States shall abide by its statutory and treaty obligations that prohibit torture," "Any U.S. person and any person within the United States who is seized or arrested outside a zone of active combat shall be detained only on criminal charges," "Any requirement that a nonjudicial demand, such as a National Security Letter, be kept secret shall be valid for only sixty days," and so on.[7]

On the surface, such recommendations appear to prioritize the protection of civil rights and liberties over the predilections of the executive branch (or military and intelligence apparatuses). However, the recommendations are

quickly qualified in their explanatory text, providing for all kinds of exceptions. The most often utilized mechanism for qualification is to change the
terms of the practices being discussed. For instance, while there should not be
any exceptions to the proscription of "torture," "highly coercive interrogation" (HCI) techniques may be completely justifiable and legal. HCI techniques could include things like "putting on smelly hoods or goggles, wall
standing for long periods of time, subjection to noise, deprivation of sleep,
deprivation of food and drink, deprivation of medical treatment,"[8] and so on.
Because these techniques, even in combination, do not necessarily "shock the
conscience" or inflict direct physical wounds, according to the report, they
do not technically count as torture.

This is an all-too-familiar discursive move made by nation-states struggling
to defend their own torture practices. As legal scholar Lisa Hajjar explains, "No
torturing regime defends or even acknowledges its own torture as torture."[9]
Instead, it deploys various forms of denial: "literal denial," claiming that accu-
sations of torture are false; "interpretive denial," saying that interrogation took
place—or can take place—but does not count as torture, which is the move
made by the report in question; and "implicatory denial," asserting that any
instances of torture are the fault of a few bad apples, not the result of state
policies, direct orders, or tacit acceptance by commanders, which is the defense
provided by the U.S. military for the actions at Abu Ghraib.[10]

Similarly, the terms used within other recommendations in this report
are wide open to interpretation and exception. What counts as a "zone of
active combat" or an "unlawful combatant?" In most cases, the answer given
is that the president shall decide (with some additional mechanisms of oversight to assess the legality or necessity of the decisions). These are not simply
matters of semantics, however, when indefinite detention, cruel or degrading
punishment, suspension of due process, or death may be the outcomes of
their subjective interpretation. In my estimation, the "war on terror" is more
ontological than geographical; its extralegal operations occur upon bodies
within "states of exception" that are quickly becoming the rule. So, while the
devil is in the details, the details of mainstream policy reports will probably
not challenge most existing state practices or power structures.

An underlying argument behind the generation of policy guidelines for
interrogation is that abuses occur because policy makers and state agents lack
clear, unambiguous guidelines. As the policy report explains:

> Rules proscribing the use of torture and other cruel and inhuman treatment
> by the United States provide little guidance as to the legitimacy of specific
> interrogation techniques and when they can be used. . . . In this context of
> uncertainty, the use of particular coercive techniques remains and has been
> subject to serious abuse. On the other hand, the controversy surrounding

interrogation tactics in Iraq and elsewhere, and the resulting criminal charges against military personnel, has resulted in a dramatic swing of the pendulum that may discourage legitimate interrogation tactics.[11]

In other words, not only is abuse catalyzed by ambiguous policies, but the public and legal backlash that occurs when abuses come to light causes an overcorrection that may detrimentally impinge upon the effectiveness of state agents. Within this explanatory framework, policy reports aim to curb abuses and simultaneously enhance the effectiveness of counterterrorism activities.

Unfortunately this logic is undermined by the fact that in the "war on terror," clear policies and laws are violated right and left, often with impunity. As Thomas Lue writes, "One glaring exception [to U.S. interrogation methods not qualifying as 'torture'] may be the treatment of prisoners at the Abu Ghraib prison in Baghdad, where the beating and sodomizing of detainees, the unleashing of dogs, and the pouring of phosphoric liquid almost certainly qualify as acts of torture."[12] And, although manifesting in a completely different geographic and discursive realm, President Bush's authorization of National Security Agency (NSA) surveillance of U.S. citizens was in clear violation of the Foreign Intelligence Surveillance Act (FISA) of 1978. The issue of accountability for illegal spying on Americans was exactly what was at stake with the revision of FISA in 2008. Judged against the old FISA law, telecommunications companies that participated in government surveillance without warrants were engaged in illegal activities for which they could be prosecuted. So with extreme pressure from the Bush administration, amendments to FISA provided retroactive immunity for these companies. This illustrates that although unambiguous guidelines may be essential, they alone cannot prevent or hold people or organizations accountable for abuses of power.

Practices of counterterrorism and interrogation are ad-hoc, particularistic, and wide open to abuse. As with much governance in the post-9/11 context, these practices are also shrouded in secrecy, and whistleblowers are often punished instead of praised. Complex rationalizations concerning necessary interventions and the semantics of torture may be politically expedient, but, more importantly, they signal an effort to enroll citizens as active supporters of the "war on terror." The next section explores the refashioning of this relationship between citizens and the state through the lens of disaster preparedness.

ENLISTING THE INDIVIDUAL

A new kind of citizen, the insecurity subject, is being constructed by the reigning discourses of homeland security. Increasingly, public programs are being reduced or restructured to place responsibility for the provision of social services in the hands of individuals, private corporations, or nongovernmental organizations.[13] This neoliberal trend in governance predates the "war on terror," of course, and is grounded in the "reinventing govern-ment"[14] movement of the Clinton presidency. What has changed since 9/11 is the militarization of government agencies and the active enlisting of indi-viduals as the first line of defense in securing the homeland. In other words, the very concept of the public sphere is being militarized. Even if breaches in security are seen as the fault of the government, the responsibility for correct-ing related conditions of human suffering or inequality are placed firmly on the shoulders of individuals, either to pull themselves out of their problems or to assist others who cannot do so on their own.

While public programs such as education, healthcare, and welfare face radical cuts and privatization, the state entrenches even further in instituting and elaborately funding security operations both abroad and at home. In the United States, a host of agencies that previously did not have "security" as their primary mandate were absorbed into the Department of Homeland Secu-rity (DHS) in 2003, where they have been restructured and reoriented to pri-oritize security functions above all others. Three telling examples of this are the U.S. Coast Guard, the Federal Emergency Management Agency (FEMA), and the agency formerly known as Immigration and Naturalization Service (INS). The Coast Guard's previous mandate was ensuring safety around costal areas, which also included rescuing refugees and intercepting drugs; it has now been recast as a security agency guarding the nation from potential ter-rorist infiltration or attack by sea.[15] FEMA originated in the 1970s as an "all-hazards planning" agency, which emphasized responding to natural disasters when under Democratic leadership and meeting the needs of civil defense when under Republican leadership.[16] It was absorbed into the Department of Homeland Security after 9/11 and restructured to prioritize response to secu-rity threats. As evinced by the catastrophe of Hurricane Katrina, the current security orientation of FEMA makes it ill equipped to handle the emergency needs of victims of natural disasters.[17] Finally, Immigration and Naturalization Service has been distributed into two divisions since it became part of DHS: Customs and Border Protection and Immigration and Customs Enforcement. Whereas the previous functions of INS did include raids and deportations, the name and mission of INS stressed managing migrant workers and guiding individuals through the process of immigration and citizenship,[18] which were "services" the agency provided. The Homeland Security incarnation of INS now prioritizes antiterrorism, including the militarization of the border through high-tech systems and the detaining and deporting of undocumented resi-dents without any of the symbolic overtones of governmental service.

Corresponding with the restructuring of government agencies, individu-als have been enlisted as security agents in a variety of ways. The first rather awkward innovation was to cultivate citizen spies. Immediately following the 9/11 attacks, the Justice Department developed a program called "Terrorism

Information and Prevention System" (TIPS), which would require postal carriers and private-sector service providers, such as cable repair persons, to carefully monitor the houses they serviced, watch for anything that might appear suspicious, and report their findings to law enforcement authorities. There was major backlash against this program by service-sector workers and the general public, so it was shelved. Similarly, under DHS's "Highway Watch" program, interstate truck drivers are recruited and trained to keep on the lookout for anyone suspicious and to phone a tip line should they spot anyone or anything unusual. Many truck drivers have joined this loose network of citizen spies, but they tend to engage in racial profiling and have not yielded useful tips. The final example in this vein was to grant the Federal Bureau of Investigation (FBI) access to library databases to spy on the browsing habits of patrons, while preventing librarians or others from notifying those being spied upon. What legislators did not properly appreciate in advance was that librarians and archivists are well-organized professional groups dedicated to freedom of information. The American Library Association waged an influential campaign to oppose these provisions of the USA PATRIOT Act, and many individual librarians refused outright to participate in the program. Along with public opposition, the effect was a partial roll-back of library spying with the reauthorization of the USA PATRIOT Act in 2006. The changes included allowances for limited disclosure and access to attorneys, and an obligation for the FBI to demonstrate "reasonable grounds" to suspect that the information is pertinent to an investigation prior to a search of library records.

The cultivating of citizen spies may not have been an effective strategy, but some citizens have responded enthusiastically to the perceived need to help others. Whereas most people perceive "national security," or the protection of the nation from attack, as the domain of the government, freedom from need or want has been carefully constructed as the domain and the responsibility of the public. Thus, philanthropic donations pour in to assist victims of terrorist attacks or natural disasters. The state typically responds tepidly, usually with contracts to private companies.[19] Absent from this arena of intervention are any serious attempts to address the social inequalities and inadequate public infrastructures that enable disasters, such as the one caused by Hurricane Katrina, to become catastrophes.

Instead, perhaps based on the model of organically generated individual aid for victims of Hurricane Katrina, the state has embraced a preparedness strategy of outsourcing management of future disasters to compassionate individuals, communities, and philanthropic organizations.[20] Take, for example, the media-publicized quotation from a 2006 report by the Department of Homeland Security on how to contend with the (purported) threats introduced by avian flu: "Institutions in danger of becoming overwhelmed will rely on the voluntarism and sense of civic and humanitarian duty of ordinary

Americans. The talents and skills of individuals will prove crucial in our Nation's response to a pandemic."[21] This is a remarkable statement given that the state and media are thoroughly invested in fostering a "moral panic" around threats like avian or swine flu. It is as if the state is saying, "Be very afraid, but don't count on us to help you out." Effective public health programs and infrastructures that might serve a dual function of treating people even without the occurrence of a pandemic are seldom funded. Instead, "national security" takes priority and is funded at a record rate. According to Reuters News Service, for instance, the United States spent over $800 billion on military operations in Iraq and Afghanistan between 2001 and 2009.[22] Other estimates that take into account total collateral costs put the price tag for the Iraq war alone at $3 trillion.[23] Exceptions for the provision of public health, however, are made especially when they support the financial gain of private companies, for example, when lawmakers directed the Department of Defense to stockpile avian flu vaccines at a public cost (and private industry profit) approaching $8 billion.[24] This was an especially troubling exception given that experts agreed that the flu would likely mutate, rendering today's stockpiled vaccines totally useless in the years to come.[25]

Perhaps the most interesting articulations of enlisting the public in security operations are those that call for preparedness. The first stage of this discourse invokes the fear of grave—and seemingly inevitable—threats. For instance, a 2006 government report on "Pandemic Influenza Planning" describes the severe mortality rates of the three influenza pandemics that occurred in the last century. One pandemic from 1918 to 1919 killed 50 million people worldwide; one from 1957 to 1958 killed 2 million people; and one from 1968 to 1969 killed 700,000 people.[26] By historicizing the threat of avian flu in this way, the report *could* draw attention to the positive trajectory of how mortality rates have decreased for each subsequent pandemic because of the rise in public health infrastructures. Instead, the stress is placed upon the unavoidability of another pandemic, which will be potentially much more severe than previous ones because of today's global nature of air travel. It should be noted that projections of massive deaths caused by avian or swine flu conveniently neglect to compare this threat to that of the SARS coronavirus, which was not all that infectious in spite of global travel. Indeed, funding for flu vaccines and preparedness infrastructures should be put into perspective: avian flu caused 114 deaths in nine years; meanwhile, malaria "kills more than 1 million people a year; tuberculosis, more than 2 million; and HIV/AIDS, more than 3 million."[27]

The second stage in the discourse on preparedness is to individualize responses and localize responsibility for contending with threats. This argument is captured in quotes by officials and in the many reports and pamphlets on preparedness that are readily disseminated by media outlets. In commenting on the need to prepare for an avian flu pandemic, for instance, President Bush said: "addressing the challenge will require active participation by individual citizens in each community across our Nation."[28] Former Secretary of Homeland Security, Tom Ridge, communicated a similar message when speaking about terrorist threats: "to defeat an enemy that lurks in the shadows and seeks relentlessly for some small crack through which to slip their evil designs—such a victory requires the vigilance of every American, the diligent preparation of every community, and the collective will of our entire nation."[29] Finally, in the context of preparing for future hurricanes, Secretary of Homeland Security Michael Chertoff claimed that preparedness by citizens is "part of the responsibility we owe to our families, and it's also part of a responsibility we owe to our communities."[30]

Just what are citizens advised to do in order to be prepared? First, they are given numerous checklists for things to buy: duct tape, bottled water, tissues, medical supplies, prescriptions, plastic sheets, canned food, flashlights, batteries, etc. Second, they are encouraged to volunteer in community preparedness programs or to initiate such programs themselves: "Volunteer with local groups to prepare and assist with emergency response" or "Get involved in your community as it works to prepare for an influenza pandemic."[31] Third, they are given detailed instructions on how to alter their current behavior to be more flexible in their work, education, and consumption patterns. To continue to be a productive member of the workforce, for example, the Pandemic Influenza Planning report advises: "Ask your employer how business will continue during a pandemic. Discuss staggered shifts or working at home with your employer. Discuss telecommuting possibilities and needs, accessing remote networks, and using portable computers."[32] And to maintain the education of children without schools, the report suggests "continuing courses by TV or the internet."[33] The so-called facts of such official messages are first that threats to the populace are absolute and inevitable and second that the government will not be able to contend with them for its citizenry.

These many checklists and instructions contribute to the construction of the insecurity subject. The insecurity subject is afraid but can effectively sublimate these fears by engaging in preparedness activities. The insecurity subject does not depend on the government for anything, least of all for safeguarding human security in the face of disaster. The insecurity subject employs the power of consumption as a shield against threats. And the insecurity subject internalizes flexible production and consumption models for work, education, and leisure, so that she or he can adapt to any instabilities without drawing upon the resources of the public or private sectors. These are simultaneously the rules that individuals need to internalize in order to be good citizens and the mechanisms by which individuals are to enlist as citizen soldiers. One implication is that those who cannot meet these expectations—because of economic vulnerability, for instance—not only fail as citizens but compromise the security infrastructure upon which the nation depends.

This construction of insecurity subjects occurs through discursive power operations. Whereas Michel Foucault is often cited for his treatment of disciplinary power, which operates on the level of the body or soul, he also stressed a corresponding biopolitical power that functions on the level of populations. Biopower's mechanisms are those of measurement and regulation of reproduction, morbidity, epidemics, and so on. These technologies of regulation fit neatly with the discourse of preparedness, which mandates detailed risk assessment on the part of the state rather than active correction of the causes of population vulnerability.[34] The plight of the victims of Hurricane Katrina in 2005 clearly demonstrates the exclusionary logics of biopower, which allow for the individualization of problems as a mechanism of population regulation.

The nature of biopower, therefore, does not rest in the state's power to kill or let live, as sovereign power did, but instead to allow certain populations to fall through the cracks, to let them die. Unlike the national security "cracks" that Secretary Ridge warned people that terrorists might be hiding in, and which the state directs its attention to with surveillance and counterterrorism programs, the fissures in social welfare are deepened by the diversion of state funding elsewhere. In his lectures titled "Society Must Be Defended," Foucault said: "Sovereignty took life and let live. And now we have the emergence of a power that I would call the power of regularization, and it, in contrast, consists in making live and letting die."[35] The current manifestation of population regulation naturalizes the "letting die" of those who are inadequately prepared. Biopower absolves the state (and others) from blame for their death through the codification of institutional racism. Foucault continues:

> In a normalizing society, race or racism is the precondition that makes killing acceptable. . . . Once the State functions in the biopower mode, racism alone can justify the murderous function of the State. . . . When I say "killing," I obviously do not mean simply murder as such, but also every form of indirect murder: the fact of exposing someone to death, increasing the risk of death for some people, or, quite simply, political death, expulsion, rejection, and so on.[36]

The construction of insecurity subjects as defenders of security, therefore, indicates new relationships among states and populations. Individuals are conscripted and blamed, in advance, for failures in social infrastructure. The demise of social services and programs, in turn, normalizes the fact that the "right to let die," as a form of governance, infects the state with the pathogens of racism. The vulnerable are made more vulnerable in the pursuit of preparedness.

CONCLUSION

Despite efforts by the United States to achieve national security, and perhaps because of these efforts, conditions of vast human insecurity persist. Torture practices, restrictions of due process, and government spying introduce new layers of insecurity, on one hand, while the militarization of government agencies, costly wars, and privatized security forces deplete resources sorely needed for public programs, on the other. All the while, moral panics about "not being prepared" for any sort of looming disaster are both cultivated by and answered with disaster preparedness plans. Such plans construct an ideal type of citizen-soldier—and insecurity subject—in the ongoing battle to secure the homeland. This citizen is constantly terrified but bravely embraces responsibility for contending with all known and unknown threats, leaving the government to deal with national security matters elsewhere, as it sees fit. The resulting macro-power structure is one where decision-making is consolidated high up on the hierarchy of the state, while the burden of those decisions falls squarely upon the most vulnerable populations in society, populations whose only recourse lies in individualized efforts to absorb the asymmetrical "responsibility" and "accountability" meted out to them.[37] Interwoven with the various extremes of modern insecurities is the emergence of a new mode of governance predicated on social inequality and individual responsibility.

CHAPTER 2

Twenty-Four-Hour Exceptions

POPULAR ENTERTAINMENT CONTRIBUTES significantly to public
fear of not being prepared for future disasters. The television series *24*, for
example, depicts a world in a state of constant flux and crisis. It is a uniquely
globalized world that demands skills of rapid assessment and adaptation, along
with technological acumen. Because nothing less than the survival of entire
cities or nations is at stake in each moment of conflict, every interaction is one
of heightened tension and instability, both for the characters and the viewers.
The world of *24* is also incredibly brutal: it demands the blurring of individual identities, social relations, and state legalities. This constant crisis of identity and of "truth" takes its toll on the characters, who not only subject
themselves to grave physical and psychological harm but also must harm and
even kill their friends and colleagues for the ever-elusive goal of achieving
national security.

The first season of *24* aired in 2001, after the attacks of 9/11. Starring
Kiefer Sutherland as counterterrorism agent Jack Bauer, the show gained
widespread acclaim for its innovative split-screen format, real-time depiction
of events, and suspenseful plots. The remarkable success of this show must be
credited to more than its ability to speak to the fears of Americans and others
about constant plotting by terrorist sleeper cells or enhanced vulnerability to
attack. More than this, *24* has played an active role in reshaping public perceptions and political discourses about terrorism and counterterrorism, especially by normalizing practices of torture as necessary and supposedly effective
tactics in the "war on terror."

In many ways, *24* functions as a metaphor for our times. It presents, in
highly crystallized form, the emerging social orders and contradictions of globalization. Global flows of people and goods are perceived as necessary for
national economies and for democratic ways of life, yet these flows also catalyze
vulnerabilities: terrorism, military intervention, and economic instability, to
name a few. The neoliberal state heightens its security apparatuses while dismantling its social programs. Whereas neoliberalism is typically understood to
indicate the privatization of public services or resources, it now takes on an
added disciplinary dimension with the simultaneous augmentation of security

forces throughout societies. Thus, the state-run Counter Terrorism Unit (CTU) in the show is well funded and stocked with the latest high-tech surveillance systems, but some of the show's characters must contend with conditions of pressing poverty and insufficient child support. There is some evidence, in fact, that the unwitting "bad guys" in the show are driven into collusion with "real" terrorists because of their economic insecurity. The window that viewers are given to state agencies, such as CTU, paints them as bureaucracies burdened by unnecessarily strict rules, procedures, and chains of command. These agencies function, it seems, in spite of themselves, due in large part to flexible individuals who can work between agencies and in the margins of acceptable behavior. In this way the show echoes and reinforces dominant neoliberal sentiments expressed by the media and others in the current political environment. Finally, the structure of show as a real-time, twenty-four-hour day effectively symbolizes the nonstop, just-in-time production models of economic globalization, but with an added emphasis on the need for constant, self-sacrificing labor and responsibility. The future of the world depends on it.

This chapter interrogates the dominant political messages of *24*. It perceives the show simultaneously as a form of captivating entertainment and as a disturbing representation of dominant perceptions of insecurity. First, the chapter demonstrates how security threats are constantly mobilized in absolute terms, such that they seemingly necessitate the suspension of the law, direct masculine action, and the reduction of people to mere bodies that can be manipulated by the state. Second, it analyzes the relationship between the neoliberal dynamics depicted in the show and those reproduced in the ongoing "war on terror," especially by the United States. The scaling up of surveillance and security apparatuses and the dismantling of the welfare state are two intertwined expressions of neoliberalism that are justified by entertainment programs such as *24*.

Absolute Insecurities

Absolute and ubiquitous threats characterize the world of *24*. Questions of scale and scope implode as all dangers take on the significance of finality. Thus, the plot is driven by assassination attempts upon the president, nuclear attacks upon major U.S. cities, bioterrorist releases of deadly viruses into the population at large, the meltdown of nuclear reactors across the United States, and the dispersal of nerve gas in public and military zones. Each threat gives way to another, just when the characters and viewers long for—and expect—resolution and safety. The best that can be hoped for is temporary management, containment, or postponement of the indiscriminate annihilation of civilian populations. Even individualized threats and sacrifices symbolize absolute ones because any loss of positional advantage against terrorists could destabilize the tenuous state of security.

The initial threat is upon the sovereign himself,[1] who in the initial seasons is cast as the first African American president of the United States: David Palmer. Palmer is caught within the constraints and contradictions of his office as the symbolic head of state and the embodiment of democratic and merito-cratic ideals. Agents of the state, such as the primary protagonist Jack Bauer, implicitly recognize their role within this disintegrating functionalist paradigm as shielding the president from any attack, physical or symbolic, and thereby ensuring the stability of the nation for just a few minutes longer. While assas-sination attempts upon Palmer's life are always present, his involvement in and approval of ethically questionable security interventions could also ramify back upon him (and his career) with similar deadly potency. The sovereign, in essence, must be protected from himself, from the self-defiling orders that his office demands, and from the moral nihilism that is his constant risk.

Examples of such unsavory and morally damning involvements prolifer-ate throughout the show. They include Palmer's authorization of covert operations in Kosovo, in which Jack Bauer led a team of agents on an extrale-gal assassination attempt of a war-crimes suspect; this operation took innocent lives, failed in its mission, and catalyzed a revenge plot. The routine interro-gation and torture of suspects also figure prominently as tacitly condoned methods, especially when immediate information extraction is necessary for ensuring public safety, which is always the case. Other sanctioned actions include things like jailbreaks by criminals in order to prevent biological attacks (in the form of a deadly virus); in this case, as with many of these, Bauer presents the scenario to the president and interprets his lack of objec-tion as support: "If you don't say anything, Mr. President, I will accept that as a go for this mission." The president answers with his silence. Finally, in what might be the most extreme of circumstances (in Season Three of the show), the president provides an off-the-record order for Bauer to kill his supervisor, also a CTU agent, with the aim of preventing a biological attack upon civil-ian populations. Bauer complies, with some remorse but no hesitation, by shooting his boss point-blank in the head.

These extreme actions are necessitated by circumstance because threats to the sovereign are interlinked with absolute threats to society, such as nuclear or biological attacks on American soil. In the face of catastrophic events of this nature, the future itself depends upon radical intervention and individual sacrifice, or so the logic goes. The characters respond by creating what Giorgio Agamben would call "states of exception," which quickly propagate. Agamben writes: "The state of exception is not a special kind of law (like the law of war); rather, insofar as it is a suspension of the juridical order itself, it defines law's threshold or limit concept."[2] So, although it may not be legal to suspend the law, the preservation of a functioning legal society may depend upon it, or so it appears in the context of the show. By suspending the law for the purposes of security, however, legal structures and principles are eviscerated, losing their importance and force as mechanisms for maintaining social order.

Any actions can be justifiable when they occur by means of the suspension of the very rule of law, facilitating—in turn—the subjection of humans to fundamental operations of power, stripping them of identities, citizenship, and value within emerging "zones of indistinction."[3] Torture is always an exercise of power, not just one of information extraction;[4] it is about the assertion of dominance over others in a way that eats at both parties like cancer. By reducing people to instrumental objects, which are seen either as pawns to be manipulated or as receptacles of information that must be extracted, humanity is excised from the object *and* the subject, the interrogated and the interrogator. Paradoxically, such practices are done in the name of preserving their opposite: civil society, human rights, political accountability, and democratic processes.

Individual choices in this arena are always false choices. The stakes are simply too high for characters to resist—for too long—the injunction to prioritize the demands of political structures and the survival of nations. Even terrorists and their accomplices seem tightly bound to structural logics and clan biographies that strip their autonomy, predisposing them to plot against the state, sometimes in spite of their personal interests and vendettas. In "states of exception," individuals must make personal sacrifices. Thus, Jack Bauer's wife is murdered in Season One, while he is preoccupied with matters of national security: eliminating those who made an attempt upon the president's life. In Season Three, we find that Bauer has developed a heroin addiction, which he "needed" to do in order to integrate himself sufficiently into and bust a drug ring. Bauer's partner, Chase Edmunds, is also brutally tortured in Season Three, while Bauer refrains from interfering, lest he blow his own cover; Bauer even puts a gun to Chase's head and pulls the trigger, unaware that the gun was not loaded, to prove that he had totally rejected his former identity as a morally incorruptible agent. In the same season, Tony Almeida and Michelle Dessler, characters who are married and both work at CTU, must refrain from rushing to the others' aid when Tony is shot in the neck and Michelle is trapped in a virus-infected hotel, respectively; they are needed on the job, and they submit—at least in the short term—for the "greater good." In Season Four, Bauer forces a surgeon at gunpoint to save the life of an informant while the estranged husband of Bauer's love interest dies on a nearby table. Of course, there are gender stereotypes at work here too, whereby those who cannot sufficiently sacrifice are emasculated by the discursive practices of others, implying that if they cannot "cut it" then they should leave and go join the uninformed, hapless public.

While personal sacrifices abound, the law need not be preserved, so opportunities for revenge are taken, which then serve to reify the ongoing states of exception that govern this world. From this standpoint, Bauer does kill freely and consciously, sometimes without immediate need for doing so, because terrorists and traitors, once loose, may return to kill again. Bauer learned this lesson the hard way in the case of Nina Myers, who killed his wife in Season One and then returned to insinuate herself into the next two seasons before he unceremoniously shot and killed her. As theorist Paolo Virno relates, this is the nature of responses to dilemmas constructed in absolute terms: "There is always something indefinite about the world: it is laden with contingencies and surprises; it is a vital context which is never mastered once and for all; for this reason, it is a source of permanent insecurity. While relative dangers have a 'first and last name,' absolute dangerousness has no exact face and no unambiguous context."[5] The show *24* confounds this interpretation, however, in the sense that few dangers are "relative" in nature, and even those that may seem purely personal imbricate with large-scale, complex systems to eclipse relative relations altogether in the final analysis. The relative has become the absolute; the absolute has become the dominant; the state of exception has become the rule.

Furthermore, gender roles and gendered actions take on added significance in the land of absolute, twenty-four-hour danger. Women are expected to take care of children and adults; male administrators predominate; and female characters, more often than not, jeopardize missions of critical importance through their relative emotional and physical weakness (seen clearly with the penchant of Jack's daughter, Kim, for getting kidnapped) or through their meddling (seen with President Palmer's [ex-]wife's constant plotting). Even when Chase, Bauer's partner and arguably the toughest male character in the show, has a romantic relationship with Kim Bauer, he is advised to resign as a "field agent," demonstrating that the relationship has a feminizing effect upon him, rendering him unfit for dangerous work.

Beyond sexist stereotypes, *24* exudes hypermasculinity through its constant valorization of direct action. Decisiveness is valued, reflection is not. The temporal pressures of second-by-second insecurities mandate and naturalize frontier mentalities of shooting first and asking questions later. In this light, governmental agencies and (inter)national laws are feminized bureaucracies and conventions, respectively, out of touch with the field and as such insufficiently adapted for the rapid responses necessitated by absolute dangers. Entrepreneurial agents, especially rogue ones who create and operate within zones of indistinction, are the only ones who can act sufficiently. The underlying implication is that the protagonists would certainly prefer to think things through, follow rules, and obey the law, but that the circumstances of modern risk societies foreclose such time-consuming endeavors. Thus imperatives for speed and decisive action become social facts and everything else anachronism.

24's projection of constant, dire security threats invokes states of permanent exception. Individuals, whether characters or viewers, are told that they are now—and forever will be—vulnerable to external *and* internal threats to their well-being, and that external/internal distinctions have all but collapsed. Individuals should distrust the capabilities of the state for meeting the needs of the people and should take matters into their own hands, by whatever means necessary. At the very least, individuals need to forgive the human and legal violations of rogue agents or politicians who seemingly have no choice but to bend or break, exceed or suspend, rules to ensure the safety of the populace. The irony of this message, which is a message of the show as a whole, is that "common people" may never know the rationales behind legal infractions or about major catastrophic events; in fact, they *must not know*, because that would engender even greater fear, insecurity, and social instability.[6]

NEOLIBERAL CRISES

Behind *24*'s terrorist plots and security (re)actions loom social crises of growing magnitude. Parenting is one of the first observable casualties in this battle against absolute threats. In the first show of Season One, for instance, Bauer's wife calls him to say that she found marijuana joints in their daughter's desk; his response is an apology for not being there, but given his job expectations, the viewers are made to understand that he simply cannot ever meaningfully be there. This theme recurs throughout all seasons of the show as a more general sacrifice required of counterterrorism agents, no matter what their rank or standing. This could not be more apparent than in Season Four, where the theme of sacrificing children and parenting is amplified to dramatic proportions. In this case, the daughter of CTU head Erin Driscoll commits suicide in the building's medical facility while her conflicted mother attends to pressing security threats. A variation on this theme also emerges in Season Two. When special agent George Mason discovers that he has been exposed to a lethal dose of radiation and will shortly die, he has the police bring his neglected son to him by force, attempts to apologize for his absence and aloofness, and soon thereafter gives what remains of his wasting body to the state by knowingly piloting a plane with a nuclear device on board to its fiery conclusion.

Other social devolutions reveal stark contrasts between CTU's technologically scaled-up world of just-in-time security and the characters' lack of basic human necessities. The state invests heavily in the former and not at all in the latter. The plot in the first half of Season Three, for example, is driven by the terrifying prospect that a teenaged boy returning from Mexico may carry a virus capable of killing millions of people—all because he was trying to help his struggling family pay the rent on their low-income apartment. Viewers are led to sympathize with this character, who is, after all, a white kid trying to do the right thing and is even willing to take his own life when he discovers that he may be a vector for this deadly pandemic.

In another, less critical example, various female characters are charged with caring for and hiding Chase's baby throughout Season Three when he is off in the field helping to save the nation. While clearly a subplot designed to create tensions among characters, the subtext is profound given the vast resources obviously poured into CTU, the temporary holding facility for the child. Child care is simply not available in this story, so one must rely upon other individuals, all of whom happen to be women and some totally unreliable. The constant work hours demanded of employees at CTU, at least in periods of twenty-four-hour crisis, communicate the irresponsibility of having children or families to begin with. When agents are distracted by these external obligations, whether they are the parents or not, then entire missions may fail, elevating all personal distractions or relationships to the level of potential catastrophe for everyone. This, in fact, was a major plot device of Season One where Jack Bauer was given a choice between saving either his family or the president—for the good of the nation, he had the cold determination to choose the latter.

Although intentionally blurred in the show, it is productive to reflect upon distinctions between human security and national security. One might expect calls for social intervention into some of the root causes of human insecurity that facilitate (and probably fuel) terrorist activities; instead, the answers are technological fixes in the form of CTU surveillance and rapid response to contain threats, not cure their causes. As with the earlier discussion of gendered action, attention to social problems is too soft in its approach, too systemic in its demands, and too time-intensive to even warrant mention. High-tech containment is possible because it is finite, immediate, and largely individualized; anything else is understood to be implausible in the context of national security crises. In this way, human security is simultaneously delegitimized as a worthwhile endeavor and subordinated, financially and symbolically, to the growing national security apparatus.

REAL-WORLD POLITICS

At this point, it becomes increasingly clear that the logics of 24's fictitious world reflect, legitimate, and co-construct those of nonfictional neoliberal police states. As with the president in 24, President George W. Bush was a head of state who insulated himself at all costs. Those around him willingly sacrificed themselves or their careers to preserve the ostensible purity of the presidential office, even if purity could be achieved only through the active manufacturing of ignorance (about the occurrence of torture or extraordinary rendition, for instance). When extended to cases of "natural" disasters, such as Hurricane Katrina, which killed at least 1,577 people[7] in New Orleans and along the Gulf Coast in 2005 while Federal Emergency Response Agency (FEMA) stood idly by, agency heads fell—and justifiably so—but unequal power structures remain tightly secured.[8]

In the face of real and imagined insecurities, television shows like *24* and other media programs celebrate consumption as the privileged mechanism of public response. The explicit rationale behind this was articulated by none other than President Bush after the 9/11 attacks when he argued, remarkably, that supporting the economy (by transferring individual wages and public funds to the private sector) would strengthen the country, making the United States resistant to future attacks.[9] Consumption of television programming, when done in lieu of other forms of democratic participation or information gathering, also serves to secure existing power structures by depoliticizing the body politic.[10] It should not be seen as coincidental that the content of news programming by the Fox Broadcasting Company, which airs *24* on its network, is almost indistinguishable from the entertainment: with few exceptions, both express conservative ideologies and cultivate cultures of fear that can be at once pleasurably entertaining and disturbingly disconnected from daunting human insecurities in the world.

Shows like *24* also function as nonstop commercials for information and communication technologies (ICTs), where cell phones play a central role in almost every scene, and Fox conveniently sells downloadable programming and ring tones for cell phones, in addition to a computer game and other merchandise. The point, here, is not to condemn business practices but instead to flag the myriad ways that fear of insecurity is commercialized, largely to the benefit of private companies and the detriment of populations in need of the social programs being dismantled and privatized, such as health care, education, and child care.

The ultimate consumption, however, is that of bodies themselves, which the state increasingly calls upon in order to satiate its desire for life-threatening military actions overseas. The aggressive infiltration of military recruiters into poor public schools and throughout public life is a crucial strategy for the consumption of bodies, at least in the United States.[11] So too is the preying upon financially burdened adults by hiring them as "security contractors," which is the all-new sanitized term for what used to be called mercenaries. Conveniently, contractors can be deployed in "hot zones" throughout the world or in disaster zones like New Orleans to police the public, but contractors are not subject to the burden of due process and equal protection required of real law enforcement agents.[12]

24 has also influenced the very framing of political problems and discourses, if not official policies. For instance, the "ticking time bomb" scenario, which is the central organizing conceit of the show, was invoked repeatedly in the U.S. presidential primary debates in 2007. In these debates, candidates were compelled to say whether they would sanction torture under extreme circumstances of the likes that occur on *24*. Thus, in a Democratic primary debate, moderator Tim Russert hounded the candidates with this question:

> Imagine the following scenario. We get lucky. We get the number three guy in Al Qaida. We know there's a big bomb going off in America in three days and we know this guy knows where it is. Don't we have the right and responsibility to beat it out of him? You could set up a law where the president could make a finding or could guarantee a pardon. President [*sic*] Obama—would you do that as president?[13]

Barack Obama responded confidently at first with a firm negative but then qualified his position in order not to appear soft on national security: "Now, I will do whatever it takes to keep America safe. And there are going to be all sorts of hypotheticals and emergency situations and I will make that judgment at that time."[14] Russert did not let the other Democratic candidates off the hook, either, but persisted with his highly unlikely scenario, lending it more credibility with each repetition. Being more aggressive with Hillary Clinton, Russert demanded: "Senator Clinton, this is the number three man in Al Qaida. We know there's a bomb about to go off, and we have three days, and we know this guy knows where it is. Should there be a presidential exception to allow torture in that kind of situation?"[15] Clinton also responded with a "no," but in a way that left an opportunity for exceptions: "As a matter of policy it cannot be American policy, period."[16] Torture cannot be a part of U.S. policy, period—but this deftly avoids the question of potential exceptions to policies. And although the question of legality was somehow seen as too academic for the debate format, the law is clear in this regard. Under the United Nations Convention Against Torture, which was ratified by the U.S. Senate in 1994: "No exceptional circumstances, whatsoever, whether a state of war or a threat of war, internal political instability or any other public emergency, may be invoked as a justification for torture."[17]

Obviously, revelations about U.S. practices of torture and the Bush administration's claims of executive power to suspend the law provide an important part of the context for these debate questions. Still, there should be little doubt that popular culture, *24* in particular, similarly structures the types of questions asked and responses given. A similar line of questioning in the Republican primary debates, for example, elicited direct references to the television show. Tom Tancredo, a Republican congressman from Colorado, replied:

> Well, let me just say that it's almost unbelievable to listen to this in a way. We're talking about—we're talking about it in such a theoretical fashion. You say that—that nuclear devices have gone off in the United States,

more are planned, and we're wondering about whether waterboarding would be a—a bad thing to do? I'm looking for "Jack Bauer" at that time, let me tell you. (Laughter, applause.)[18]

It is incredible that the conceit of the ticking time bomb, which experts agree is completely fictitious, has become a litmus test for measuring presidential candidates' qualifications to lead the country. Bob Cochran, a co-creator of the show, admits: "Most terrorism experts will tell you that the 'ticking time bomb' situation never occurs in real life, or very rarely. But on our show it happens every week."[19] Because of the popular resonance of *24* and the mainstream media's appetite for drama, presidential candidates, along with others, are forced not only to accept the terms of fictitious representations but also to be judged by their rules.

Although questions about torture are important ones to ask presidential candidates, the way that such questions are asked privileges masculinist responses, the likes of which would suit Jack Bauer perfectly. Candidates are not asked how to safeguard civil liberties and uphold the Geneva Conventions in the face of terrorist threats. Instead, they are asked about ticking time bombs and knowledgeable detainees, which naturally valence responses toward immediate, tough action. This is especially apparent in debate moderators' impatience with nuanced answers, as when Democratic candidates attempted to explain to Tim Russert that torture does not work and even U.S. generals say it yields false information and is ultimately counterproductive. The truth of *24* is that torture *does* work, so numerous findings to the contrary are simply unwelcome data that needlessly complicate what should be simple.[20] This, anyhow, is an effect of the show upon what should be serious political and public discourse.

Disturbing connections have emerged, as well, between the television series and actual military practices. U.S. soldiers in Iraq and Afghanistan widely share DVDs of *24* among themselves and eagerly try out the new torture techniques they learn from the episodes. According to Tony Lagouranis, who was an interrogator in Iraq: "People watch the shows, and then walk into the interrogation booths and do the same things they've just seen."[21] Concerned military commanders have visited the studios of *24* and unsuccessfully appealed to the show's producers to temper the torture scenes with elements from reality: that torture of all sorts is illegal, elicits incorrect or already known intelligence, can cause detainees to clam up, taints the reputation of the United States, and psychologically damages interrogators.[22] U.S. Army Brigadier General Patrick Finnegan, who spoke with the producers, said of the show: "The kids [future commanders] see it, and say, 'if torture is wrong, what about "24"?'"[23] Building rapport with detainees is actually a more effective intelligence-gathering technique, but depicting such a time-consuming activity simply would not fit with the twenty-four-hour constraint—and hook—of the show.[24]

One must also consider the potential impact of *24* upon politicians, judges, political pundits, and others in a position to affect public policy. The show's co-creator, Joel Surnow, boasts: "People in the [Bush] Administration love the series, too. It's a patriotic show. They *should* love it."[25] Surnow has gained incredible access to the powers-that-be as a result of the show. He had a private dinner with Supreme Court Justice Clarence Thomas at Rush Limbaugh's home, socialized with former Homeland Security Secretary Michael Chertoff, who says the show "reflects real life," and had a private luncheon at the White House with the late Tony Snow (the former press secretary), Lynn and Mary Cheney (the wife and daughter, respectively, of former Vice President Dick Cheney), and Karl Rove (the former deputy chief of staff), with whom Surnow also spent more than an hour in private conversation.[26] When the legal, military, and international consensus is that torture is both unethical and ineffective, yet governments hold tightly to their right to employ "enhanced interrogation techniques" considered by most to be torture, then it may be the case that *24* and its politics are contributing to real-world policies. Fiction has become fact, but the ramifications are much more complex and unruly than that which can be dramatized on television.

WINDING DOWN THE CLOCK

The show *24* actively contributes to the construction of security cultures. The economic vulnerabilities of globalized and informatized modes of capitalist production merge with national and political insecurities brought about by terrorist attacks. In the enfolded representational space of the show and real life, both of these forces are mobilized by political actors and the media to mandate the evacuation of public resources, democratic process, and (inter)national laws. Speed is the imperative of the contemporary political and economic landscape.[27] The actively constructed social fact of rapid response as an ethical obligation forecloses alternative possibilities and legitimates the status quo of neoliberal security and individualized public sacrifice for the public good. This situation further catalyzes the creation of zones of indistinction and states of legal exception whereby the torture and consumption of human bodies appears to be merely collateral damage in the war for national security. In fact, spatial distinctions start to disappear so that these "external" practices communicate the very "internal" operating logic of governance regimes in our time. As Avital Ronell articulates, "The worst moment in the history of technology [which is 'the concentration camp'] may not have an off switch, but only a modality of being on."[28] The mitigation of that modality is itself an ethical demand for action. Time, as the show reminds us, is running out.

CHAPTER 3

Situational Awareness of
the Security Industry

WHEREAS TELEVISION SERIES such as *24* normalize torture in the public imaginary and shape political discourse, U.S. government agencies actively partner with the security industry to propagate fear of terrorist attacks and cultivate a desire for prevention through technological means. This partnership is a component of larger trends in the privatization of national security, which spreads across many theaters of operation. It can be witnessed in the growth of military contractor organizations that operate with little oversight or accountability and are sometimes given "shoot to kill" authorization by the Federal Bureau of Investigation (FBI) for domestic security provision.[1] It can be spotted at mega-events—such as Olympic Games—where security companies profit amazingly from what are essentially grand commercials advertising their wares to other governments and private industries, while the needs and rights of citizens are neglected or trampled.[2] It can be detected in the not-so-new awarding of government defense and security contracts to universities that then seek patents, public-private partnerships, and private company spin-offs to gain financially from what was originally a "public" investment.[3] It manifests, sometimes most acutely, at border zones with the implementation of biometric identification systems, x-ray machines, metal and bomb-residue detectors, "backscatter" body scans that view beneath clothing, motion sensors, unmanned aerial vehicles, video surveillance, and so on—most of which are purchased by government agencies but supplied by private companies.[4]

The privatization of security entails much more than the awarding of government contracts to private companies, however. It is fundamentally about the realigning of national security interests with the profit motives of private companies. Thus, a first step in this development is the restructuring of governmental agencies and reorienting their missions to stress security provision, as was discussed in chapter 1. Once reoriented toward security provision, all agencies—and potentially all organizations—are positioned as in need of security equipment and relationships with security companies. With these developments, the stated national security goal is to achieve "situational awareness" in order to protect the country and its critical infrastructures better. In the parlance of Homeland Security, situational awareness means an accurate understanding of what is happening on the ground. With the use of advanced technologies of motion sensors, video surveillance cameras, mapping and visualization applications, and so on, commanders can achieve situational awareness so that they can respond intelligently and effectively in crisis situations.

Because national security imperatives trump all others in this governance era, not only are individuals expected not to complain about these changes, they are compelled to participate in the consumption binge. As Nikolas Rose argues, "modern individuals are not merely 'free to choose,' but instead *obliged to be free*, to understand and enact their lives in terms of choice."[5] Choice, in this context, means choosing market-based solutions to individual needs or social problems. Governance mutates into the disciplining of those who are not adequately consuming or whose very existence threatens the logics of neoliberalism. The consumption of security serves as a universal response to any given need, from the level of the state to the individual, and thereby becomes the ultimate need and ultimate commodity, seldom achieved yet rapaciously sought after.

Security cultures, therefore, are inflected by the ongoing privatization of national security. Lest these seem to be overly abstract or functionalist observations, it is worth attending to the agential shaping of these governance regimes, especially to the mobilization of security discourses. To this end, I will now turn to an analysis of one such theater of operation—the security conference—where private companies, government agencies, and "first responders" (police, firefighters, and rescue workers, for example) meet to collectively construct national security needs through the consumption of the latest security technologies.

RECONNAISSANCE AT A HOMELAND SECURITY CONFERENCE

Security conferences are highly ritualized insider events that offer a window into the values and assumptions of national security provision. As I arrived at the 9th Annual Technologies for Critical Incident Preparedness Conference and Exposition in San Francisco in 2007, the woman at the registration desk had some difficulty with my name, so I joked with her that it is hard to make up a name like mine. Without cracking a smile she stared me straight in the eyes and asked if it was a fabricated name; her tense body posture indicated that she was all too ready to call for backup should I say anything other than "no, ma'am." Uncomfortable, I struggled to explain: "I mean, unlike Bob Smith." But it was obvious that she was neither amused nor willing to banter with me about something as serious as one's true identity at a conference that most likely ran background checks on all participants.

With others I filed down several hallways lined with booths representing the conference's primary government sponsors: Department of Homeland Security, Department of Defense (DOD), and Department of Justice. Vast exhibition halls showcasing private and government technologies were visible through side doors, but for the moment I made my way faithfully to the main auditorium for the opening ceremony. Over one thousand people were present, mostly white, middle-aged or older, but with a surprisingly good representation of women, probably close to half. The event commenced with an ostentatious "presentation of colors" as strident bagpipes cut through the din, silencing everyone and turning all eyes to the kilted bagpiper marching up the center aisle followed by an honor guard of uniformed bearers of the flags of the various sponsoring agencies, and the national flag, of course. Although most people were in plainclothes, it was immediately apparent who was military or ex-military when their bodies snapped to rigid attention, with no one "at ease." After a white fireman soulfully sang the national anthem, a representative from the Department of Justice explained that the primary objective of the conference was for first responders to learn about existing and new technologies being developed with their tax dollars for homeland security purposes.

Heather J. Fong, the chief of police for San Francisco, next set a grave tone by declaring: "It's not a matter of if; it's a matter of when [the next terrorist attack will occur]." Throughout the conference, this expression would be repeated in a variety of forms, becoming one of the mantras of the event and an unquestioned truism justifying the use of almost any new technology, industry collaboration, or form of intervention. Presenters at this conference creatively mobilized—but never critically unpacked—a wide swath of examples supporting the inevitability of absolute threats from marginal actors in the "war on terror." For instance, "All it takes is a brain, a microscope, and a basement" for potential terrorists to make a biological weapon today, or "IEDs [improvised explosive devices] are coming to a theater near us," soon moving from roadsides in Iraq and Afghanistan and into U.S. urban communities.[6] Political or economic motives for these so-called inevitable attacks were neither raised nor debated. It was apparently sufficient to say that terrorists are "different kinds of people [than us]," who are essentially uncivilized and whose actions are monstrous, as Mike Matthews from the Department of Homeland Security (DHS) communicated to an audience that nodded in sober agreement.[7]

The statements about terrorists mobilized at this event were often in tension with each other or downright contradictory. On one hand, terrorists were positioned as uncivilized and technologically backward "others" who are so unlike normal people that it is a waste of time to try to understand them. On the other hand, DHS representatives averred that their "human factors"

division is actively creating psychological and physical profiles to better understand the terrorist mind and body, and military spokespersons, such as Lt. Col.
Mark Wickham of the United Kingdom, complained, "The terrorists share on
the Internet, in cyberspace, everything they've got," effectively living in a
"cybersanctuary" that intelligence agencies are not very good at infiltrating.[8]

SECURITY OF COMMERCE
IS NATIONAL SECURITY

Even after terrible disasters such as the attacks of 9/11 or Hurricane
Katrina cause human suffering and loss of life, the immediate policy response
from many politicians and government agencies is to protect—or advance—
corporate interests. This approach, which Naomi Klein has labeled "disaster
capitalism,"[9] was especially true in the neoliberal and neoconservative climate
nurtured by the Bush administration. Whereas politicians are sometimes savvy
about hiding this agenda behind media sound-bites and staged visits to disaster zones, the corporate and government personnel at this security conference
jumped with ease from the fact of human suffering to the explicit conclusion
that they must assist the private sector. Making logical arguments to connect
these things was apparently unnecessary because most people were already in
agreement that only the private sector was nimble enough to protect the public, provided that the government safeguarded corporations' economic needs
by limiting regulation and awarding them contracts.

The conflation of national security with commercial prosperity was
detectable in both off-the-cuff examples given by presenters and in formal
arrangements being developed between these sectors. For instance, in a ple-
nary presentation, Bill Brian of the Department of Defense argued that
twenty-four-hour Wal-Mart stores should be classified as "critical infrastructure" in need of government protection because when he loses luggage and
needs clothes for speaking engagements, he can always go there. This example
was only partly delivered as a joke. Brian's point was that the category of
"critical infrastructure" must be as mutable and inclusive as possible because
what is considered "critical" will vary by context and person. Similarly, during a session about public-private partnerships, panelists equated Starbucks
with other essential "public utilities," such as water and electricity, in need of
priority DHS protection. Ironically, DHS representative Matthew Skonovd
claimed that the department's security protocols for shipping containers
lagged significantly behind those of Starbucks and that it had a lot to learn
from that company. Finally, U.S. Airport and Seaport Police representative
Jay Grant argued that because America's ports are central to the national
economy, severe economic risks could ensue if they were attacked or shipping was disrupted, resulting in no toys making it to the shelves by Christmas.
The ports are critical infrastructures because corporations depend on them for

profit, and the rest of us depend on them for products. In Grant's allusion to "disruption," however, he problematically equated legal planned disruptions by unionized dockworkers, for instance, with unanticipated terrorist attacks, implying that the two might not be so different in their effects. On the last day of the three-day conference, DHS representative Mike Matthews effectively summed up the sentiment of prioritizing business interests, saying that achieving a "resilient community" demands that we all pay more attention to the "business community" because it is driving the economy.

The role of public safety organizations is to develop strategic plans for providing security on the local level, with little if any help from the federal government, and reaching out to business by supporting "technology parks." Matthews concluded: "The communities are going to develop this. We're not going to come down and say, you know, we're Big Brother and we're DHS [and you should do this]. No, they have to do it. It's their community, so they're going to be doing this. [uncomfortable pause] With our help." In other words, if communities want security beyond that of security for business, they had better learn to provide it themselves.

CORPORATIZATION OF NATIONAL SECURITY AGENCIES

Once the market logics of the private sector are glorified and the traditional functions of government agencies providing "public services" are demonized, it is a seemingly natural progression for public institutions to emulate corporations. For some time, scholars have been noting the inimical effects of this neoliberal trend across the spectrum of public programs, from welfare, to education, to healthcare.[10] Although extraordinarily well funded compared to their agency counterparts, government security agencies have similarly moved their missions away from service provision for the general public and toward service provision for corporations, whose interests come to stand in for those of the public. In the process, the language of business transplants that of the public, transforming everyone, even firefighters and police personnel, into "customers" of security equipment or intelligence. Government agencies such as DHS and DOD then serve as facilitators in the transaction, commissioning products from industry or buying products "off the shelf" and then delivering those products to its customers on the front lines. Thus, the DHS undersecretary of science and technology, Jay M. Cohen, explained that when DHS pulled together twenty-two different agencies, it was "an experiment in mergers and acquisitions" that is still "a work in progress."[11] But as a result of that corporate-like takeover, he said with a smile, DHS is better able to serve "the customers of the customers," meaning that DHS is the customer of industry products and local fire and police departments and emergency medical technicians (EMTs) are customers of DHS.[12]

Government officials presenting at this conference asserted that they would provide the imperatives for the purchase of new equipment and that they would take care of the politics behind those demands, but that industry would take the lead in making and marketing the technologies because "they do a much better job." In this context, though, industry representatives moderated panels where government officials touted the remarkable benefits of the particular systems being sold by the very same companies moderating the panels. For example, Aimee David, an employee of the company TRIPwire, sat back and let a DHS representative, Charlie Payne, describe the capabilities of the TRIPwire system for scouring Internet chat rooms and Web sites to seek out terrorist plots. She was there to answer questions and assert her authority as an experienced "counterterrorism contractor," but she let the DHS spokesperson make the case for her company's products and bumble through the technical difficulties of playing a promotional video for her company. Payne went on to say that DHS is involved in running a number of "awareness campaigns" because policy makers and agency heads do not sufficiently understand needs for equipment on the ground. For instance, they might feel that one $250,000 robot was sufficient for each bomb squad when in fact they should have multiple ones, just in case, because IEDs are now the "weapons of choice" for terrorists, so the United States is going to have to be prepared for them. The implication was that the roadside bombs of Iraq will arrive on U.S. streets—it is only a question of time. So, all localities should have expensive, redundant equipment on hand in anticipation of that alleged inevitability.

Here we see that the injunction to prepare for attacks necessitates investments in high-tech equipment. What remains unstated is that governments are working with finite resources, so funds for the purchase of security technologies typically mean cutbacks in other areas, such as public transportation, environmental protection, and occupational safety. Moreover, because policy follows from discourse, articulations about public responsibility for corporate well-being translate into government contracts that are essentially forms of corporate welfare, to the detriment—again—of conceiving of and supporting social services as public rights.

CULTIVATING CONSUMER IDENTITIES

This conference was ostensibly geared toward "first responders" at local sites around the country, so that they could learn about thousands of products available from the hundreds of vendors showing off their systems in the "exhibition" halls and make purchase requests at their home departments. The high-tech surveillance and security equipment on display was simply dazzling. Visualization products by the company Pictometry merge geographic information systems (GIS) and oblique and orthogonal digital images taken by airplanes to allow security experts and emergency personnel to see three-dimensional overhead representations of any critical infrastructure. The company brochure, replete with convincing sample images, states: "With only minutes of training you can thoroughly inspect and analyze every square foot, from up to 12 different views, of every airport, chemical refinery, dam, school, port, bridge, power plant or building. With stunning clarity you can see manholes, power lines, windows, doors, and other features within your jurisdiction."[13] The company's booth in the exhibition hall, like the others surrounding it, allowed conference participants to try out the software on computers set up for that purpose. Other companies offered military-grade "smart" surveillance systems for places like airports. One such company, ICx Surveillance demonstrated the easy slippage between military language of "targets" for domestic sites: "The ICx line of radars is capable of detecting moving vehicles and intruders—walking or crawling—as well as tracking their progress across the terrain in question. Once a target moves within a designated distance from the perimeter, ICx cameras slew to cue in order to identify and assess the target."[14] A host of other products were on display for people to try out: PDA systems with GPS functionality to allow firefighters to see schematics of buildings and real-time indicators of the location of emergency personnel in buildings; thermal-imaging surveillance systems for viewing people behind walls; protective clothing and gas masks for emergency personnel working in dangerous situations with potentially hazardous materials; chemical and biological decontamination equipment; a variety of robots for finding victims and assessing structural conditions in disaster zones; self-heating meals for mobile, rapid distribution to emergency responders; and so on.

In addition, various hands-on activities had been planned to allow individuals to experience the pedagogical potential of government-funded simulation games. In one, designed by the U.S. Naval Air Warfare Center in partnership with private company Boston Dynamics, Inc., participants strapped on modified Taser stun guns, mock handguns, and headsets with microphones and confronted a large video screen displaying computer animations of people in conflict situations.[15] The objective of the simulation was to teach appropriate "use of force" to police officers. I gave it a try while other conference participants watched. I found myself in a parking lot behind a building facing an aggressive man with a stick. As the first "officer on the scene" of this disturbance, I talked to the man, asking what the problem was, and verbally responding as best as I could to his ranting. I was able to talk him down without any sort of hostility. But the woman running the simulation evidently felt that this was not entertaining enough, so she punched a button and directed the man to attack me. I was obliged to fire my Taser gun to subdue him. The next person to try the simulation volunteered that he was a U.S. Secret Service agent. In the simulation, he arrived at the scene of a domestic dispute between a man and a woman. He failed miserably at talking to the couple, and the woman ended up grabbing a hammer and attacking him. The Secret Service agent grabbed his handgun, instead of his Taser, and shot both the man and the woman.

In another game, called "Incident Commander," fourteen people sat at networked desktop computers and performed roles of various emergency responders: fire, police, EMT, public works, and so on.[16] The stated objective of the game, funded by the National Institute of Justice and developed by the private company BreakAway, Ltd., was to teach players the correct "incident command structure" so that people learn who they should be taking orders from to work most effectively as a team. With decidedly clunky graphics and interfaces, the game presented the room of players with a scenario of a hostage situation in a school. Chaos ensued: bombs went off, fires blazed, students died, and the media swarmed the school, documenting it all while most of the players struggled to figure out how to get their characters into vehicles so that they could move to the scene. The players, myself included, tried our best to coordinate our actions and address the crisis. Most people yelled out to each other in the room—"We need more firefighters!"—instead of communicating through text messages in the game, as intended. Although it was unclear that anyone learned anything about the "incident command structure" from the session, the game betrayed a somewhat transparent value system through its programmed assumptions. For instance, uniformed and armed school resource officers (SROs) were on site at the school as an *expected* force, as is increasingly the case in many U.S. high schools and middle schools.[17] Also, teams were evaluated with a "media score" and a "public safety score," conveying the fact that manipulating public perceptions of crises is also an important component, regardless of how well a crisis is managed in terms of public safety. As the woman leading the demonstration related, her son plays the game and finds the media so pesky that he intentionally leads them into buildings rigged with bombs just to get rid of them. The message behind this statement, which was shared as a joke with this audience, is that first responders wish that they could ignore media perception, but the reality is that managing it is an integral part of their jobs.

In the context of the conference, then, participants were expected to learn from government officials and industry representatives. They eagerly engaged in hands-on activities and simulation games and milled about vendor booths inquiring about the latest gadgets available or in development. The primary lessons were for them to cultivate consumer identities and share in the ongoing construction of a market for security goods.

Forming Partnerships: DHS Fusion Centers and Google's "Virtual Alabama"

If government agencies are being modeled after corporations and emergency response personnel are being molded into consumers of security products, it stands to reason that public institutions would reach out to industry in whatever ways possible to accelerate that process. Public-private partnerships are perhaps the most expected though extremely well hidden arrangements in the ongoing privatization of national security. Take, for example, the advent of DHS Fusion Centers, which according to DHS are designed for state and local governments to "blend relevant law enforcement and intelligence information analysis and coordinate security measures to reduce threats in their communities."[18] As of early 2008, there were fifty-eight such centers across the United States funded by DHS at $380 million.[19] One is hard-pressed to find out any public information about the function of these centers—neither who, exactly, is participating nor what information they are sharing. According to Robert O'Harrow Jr., who is an investigative journalist at the *Washington Post*, these centers are sifting through driver's license records, identity-theft reports, financial information on individuals, firearm licenses, car-rental information, top-secret FBI databases, and more, all in partnership with private sector "data brokers" such as "Entersect, which claims it maintains 12 billion records [on] about 98 percent of Americans."[20] There are no clear mechanisms for oversight or accountability with Fusion Centers, in spite of the fact that private companies and government agencies are likely sharing unprecedented amounts of potentially sensitive data on individuals.

In attending meetings about Fusion Centers at the conference, I was able to hear some of the rationales for these organizations and question DHS representatives about them. Unlike DHS press releases, which are evasive about the functions of Fusion Centers, DHS spokesperson Matthew Skonovd was quite clear that the purpose is to obtain data from the private sector and to share government intelligence with them so that private companies could become full partners in security provision.[21] Fusion Centers, he explained, are part of the federal government's efforts to respond to recommendations by the 9/11 Commission, which is a point seconded by a congressional report from which he quoted: "[T]he DHS State, Local, and Regional Fusion Center Initiative is key to Federal information sharing efforts and must succeed in order for the Department to remain relevant in the blossoming State and local intelligence community."[22] State funds invested in the private intelligence community, broadly speaking, are stunning: "Washington spends some $42 billion annually on private intelligence contractors, up from $17.5 billion in 2000. That means 70 percent of the US intelligence budget is going to private companies."[23] This, in turn, depletes talent from federal agencies, as the best analysts from the CIA, for example, are lured away by private companies.[24]

In this "blossoming" intelligence-sharing field, "harvesting" and "sharing" information, Matthew Skonovd explained, is necessary to enable the community to "connect the dots" in order to avoid future terrorist attacks. When I asked what kinds of information are shared and with what private industries, he responded that any information about risks to critical infrastructures, such as electricity plants and water-treatment facilities, which are increasingly privately owned utilities in the United States, would be conveyed to those companies, and DHS would request cooperation in return. (It should be noted that this is a clear departure from public DHS documents, which emphasize coordination with local law enforcement agencies, not with the private sector.) If industry partners in Fusion Centers do not have appropriate classified clearance levels, Skonovd indicated that there are always "work-arounds" to facilitate sharing, such as having individuals sign "nondisclosure agreements." Industry representatives on the panel added that their companies were in a good position to cooperate with DHS because the U.S. SAFETY Act of 2002 protected them from liability if they did so. Therefore, businesses will likely be shielded from liability in sharing with Fusion Centers or any other government organization.

In a different vein, private companies, such as Google, are now building custom applications for intelligence and public safety organizations, thoroughly combining their data-management operations and brand name with security functions. According to James M. Walker Jr., the director of the Alabama Department of Homeland Security, Google's "Virtual Alabama" project is one such application that "shows the value of a public-private partnership."[25] Virtual Alabama is a complex database replete with three-dimensional imagery of most of the state (including, for example, buildings, roadways, power plants, refineries, and airports), GIS overlays for additional contextual information, building schematics, video surveillance access for all public cameras, algorithmic scenarios for likely direction of chemical plumes in case of a toxic release, and so on (see figure 1). Modeled after the Google Earth platform, this science-fiction-like surveillance system allows real-time access for all first responders in all counties within the state. James Walker explained that at first DHS had a very difficult time convincing local sheriffs that they should participate and share their data. This obstacle was overcome, however, when DHS promised to include a GIS overlay for all registered sex offenders in the state, showing exactly where each of them are supposed to be residing.

As James Walker proclaimed, one of the best things about applications like Google's Virtual Alabama is the low cost. With a $150,000 license from Google, Alabama is able to "populate" the database for free by convincing local firefighters, police officers, and others to add elements that they want to the open-source-like system in their spare time. In other words, if firefighters feel that having full building schematics is desirable before they venture into a building that is on fire, they should invest their own time and energy programming those schematics into the system. Instead of being seen as a form of exploitation or responsibilization when the state fails to fund or develop essential tools for public safety providers, the DHS director justified the

1. Virtual Alabama: Mapping of anticipated plume over city. Image courtesy of Alabama's Department of Homeland Security.

arrangement—with a telling combination of business and military discourses—as being "value added to the folks at the tip of the spear."[26]

The vision for Virtual Alabama, and for similar applications in other states, is to map everything and share data liberally. DHS envisions being able to share data regionally and nationally so that all emergency responders have access to the system, from local public safety providers to the National Guard—and, one must suspect, private contractors as well, especially because in addition to security contractor companies like Blackwater, which has been rebranded as "Xe Services," fire departments have jumped on the privatization bandwagon too.[27] DHS would like to achieve total "situational awareness" from the system, including real-time GPS data on the location of all state troopers, real-time readouts of available beds in hospitals, and GIS overlays for hunting licenses issued and chicken farms (in case of an avian flu outbreak). There may be perks for businesses too. James Walker said that he would like to make the data available to corporations as an incentive for them to relocate to Alabama. Or, he continued, insurance companies and FEMA might like to have access to before-and-after aerial photographs of disaster sites so that they can determine who should really qualify for reimbursement to repair damaged property. In other words, this high-tech security application can be used to protect the assets of private companies or the state from the "security threat" of fraud. As with other articulations of neoliberalism, the suspicion of those accessing public resources (such as FEMA) or making insurance claims is categorized alongside other national security or public safety threats and may be mitigated using the same high-tech security applications.

What is glaringly absent here is any discussion of the extent to which sys-tems like Virtual Alabama could create new security threats. The detailed mapping of critical information can be as dangerous as it is useful if it falls into the "wrong hands." This possibility, however, is not on the agenda of those advocating for such systems, which reveals that the goal of generating prof-itable data may be just as important as protecting the public, if not more important.

CONCLUSION

This chapter has called attention to a few dominant security discourses, practices, and organizational arrangements that deserve further investigation and critique. The first is the equating of national security with commercial prosperity. It is clear that the neoliberal political economy shapes and supports such beliefs under the assumption that what is good for private industry is good for society. Unfortunately, much is elided by this rationality. Obviously the provision of human security may be perceived as too risky or unprofitable an investment for government or industry, but certain elements of national security may be neglected as well, such as protecting water supplies from con-tamination (whether by terrorists or industry polluters) or hiring adequately trained and competitively paid airport personnel to screen people, bags, and cargo. Although technological fixes seldom achieve desired results and often create more problems, government support of technological systems is clearly lucrative for private companies, so technological responses to security provi-sion almost always prevail.[28]

The corporatization of national security and its cultures similarly grows out of a modernist orientation toward risk management. Not only do gov-ernment officials feel that it is their duty to provide the political support and government contracts for industry's security "solutions," they also internalize a market ethos that transforms government agencies and first responders into compliant customers of industry products. The unacknowledged flip side is that this consumerist orientation holds local governments accountable for acquiring and incorporating into their daily lives advanced security technolo-gies; if they do not, they are neglecting their responsibility to the people in their jurisdictions and possibly to the country as a whole, because local vul-nerabilities are now national vulnerabilities, as the hijacking of airplanes on September 11, 2001, so convincingly demonstrated. The transformation of subject positions of government employees, from public servants to industry consumers, does not bode well for marginalized and economically disenfran-chised populations in the United States, whose interests and needs are seldom sufficiently represented or met by public institutions even in the best of times.

For government security agencies, public–private partnerships may repre-sent a way to tap the expertise of private companies, minimize labor and cost, and increase situational awareness. Even if these objectives were met through such arrangements, they give rise to other serious concerns. First, the privacy of individuals is at significant risk with current levels of liberal data sharing among private companies and government agencies, along with the absence of serious privacy regulations in the United States.[29] DHS Fusion Centers promise to institutionalize the data sharing that has been ad hoc to date. Second, while it is unclear if Google or similar companies will have access to data entered into security applications like Virtual Alabama, the centralized stockpiling of diverse data elements will certainly allow for intensified surveillance of people, whether for purposes of public safety, consumer marketing, fraud detection, or other unimagined possibilities enabled by these systems. The limited information currently available on these nascent systems indicates that DHS is more than willing to approve the sharing of public data with private companies to encourage them to relocate their businesses or help them detect fraud. It is only a matter of time before other mutually profitable—but probably liberty-decaying—arrangements are discovered.

In these ways, security cultures are formed and re-formed, through discourse and practice, at specific sites like security conferences. Security cultures, in turn, become the lenses through which first responders, government officials, and others come to see the problems of insecurity as those that can be met with industry products, services, and partnerships. As the next chapter will develop further, this general pattern is reproduced on the level of the individual too, where the expected response to perceived vulnerability is to adopt the identity of insecurity subject.

CHAPTER 4

Vulnerable Identities

CONTEMPORARY INSECURITY NOW EXTENDS WELL beyond individual bodies, national borders, and material infrastructures. It includes, as well, the electronic data required for people to function in societies. Given the enhanced vulnerability of people's data, identity theft has become a critical concern, as it now represents the largest category of fraud-related complaints in the United States. According to the Federal Trade Commission (FTC), roughly 9 million U.S. adults are victims of identity theft each year.[1] These include cases of credit card theft, illegal wire transfers, Internet scams, phone and utilities fraud, and theft of business data. Police agencies have responded to this new crime threat by launching coordinated public education programs to teach consumers to "protect themselves" better. Some police recommendations include buying paper shredders for home use, shielding the keypad when using an ATM, not disclosing any personal information over the phone or the Internet, and setting up network "firewalls" to safeguard electronic data. While self-protection is important within the current climate of enhanced data vulnerability, this victim-centered response neglects the political and economic forces and systemic vulnerabilities that may be contributing to this form of insecurity in the first place.

This chapter investigates the ways that identity theft integrates with dominant security cultures and supports their logics. The creation of insecurity subjects who adopt responsibility for certain police and government functions is one theme. This involves the construction of threats against which individuals must protect themselves. The veracity of these threats or the underlying causes of them are typically ignored because consideration of them would likely imply state intervention through social programs and regulation of industry, both of which would be dissonant against today's dominant neoliberal tones.

The political and economic context for identity theft is one of postindustrialization, particularly within regions that have lost their stable industries and have gained a host of social instabilities, such as the manufacture and use of methamphetamines. Another geography where identity theft thrives is in regions of heightened economic polarization and sociospatial segregation, such as large cities in the southwestern United States. Meanwhile, the technological systems that facilitate identity theft are those of large-scale databases that are poorly regulated and vulnerable to attack. Most of these are operated by credit and telecommunications industries that hold profit motives over those for social good, such as privacy, but government databases are similarly vulnerable to compromise. The combination of economic vulnerabilities caused by post-industrialization and relaxed regulations for data protection may facilitate neoliberal forms of capital accumulation but also increase data vulnerability.

CREATING IDENTITY THEFT

Identity theft can be understood, at least initially, as a set of practices for stealing someone's personal information. This is usually done for the sake of receiving profit from a third party, which is a practice known as "financial identity theft"; other forms include "criminal identity theft," where one provides law enforcement agents with someone else's information, and "identity cloning," where one adopts someone else's identity to begin a new life or become a virtual doppelgänger of the victim.[2] For the purposes of this chapter, the term *identity theft* will be used primarily to indicate financial identity theft, which is its most widely publicized form. Such identity-theft practices can include dumpster diving for personal information; stealing laptop computers, wallets, or physical files; hacking into computer databases; planting "Trojan horse" or keystroke-tracking programs on personal computers (which will then "phone home" to send information back over the Internet); "skimming" credit card or ATM information with magnetic strip readers; "phishing" for valuable information through e-mail solicitations that appear to come from legitimate sources; "pharming" information by redirecting Internet traffic to illegitimate sites that appear credible and then asking users to enter or "update" credit card numbers, passwords, or other identifiers; and so on.

Beyond these practices, identity theft must also be understood as a "moral panic" and as a powerful myth that enrolls individuals, whether victims, criminals, state agents, or industry employees, into new social relations and forms of life. Moral panics are widespread—but largely spurious—beliefs in threats to the social order posed by dangerous groups, such as identity-theft perpetrators. The media act as "moral entrepreneurs" that foster fear in the public of its vulnerability to identity-theft attack by online hackers capturing credit card information, drug users sifting through one's trash, or scam artists calling to request sensitive personal information. By referring to identity theft as a "myth," I do not mean to deny its occurrence or experiences of it. Instead, I am calling attention to the fact of its social construction and its symbolic force to organize social life and contribute to security cultures. Identity theft is said to be the "fastest growing crime in America,"[3] and while reported cases are growing rapidly, the rate of those arrested for it is simultaneously decreasing.[4]

Fear of identity theft is inculcated by the media, police agencies, banking and credit industries, and personal stories of friends, relatives, or neighbors who have experienced the taxing ordeal of trying to restore their identity documents or their good credit. Simon Cole and Henry Pontell relate:

> The true damage and real victimization lies in the sense of personal violation, psychological trauma, possible medical care, family issues, and other ill effects, which of course include the time and expense involved in trying to restore one's financial identity. . . . Identity theft is thus analogous to the theft of a key. The key itself is not particularly valuable, but the theft engenders insecurity disproportionate to the value of the key, which entails further costs (i.e., changing the locks).[5]

Because fear of being a victim of identity theft far outstrips its actual occurrence, and because extreme actions are taken to mitigate it, it can properly be called a moral panic.[6] This conclusion is supported by the fact that most credit agencies and retailers currently cover expenses associated with fraudulent purchases; thus, the concern felt by individuals is out of proportion to the risk they face.

Identity theft also represents an ongoing shift in the way people and institutions perceive individual "selves." Brought about in large part by the proliferation of networked information infrastructures, identities are increasingly constructed through the selective concatenation of disparate, external representations of personal information, rather than being perceived as a unified, coherent cores residing within people. Mark Poster explains:

> The practice of identity theft is conditional on the heterogeneity of identity, the inextricable mixing of consciousness with information machines, the dispersal of the self across the spaces of culture, its fragmentation into bits and bytes, the nonidentical identity or better identities that link machines with human bodies in new configurations or assemblages, the suturing or coupling of pieces of information in disjunctive time and scattered spaces.[7]

Poster pinpoints a phase shift in cultural perceptions and valuations of identity as fragmented data, the likes of which spark new struggles for control.[8] In other words, the cultural externalization and circulation of identity—as data—afford its theft.

Government institutions and the media have played a significant role in catalyzing this new orientation to the self. With the passage of the Identity Theft and Assumption Deterrence Act of 1998, the U.S. government codified a disparate set of practices into a new crime category, which could then be transformed by the media into a moral panic. (In this respect, identity theft carves out a unique development trajectory because most moral panics move in the opposite direction: from media coverage to government action.[9]) This law brought the crime to life in the public imaginary, so to speak, whereas prior to this the media and general public had largely ignored such crimes.[10] Furthermore, many crimes that were previously classified as "fraud" were absorbed into—or colonized by—the new crime category of "identity theft," especially for theft of individual data with information technologies.[11] The label of "fastest growing crime," therefore, is itself a misnomer that has become a social fact, generating further concern.[12]

SELF-PROTECTION OR SELF-POLICING?

The central message for people concerned about identity theft is to protect themselves. But something interesting happens through the mobilization of arguments for individualized solutions to identity-theft risks: citizens are reframed as insecurity subjects who can best combat crime through consumption. Take, for example, a story in 2005 about the theft of Lexis-Nexis consumer data by what the reporter calls an "online gang" known as Defonic Crew. After describing the theft, the story concludes with the sage advice: "Let this serve as a potent reminder that we should all take precautions to safeguard our PCs. Who knows? You might have already inadvertently aided and abetted a criminal by not removing a Trojan horse."[13] In this case, individuals are metaphorically accused of aiding and abetting criminals by not purchasing antivirus software or taking other precautions; by this logic, the victim of identity theft is not only blamed for being an easy target but is guilty of participating in the crime.

In the discourse of self-protection, the "choice" not to consume is not only irresponsible—it is criminal. When citizens are recast in this way, the relationship between citizens and the state changes. Instead of the state being responsible for ensuring the safety of people, insecurity subjects are charged with regulating their localized territories through consumption. Additionally, government Web sites stress that the credit industry is the primary victim of identity theft, so if individuals are irresponsible enough not to protect themselves, by implication they are damaging the national economy upon which everyone depends. The City of Phoenix illustrates this logic by subordinating the violation of individuals to that of industry: "Identity Theft is a 'dual crime'—besides the financial institution that extended the credit being a victim, you are also a victim."[14] Such a framing of rights and responsibilities, which is by no means unique to identity theft, advances a neoliberal form of insecurity.

Although consumption may be presented as a requirement for individuals who choose to take data security seriously, it is analytically important to separate out three dominant modes of consumption in this context. The first, already mentioned, is the purchase of products and services: paper shredders, Internet firewalls, antivirus programs, home safes, home alarm systems, credit-monitoring services, and so on. For example, one such fraud protection service called "Identity Guard" is offered by the Web site www.stopijacking.com. The site lures customers through well-placed, fear-inducing banner ads, which are disseminated widely across the Internet. They brand identity theft as "iJacking," which they define as "an emotionally devastating crime that drains your accounts, hurts your reputation, and leaves you financially paralyzed when thieves assume your identity or use your social security number [to] commit fraud crimes."[15]

The second mode of consumption is that of consumer-protection information in the form of police workshops, university information sessions, government pamphlets, and numerous government, industry, and consumer advocacy Web sites. The stress of these information resources is always on individual responsibility. The FTC, for instance, has a "Deter, Detect, and Defend" campaign that places all of the burden upon members of the public to protect themselves and act quickly to report identity theft as soon as they detect it.[16] The FTC offers detailed instructions about the steps individuals should take immediately upon detecting that their identities have been compromised: "1. Place a fraud alert on your credit reports, and review your credit reports. . . . 2. Close the accounts that you know, or believe, have been tampered with or opened fraudulently. . . . 3. File a report with your local police or the police in the community where the identity theft took place. . . . 4. File a complaint with the Federal Trade Commission."[17] In addition, individuals are explicitly told that they must "prove" that they are identity theft victims.

Similarly, on local levels, the resources offered by city governments and police agencies clearly communicate where responsibility lies, such as Phoenix's campaign titled "Identity Theft: Learn to Protect Yourself." In this campaign, citizens are provided with an overwhelming list of precautions to take, ranging from implementing home-security systems, to "cross-cut" shredding of all potentially sensitive documents, to driving out of their way to place outgoing mail in secure postal boxes, to reviewing credit reports annually.[18] The inclusion of credit reports is especially instructive for this analysis. Because U.S. law mandates that credit agencies provide complimentary annual credit reports, this effectively structures in additional responsibility for individuals to possess and mobilize the information literacy and time required to access and scrutinize credit reports and act on any suspicious information they find. The law is couched in terms of empowerment and rights, but it is a form of empowerment whereby the state delegates data-security responsibilities to citizens. These examples illustrate that in addition to the demand for citizens to purchase goods and services and alter their practices, they are also charged with seeking out and consuming the information needed to protect themselves wisely. In this way, these two modes of consumption both overlap and reinforce one another.

The third mode of consumption is the consumption of fear. Although less tangible than the purchasing of products or services or the active collection of safety information, the consumption of fear describes a critical component in the social construction of identity theft as a moral panic. Fear is not simply transmitted from the media to the public. Instead, it involves the collaborative cultivation of subjects who are receptive to moral panics as compelling explanations for everyday insecurities. A consumerist orientation to messages of fear facilitates this process. The obvious source for these goods is the mainstream media, with their many horror stories about personal trauma inflicted by identity theft. These stories frequently lead with sensational experiences by innocent victims who are desperately trying to restore their credit. The convenient linking of identity theft to illegal drugs—or more recently to illegal immigrants—helps to fuel the fears that people might have about vulnerability because the perpetrators are constructed as transgressing social norms and spatial boundaries in pursuit of short-term economic gain at the expense of law-abiding individuals. For instance, an MSNBC story begins:

> Police in the small Olympic Peninsula town of Port Orchard, Wash., sensed something was wrong when they approached the pickup truck sitting in the town's RV park. To begin with, its occupants were naked. Inside the truck, an even more bizarre scene: Piles and piles of mail. The truck's occupants quickly confessed: The mail was stolen, lifted from mailboxes in the hopes of trading it for hits of methamphetamine at a nearby mobile home.[19]

The "facts" are presented in such a way as to highlight the supposed irrationality and otherness, if not dangerousness, of identity thieves: the perpetrators are sitting naked and poring over stacks of other people's mail in search of information that could be traded for hits of methamphetamine.

Identity theft has now been yoked to illegal immigration and national security concerns as well. This has occurred in large part courtesy of U.S. Immigration and Customs Enforcement (ICE) Agency raids on meat-processing plants in Colorado in 2006 and Iowa in 2008,[20] and subsequent news briefings by the Department of Homeland Security (DHS) and reports by the mainstream media. Because undocumented workers in the meat-processing plants borrowed social security numbers in order to receive paychecks (and pay taxes), DHS characterized them as identity-theft criminals who were compromising the security of the country and well-being of its citizens.[21] DHS Secretary Michael Chertoff explained: "This is not only a case about illegal immigration, which is bad enough . . . it's a case about identity theft and violation of the privacy rights and the economic rights of innocent Americans. . . . The issue of fraudulent identification is one which, as the 9/11 Commission recognized, poses a homeland security challenge [because terrorists could use false documents to board airplanes].[22] The tone for new cultures of control is set in conjunction with the media,[23] which in this case readily picked up and circulated the official framing of personal and national security risks associated with supposed identity theft by undocumented workers.[24] What is interesting here are the levels of conflation at work in this state and media production: first, the borrowing of social security numbers is framed as identity theft, somehow in the same category as running up the debt of others; next, this form of identity theft is folded into national security concerns, such that it would be ethically irresponsible for state agents not to employ the most puni- tive of measures. The combined result is a message of individual risk (eco- nomic insecurity) and absolute threat (national insecurity). Thus, one of the emerging dimensions of neoliberal crime control is harsh, disciplinary state action for overtly political issues, such as "illegal immigration," along with heightened individual responsibility for most other cases. It is the conver- gence of neoconservative with neoliberal rationalities, respectively, with the former asserting a moral-political force and the latter a market-political one.[25]

Apart from high-profile roundups of undocumented workers, which are only tenuously about identity theft, the neglect of institutions to address this crime signals a dramatic shift in modes of governance and policing. The pre- ferred response is the delegation of responsibility to citizens, as insecurity sub- jects, in the battle against identity theft. One might still say that there is a reactive form of law enforcement at work because police agencies and law- makers are apparently responding to the demands of citizens to crack down on identity theft with harsher laws. It is my contention that the reactive law- enforcement mode is present but largely symbolic, especially in the United States. For instance, a common complaint among law enforcement agencies is that they lack the personnel and resources to contend with the flood of com- plaints, let alone to intervene in any meaningful way. A U.S. General Accounting Office report supports this conclusion: "[P]olice departments are more inclined to use their limited resources for investigating violent crimes and drug offenses rather than handling complicated identity theft cases that, even if successfully prosecuted, often lead to relatively light sentences."[26]

As previous chapters have illustrated, the role of the state is becoming one of minimized social programs coupled with demands upon citizens for meet- ing the needs of society, whether in the form of consumption to drive eco- nomic prosperity, philanthropy or voluntarism to provide for the needs of the community, or policing to ensure personal safety and security. Of course, at the same time that the state is crafting a new relationship with the public in terms of social services, it is advancing mechanisms of control through military, security, and prison apparatuses. The field for possible responses is therefore restricted to those that support neoliberal governance of minimized social serv- ices and increased punitive measures—or, as Loïc Wacquant provocatively characterizes it: the invisible hand of free-market solutions coupled with the iron fist of discipline and control.[27] This is a larger pattern that is contributed to (and in part rendered visible) by mainstream approaches to identity theft, but it has been well documented and theorized in other domains as well. David Garland, for instance, writes: "The last few decades have seen important changes in the objectives, priorities and working ideologies of the major criminal justice organizations. The police now hold themselves out less as a crime-fighting force than as a responsive public service, aiming to reduce fear, disorder and incivility."[28] Policing, Garland asserts, has become geared toward risk-management and the redistribution of crime control functions to communities and private security forces.[29] The official law-enforcement response to identity theft supports this observation: the police will provide information to help the public "contain" the problem, but it is up to insecurity subjects to engage it more or less on their own.

Ultimately, individual self-protection against identity theft functions through self-policing. The state may monitor the crime and provide information, but citizens are required to take matters into their own hands. If they do not, then the media tells them that they are aiding and abetting the crimes, and the state tells them that they are hurting credit industries and the economy. The privileged mode of individual self-protection is consumption, or the self-transformation of citizens into insecurity subjects. The modes of consumption are purchasing products and services, participating in workshops and other information-gathering activities, and actively exposing oneself to and internalizing fear. The modality of self-protection is disciplinary. It requires individuals to regulate their practices, their homes, their loved ones, and their data. It conscripts them as citizen-soldiers in the wars on crime, drugs, terror, and weak national economies. Such citizen-consumer-soldiers really are armies of one. If they fail in any way, they will be blamed and—at least discursively—held guilty for their shortcomings. In the final analysis, however, self-protection against identity theft or any other social problem is part of a much larger transformation in state functions and purposes, away from the provision of social goods and services and toward industry profits. All the while, this form of governance advances cultures of control that ignore the factors behind crime and insecurity.

POSTINDUSTRIAL CONTEXT

Tweakers, meth heads, dope fiends. These are some of the descriptors applied to identity thieves by law enforcement and the media. Methamphetamine addiction and identity theft go hand in hand, so it seems, because of the specific nature of the "high" achieved by meth use. Meth users stay awake for days on end; they are risk averse, low profile, and often technology savvy; they are obsessive compulsive and so incredibly detail oriented that they can

focus intensely for hours on tedious tasks.[30] This makes them perfectly suited—
so authorities contend—for the daunting challenges of sorting through vast
quantities of people's mail for valuable information; cracking into protected
computer networks; sending out "Trojan horses" to people's computers and
sifting through data sent back; painstakingly removing ink from used checks
with special acid washes; and creating near-perfect counterfeits of checks, driver's licenses, and other documents.

The underlying message of most news stories on methamphetamine
addiction and identity theft is one of demonizing the users/criminals, bemoan-
ing the constraints placed on law enforcement, and stressing the vulnerability
of innocent people who must take precautions to guard their information.
Rarely, if ever, is there any discussion of the politics behind recent interpretations of meth use or the specific economic conditions within which meth use
and identity theft flourish. The overlaps between meth use and identity theft
reveal a contemporary economic dimension of the United States' ongoing
"war on drugs." In the 1980s and early 1990s, meth—or "crank"—was explicitly feminized and racialized white (vis-à-vis crack cocaine). Nancy Campbell
writes of the main constructions of drug use during this time period:

> Crank [meth] enables white women to meet their obligations as mothers
> and workers—the drug helps them juggle service jobs and child-care
> responsibilities. Crack using women [by contrast] are not afflicted with
> the compulsion to clean, work, or care for their children—they are rep-
> resented as sexual compulsives, bad mothers, and willing prostitutes who
> lack even the capacity for remorse that might redeem them.[31]

Methamphetamine has now been recast as a dangerous, homemade narcotic
manufactured and used predominantly by people in low-income white rural
communities. It is now one of the primary targets in the "war on drugs." The
detailed multitasking capabilities engendered by the drug still compensate for
the decline in state support for social reproduction, as Campbell writes, but
the activities of drug users are now directed externally toward illegal capital
accumulation, rather than internally toward child care and household management. As a result, the discursive linking of meth use and identity theft
stimulates a moral panic wherein potential concern for meth users is sup-
planted by fear of them.

While quickly spreading throughout the United States, meth labs appear to
crop up first in economically depressed working-class regions where community-
sustaining industries have been downsized or eliminated, such as the towns of
the Midwest that historically relied on farming, truck driving, factory work,
and coal mining for reliable jobs or those in the Northwest that have depended
upon logging and farming.[32] The second area where meth labs and identity
theft thrive are cities with extreme social and economic polarization, such as

Phoenix, Arizona, which has the highest number of reported identity theft complaints per capita in the country.[33]

There are links worth exploring, therefore, between the social problem of identity theft (and identity thieves) and changes in the political economy. These links represent aspects of insecurity that are often absent in popular discourses. The contours of postindustrialization and globalization are an obvious starting point. More than simply indicating the loss of factory jobs or the outsourcing of them to other countries, postindustrialization signals a shift in the mode and logic of capital accumulation.[34] The hierarchical and stable industrial models of the past have been transformed, since the early 1970s, into decentralized, mutable organizations operating through rapid exchange of goods and services.[35] Capital accumulation is now facilitated by telecommunications infrastructures, just-in-time production models, and "flexible" employees with few benefits and little job security.[36] Accompanying these industrial changes are alterations in public institutions and social policy, such that public programs are minimized, privatized, or otherwise harmonized with the needs of industry.[37] Finally, large private industries (for example, energy and telecommunications) have been deregulated in such a way that services are increasingly "unbundled" for those who cannot afford to pay additional fees,[38] which is a condition that is also apparent with consumerist approaches to security provision. For the discussion of identity theft, therefore, key results of these transformations include (1) increased economic instability and social polarization and (2) the emergence of database infrastructures, such as those being celebrated at security conferences, that serve as resources for capital accumulation both for industry *and* for identity thieves.

In addition to these structural changes seen on the level of the political economy, a certain cultural logic accompanies postindustrialization, further entrenching it in social practice.[39] It should not be seen as a coincidence that today's descriptions of ideal workers and methamphetamine users are remarkably similar. They both thrive on instability, work long hours on tedious projects, multitask, adjust flexibly to changing conditions, and are technologically proficient. As Emily Martin has written about manic depression and attention deficit hyperactivity disorder (ADHD), not only does postindustrial work reward certain psychosocial pathologies, it actively cultivates them.[40] The most successful people in today's marketplace are "always adapting by scanning the environment for signs of change, flying from one thing to another, while pushing the limits of everything, and doing it all with an intense level of energy focused totally on the future."[41] The ideal flexible worker does not expect job security or state assistance; instead, he or she gets "high" on the danger associated with having everything to lose. But, as a result of the prevalence of this cultural logic of individual adaptation and responsibility and nonaccountability of government or industry, many are left in dire straits. Those, such as identity thieves, who deftly exploit the system by embodying the values of postindustrialization but who do not increase the profit of companies, are demonized and criminalized.

One could view identity thieves instead as entrepreneurs with highly specialized skills. They are individuals who have carved out niche markets for sustaining themselves by appropriating the dominant rationalities of flexible accumulation and the technologies of network interconnection. Identity theft is not entirely unlike the occult economies created by others throughout the world in response to economic vulnerabilities. Jean Comaroff and John Comaroff, for instance, describe practices of gambling, pyramid schemes, witchcraft, zombie conjuring, organ theft and trade, and so on as innovative cultural responses to instabilities of advanced capitalism and neoliberal policies to privatize all collective goods and services.[42] Seen from this perspective, the demarcation between innovative identity thieves and law-abiding workers is not so clear. Many people are subjected to the postindustrial risks of social instability, human insecurity, and downward economic mobility. Only by attending to the political and economic context of this crime can it be seen as part of larger social problems that are easily obscured by simply targeting those labeled as criminals.

DATA VULNERABILITY

The very technological systems that facilitate communication, commerce, and trade also open people up to intrusive forms of electronic surveillance. This is a point often overlooked in discussions of electronic monitoring or crime. We have been told that adopting the latest technologies is necessary to stay in touch with friends and relatives, to conduct business more efficiently, to maintain competitive advantage over other countries, or to ensure military superiority over modern-day enemies. But in equating technology with progress, societies have neglected to question the ways in which information systems increase vulnerability to surveillance abuses, whether by identity thieves, government agencies, or private industries. When risks are seen through an individualistic lens, it is difficult to perceive and address the systemic vulnerabilities enabled by information infrastructures.

Nonetheless, vulnerable information databases and their related industries are key to undermining data security and increasing avenues for identity theft.[43] For instance, while hundreds of thousands of individual complaints may be filed with the FTC each year,[44] millions of data records are compromised in mass identity thefts. In one of several high-profile cases, for example, 40 million credit cards were compromised when hackers penetrated the database of CardSystems Solutions, Inc., in Tucson, Arizona, in 2004.[45] In the same year, the consumer data aggregator company ChoicePoint admitted to losing over 163,000 records to criminals, leading to more than 800 documented cases of identity theft.[46] In 2006, personal information from 26.5 million military veterans was stolen from the home of an analyst for the U.S. Department of Veterans Affairs who was not authorized to take the records home in the first place.[47] Similar cases of massive theft or loss of sensitive data happen frequently because organizations fail to implement serious data-protection protocols. For instance, in 2007 a laptop computer containing personal information, including social security numbers for 800,000 people, was stolen from the Gap clothing company, which admits that it did not have the data encrypted on the computer.[48] Also in 2007, it came to light that international retail company TJX's central databases were hacked into without the company's awareness, giving hackers access to 45 million credit and debit card numbers.[49] The British government has also had a slew of data-loss incidents recently from the private security companies to which they outsource responsibilities, including losing "next of kin details, passport and National Insurance numbers, drivers' license and bank details, and National Health Service" numbers in 2008 for up to 1.7 million people expressing interest in joining the armed forces.[50]

Whether implicating private industries or the government, these cases underscore not only the lax security for systems containing sensitive data but also the lax enforcement of policies for data protection. These are not isolated cases that any individual action, such as using an antivirus program, could have prevented. Indeed, while police authorities and the media play upon fears of methamphetamine users and dumpster divers, the truth is that most people do not know how their information was stolen.[51] It could very well have been a result of third parties who had *legitimate* access to the data. These examples point to compromised information systems and policies that extend far beyond the safeguards that potential victims can take.

Such cases of large-scale data theft are enabled by vulnerable information systems and their companies or government agencies. The fact that industries manage their networks poorly, fail to ensure proper encryption, share data liberally, and maintain records far longer than necessary compounds the problem. Given these problems, the approach to identity theft that prioritizes individual protection may unwittingly reinforce the conditions that support these crimes by diverting attention away from central technologies and practices. Because there has not been informed public debate about the kinds of technologies that are necessary to adopt, or about the important safeguards that should be implemented for the preservation of social goods (such as data security or privacy), vulnerable information systems proliferate. In effect, individual consumers, employees, or others are blamed for their own victimization, but the systems or the industries that make them such easy targets are seldom reevaluated. These systems are the massive databases of consumer information that are stockpiled by credit agencies, telecommunications companies, and others for targeted advertising and lucrative sharing arrangements among companies. Once the systems are in place, they also enable multiple uses far beyond the original intent for them, which can be seen clearly with major telecommunications companies turning over their databases to U.S. government agencies to sift through and spy on U.S. citizens, ostensibly for counterterrorism purposes. When confronted with the problems of easily compromised databases and data-security practices, the major industries respond by saying that the systems are too profitable to impose serious restrictions upon them and that customers desire the instant credit that such systems afford.[52] It is a market-based decision that has nothing to do with minimizing insecurity or protecting privacy.

Presently, the FTC can fine companies that have not taken "reasonable" precautions to ensure confidentiality of consumer data. For instance, a $15 million fine was imposed upon ChoicePoint in January 2006 for its loss of records.[53] Notwithstanding the potential for fines to galvanize better data protection by companies, this approach to regulation presupposes that violations will come to the attention of the FTC, when it is much more likely that most cases are not identified or are only partially revealed. Fines do not address the problem of data stockpiling and exchange among companies. They do not call for the redesign of information architectures to ensure anonymity and confidentiality at every step of the way with the generation and circulation of data. Most importantly, they ignore the pressing need in the United States and elsewhere for serious data protection laws. The United States, for example, does not presuppose that everyone opts out of data sharing as a default. Currently, it is almost always the opposite: everyone is opted in for data sharing, forcing individuals to contact credit companies and others to request that their information not be shared. Similarly, the United States does not have clear guidelines for who has access to personal data (especially for data not pertaining to credit or medical records), how it can be shared, and when it will be destroyed.[54] It is likely that until data vulnerability is addressed as a systemic problem, rather than as an individual one, identity theft will continue to thrive.

Because there are few regulations for data protection, industries may profit from consumer information and governments may benefit from easier surveillance of populations. One way of interpreting such practices of fluid information exchange is that they shift power away from individuals while enabling greater control of individuals for purposes of capital accumulation or counterterrorism investigations. This illustrates another property of neoliberal governance. While individuals and their data are made vulnerable by ubiquitous information infrastructures and exchange practices, the primary trade-off articulated as justification for exposure to such risk is the availability of "easy credit" for consumers. Not only is consumption depicted as the "good" that makes exposure to identity theft worthwhile, it is also the means by which individuals can protect themselves. Meanwhile the state is almost completely absent, unless it is drawing upon the vast information systems for "national security" purposes.

Conclusion

Identity theft is an everyday form of insecurity that reveals dominant shifts in modern forms of governance and highlights new dimensions of neoliberalism. As a set of social practices and as a socially constructed crime category, identity theft illustrates transformations in social control toward individual responsibility for crime deterrence through self-policing and toward the absolution of the state for providing for social needs, whether in the form of economic stability, social services, or necessary regulations upon information industries. The overall effect is one of intensified social control, which takes place with the onset of governmentalities of hyperindividualized responsibility, privatized "solutions" to identity theft and other crimes, and crime containment, risk management, and outsourcing as the primary responses of the state.

Identity theft also depends upon the presumption of digitized selves, or data doubles, that circulate within information networks as intimate, disembodied possessions that can be stolen or compromised.[55] The self is commodified as something external to people. Both law enforcement agencies and the media fan the embers of identity theft threats into moral panics such that individual vulnerabilities are reframed in absolute terms as national security threats. Responsibilization extends beyond the individual to encompass the entire body politic. The creative appropriations and innovations of identity thieves harmonize well with the flexible production ideologies of the postindustrial labor market. The fact that such tactics of flexible accumulation are criminalized while others are celebrated demonstrates some of the contradictions and contingencies in security cultures and capitalism. Flexible tactics for the sake of industry profit are embraced, while those that threaten neoliberal orthodoxy are demonized.[56] Lastly, technological systems play a crucial role in the construction and governance of vulnerability, insecurity, and responsibility. As long as technologies are seen as neutral tools, their systemic effects will be masked, thereby allowing individualizing frames to be forced over social and institutional problems.

CHAPTER 5

Leaving Others Behind

And he causeth all, both small and great, rich and poor, free
and bond, to receive a mark in their right hand, or in their
foreheads: And that no man might buy or sell, save he that
had the mark, or the name of the beast, or the number of his
name. Here is wisdom. Let him that hath understanding
count the number of the beast: for it is the number of a man;
and his number is Six hundred threescore and six.

—Revelation 13:16–18

The Second Coming evokes not a Jesus who saves, but one
who pays dividends. Or, more accurately, one who promises
a miraculous return on a limited spiritual investment.

—Jean and John Comaroff, "Millennial Capitalism:
First Thoughts on a Second Coming"

RELIGIOUS DISCOURSES CAN CONTRIBUTE significantly to
the production of insecurity subjects, especially, it seems, when they stress
personal over collective responsibility for meeting physical and spiritual
needs during times of crisis. Broadly speaking, feelings of insecurity are often
used by communities to justify harsh or unequal treatment of people considered to be different. Xenophobic responses are common, as seen with racial
profiling of Arab-looking individuals after 9/11 or with the fortification of
national borders to keep out illegal immigrants. Similarly, in religious communities belief in the forthcoming destruction of the world may be used as a
rationalization for excluding others and abdicating responsibility for the greater
social good.

Prophecies of the apocalypse circulate and multiply with incredible fre-
quency, velocity, and profitability. In some respects, concerns over the impend-
ing destruction of the world are ancient obsessions and well-worn mythological
motifs, which wax and wane according to technological changes, historical
contingencies, or significant turning points on arbitrary calendars. On the other
hand, contemporary apocalypse prophecies fuse in interesting—and perhaps
indelible—ways with capitalist economies. Whether the looming disasters are

technological, environmental, or biblical, they tend to afford rewarding opportunities for some while fueling the increasing vulnerability of others. Jean and John Comaroff label this emerging set of practices *millennial capitalism*, indicating a globalized, neoliberal form of capitalism predicated upon privatization, individual responsibility, and the right to consume (not to produce).[1] Especially for various end-of-days movements, this neoliberal logic introduces provocative dissonances between value placed on individual profit versus universal salvation, upon the medium versus the message. In some instances, religious warnings about the dangers of technology and the capitalist market are themselves highly mediated by technology and are enormously profitable ventures.

An entire industry has developed to feed the fears of Christians, and presumably others, about the imminent coming of the Antichrist and the end of the world. As part of the $7 billion market for Christian products,[2] religious fiction now occupies aisles upon aisles of bookshelves in some large chain bookstores. Much of this religious material demonstrates a significant degree of gloating by Christian authors over the presumably "condemned" lapsed Christians and nonbelievers who will remain on Earth to suffer after "the rapture" (or the taking of Christian souls to heaven) occurs. Apart from religious fiction, products in this genre include video games, board games, Web sites, DVDs, televised sermons, and a host of "nonfiction" books, which delineate in great detail the many forms that current and future threats upon souls can take, along with identifying the complicit parties involved in propagating the secular mechanisms and ideologies of damnation.

Particularly fascinating is the mobilization of discourse about the "mark of the beast," which singles out certain technologies for vilification and people for damnation. As referenced by the opening quote from the Bible's book of Revelation, the mark of the beast indicates a symbol that will be given to people during the Last Days before the Second Coming of Jesus Christ. From this perspective, whereas the mark will be required for people to engage in any form of capitalist exchange such as might be necessary for general sustenance, in voluntarily accepting the mark people will perforce align themselves with the Antichrist and doom themselves to perdition. The alternative, as many exegeses suggest, is to reject the mark, and thus commit oneself to dying miserably on Earth to enable the possibility of eternal life in heaven. Various technologies have been nominated by Christian groups as metaphorically representing or literally being the mark of the beast. Some of these include radio-frequency identification (RFID) chips implanted into individuals' arms, national identity card schemes, and even common bar codes or credit and social security cards. Given dominant cultural equations of technology with progress and social good, and especially with economic good, religious perspectives on technologies of production and consumption provide an especially rich terrain for investigating Christian modalities of millennial capitalism.

This chapter analyzes the content and context of Left Behind, a popular series of Christian novels about the Last Days. First, it provides an overview of the book series and the philosophies that undergird it. Next, it describes three thematic areas where contradictions exist between the theological framework espoused by the novels and the practices of the novels' authors and key characters. These thematic areas include relations with the capitalist economy; perspectives on technologies of production, consumption, and control; and orientations toward social problems. The overall argument is that contemporary "rapture fiction" responds to and reproduces the crises and instabilities of modernity. It enacts a politics of consumerist and technological engagement alongside one of social disengagement, and in this way corresponds with the dimensions of security cultures discussed in the previous chapters. By rationalizing wealth disparities and religious inflexibility as part of God's plan, these politics encourage the adoption of insecurity subject positions while perhaps aggravating social inequalities, religious conflicts, and cultural tensions.

RAPTURE FICTION

The Left Behind story begins dramatically with the sudden and unexpected "rapture" of saved souls, including all children, fetuses, and true Christians.[3] As people disappear from vehicles, planes, streets, schools, and homes, chaos erupts and disastrous accidents occur all over the world. Those left behind are thrown into panic and shock, desperately trying to find their loved ones, their ways back home, and viable explanations for where everyone went. The event of the rapture marks the seven-year rule of the Antichrist and the starting point for the book series. Operating to institute a "world government" and a single world currency under the auspices of the United Nations, the Antichrist, who is secretary general of the UN, seeks to dominate all nations and make life a living hell for nonraptured, lapsed, or belatedly converted Christians. According to the biblical prophecies embraced and reinterpreted by Left Behind, after seven years, Jesus Christ will return to slaughter all of his enemies at the battle of Armageddon and initiate a one-thousand-year period of world peace before ascending again to heaven with his followers.

This particular millennialist interpretation of the book of Revelation, which posits the occurrence of a "rapture" apart from the Second Coming, derives not from traditional exegesis but instead from a relatively new revision of the Bible. The origins of this belief can be traced to the visions of a woman in Port Glasgow, Scotland, who in 1830 reported having seen Christ rescuing his believers *before* a seven-year period of "tribulation," which was then followed by him returning to rule in peace for one thousand years.[4] This proved to be a very attractive embellishment of scripture because it meant that Christians would not have to endure the tribulation, which is described in Revelation as a horrific period of intense suffering. Known as "dispensational premillennialism," this version of events was popularized by preacher John Nelson Darby in the latter half of the nineteenth century,[5] disseminated by Protestant religious tracts,[6] and embraced by American evangelicals following the 1909 publication of the Scofield Study Bible, which gave credence to the rapture prophecy in its "notes."[7] This exegesis was further entrenched in the American evangelical community with the founding of Dallas Theological Seminary in 1924, which advanced this millennial perspective in its training of pastors.[8]

Whereas dispensational premillennialism, as an interpretive position and a guide for religious conduct, has gained hegemonic status among American evangelicals, it is neither a static nor an uncontested set of beliefs. As seen in rapture literature throughout the twentieth century, the mapping of prophecies onto contemporary world events, people, and technologies has shifted alongside cultural values, ideologies, and historical contingencies.[9] For example, early rapture fiction—such as Sydney Watson's books *Scarlet and Purple* (1913), *The Mark of the Beast* (1915), and *In the Twinkling of an Eye* (1916)—perceived as "signs" of the Second Coming the host of social and environmental ills associated with industrialization and urban slums; these literary works concerned themselves as well with the so-called Jewish problem and saw Jewish people as moving the world closer to a one-world economy that would be especially inviting for the Antichrist.[10] With the publication of Hal Lindsey's *The Late Great Planet Earth* in 1970, the harbingers of end times included the post–World War II establishment of Israel and the nuclear face-off of the Cold War, with the Soviet Union representing the fertile soil within which evil would grow.[11] Finally, the Left Behind series iterates these earlier mappings within the context of a modern risk society, appealing to threats of terrorism and nuclear Armageddon and to nationalist suspicions of international organizations, trade and currency harmonization, and religious difference.[12] Indeed, nationalism and opposition to organized institutions, ranging from government agencies to the Catholic Church, run strong in Left Behind, as can be observed clearly in the books with the UN and the Vatican serving as strongholds for the reign of evil.

It may be tempting to dismiss those who follow the book series and adopt its brand of millennial prophecy as a fringe element in U.S. religious circles. This would be a mistake that seriously underestimates the sheer numbers and influence of followers. While it may be impossible and likely unproductive to separate out proponents of dispensational premillennialism from those who simply read the books as fiction, there has been a notable growth in the market for apocalypse literature, or the "dark side" of religious media, which is a cultural phenomenon worthy of investigation in its own right.[13] Similarly, the number and political power of evangelical Christians in the United States has been growing steadily, especially since the mid-1990s.[14] Susan Harding relates that "dispensationalism, broadly defined, is the way most Bible-believing Christians in America read current history and the daily news."[15] Moreover, the number of Americans identifying as evangelicals is estimated to be 27 percent of the population, which today would be roughly 81 million people, up from 14 percent in 1900.[16] Allowing for the fact that evangelicals are radically diverse, both in beliefs and practices, there has not been such a profound overlap between popular and Christian markets since the early twentieth century.[17] The widespread interest in Christian media can be explained in part by the large number of evangelicals, the increasing ambiguity of religious messages in Christian media, such as "Christian rock" music that does not explicitly mention Jesus, thereby affording increased crossover from sacred to secular markets,[18] and the mass distribution of Christian products made possible by new media technologies and large retail chains.

Not Leaving Capital Behind

The Left Behind book series is perhaps the most vibrant and visible incarnation of the apocalypse industry. Over 63 million copies of the books have been sold in at least thirty-seven countries and thirty-three languages, rivaling the sales of books by J. K. Rowling, Dan Brown, and John Grisham and repeatedly topping the bestseller lists of the *New York Times*, *USA Today*, Barnes & Noble, and Amazon.com.[19] The spin-off products from this sixteen-book series are manifold: two feature films, a companion children's book series, CDs, comic books, a Web site, devotionals, greeting cards, computer games, and more. The series has made the front cover of both *Time* and *Newsweek* magazines, and, in 2002, *Entertainment Weekly* added the authors, Tim LaHaye and Jerry Jenkins, to its list of "most powerful entertainers."[20] Finally, as a result of the book series and his other religious activities, LaHaye, who is a close colleague of televangelist Jerry Falwell, has been recognized as one of the most influential figures in the religious right movement.[21] LaHaye says that "[God] has chosen to bless the series beyond our wildest dreams."[22]

Fear, of course, sells well. A major part of why the Left Behind books sell so well may be because they represent the tensions and paranoia, the crises and instabilities, of our times.[23] As Crawford Gribben observes, "The content of these novels is marketably apocalyptic because their function is to emphasize the existing dichotomies between faith communities and contemporary life, as apocalyptic literature always has."[24] Moreover, the timing for the release of the Left Behind series could not have been more perfect. With the first book published in 1995, the series ramped up for the turning of the millennium, gaining popularity and momentum as it went, with a book published each year, and two published in 1999 alone, ringing in the new year as with the trumpet of Gabriel. By 2000, the series had sold a remarkable 20 million copies, but the flood of sales did not dissipate much after that year, and if anything the enterprise branched out to saturate new markets with apocalypse media, including a feature film in 2001 and a sequel in 2002, both costing roughly $17 million to produce and market.[25] After the attacks of 9/11, sales surged again, rising by 60 percent in the fall of 2001 alone as threats of terrorism amplified the public's anxiety about individual vulnerability, national preparedness, religious difference, and social order.[26] In Tim LaHaye's words, "The tragedy of 9/11 just made everything [about the Left Behind story] so much more real and believable."[27] By 2005, the series had made more than $650 million and had completely revitalized the Christian fiction market.[28]

Shifts in the operations and constitution of capital markets effectively mutate all sectors of production and consumption, and the market for religious fiction is no exception. It would be too facile to say that increases in sales or numbers of books published indicate a corresponding rise in evangelical belief or interest in religious fiction, although these are two likely conclusions. But, as Heather Hendershot observes, "Christian products have made it into the secular marketplace not only because their religious messages are ambiguous, diluted, or absent but also because they are increasingly distributed by huge, non-Christian companies."[29] Markets along with beliefs and desires are shaped by structural forces, which must include, for this inquiry, transformations in the publishing industry.

The number of Christian book titles has grown exponentially over the past fifteen years, with some estimates indicating an 84 percent increase just in the few years leading up to the turn of the millennium.[30] Tyndale House, which is the publisher of the Left Behind series, reaped the benefits of this trend with an annual sales increase of $135 million from 1998 to 2001.[31] The corresponding profits have enabled this Christian book publisher to hire more employees, expand its warehouse space, and release hundreds of new book titles per year. In the words of Kenneth Taylor, the Founder of Tyndale House, "The difficulty is to remember that the purpose of God's call to His publishers is to bring Him glory and not to make money."[32]

By capitalizing upon their expanded size and the popularity of the Left Behind series, Tyndale House has been able to tap markets previously closed to Christian publishers, allowing them to shift the distribution of their books from the majority being sold in traditional Christian bookstores to roughly 50 percent being sold in big-box stores, such as Barnes & Noble and Wal-Mart.[33] This movement occurred at the same time that the publishing industry was experiencing a series of mergers, leading to even larger bookseller conglomerates and the increased vulnerability of niche booksellers. Prior to being sold in big-box stores, Christian books were sold almost exclusively by Christian retailers, who are now threatened by the loss of market control caused by the mass distribution and popularization of rapture fiction. Reflecting back on sales in 2002, Steve Potratz, the founder of one Christian retailer, related,

"In my 30+ years in Christian retailing, I've never seen a tougher year than the one we just experienced. The competition for independent Christian retailers was brutal."[34] Feeling the threat to the Christian retail community and the discomfort of selling to secular stores without explicit religious missions, some Christian publishers have responded by selling only to Christian retailers or by selling only more expensive hardcover books to non-Christian stores.[35] Nonetheless, as with other small retailers throughout the United States and beyond, small Christian bookstores are increasingly being edged out by the big-box market.

Religious scholars and others have noted a corresponding growth in standardized, conservative content in religious fiction as an outcome of the articulation of Christian books with the big-box marketplace. The polarization of the sacred versus the secular, the saved versus the damned, apparently sells better than books delving into the heterogeneity of Christian and other religious beliefs. Censorship of titles engaging with complexity and difference, or of titles that are simply well-crafted works of literature, is one apparent result.[36] Some have argued that there is a larger movement to homogenize and commercialize religious belief systems,[37] so the conservative agenda in Christian publishing may be mirroring that trend. Thus, many religious books are never given a chance to compete in either the big-box or the traditional bookseller markets because religious publishers are catering to a conservative marketplace, if not a conservative readership. This being said, because of the diffuse nature of contemporary religious ideology, evangelical media draw diverse audiences, and the guilty pleasures associated with rapture fiction are undoubtedly supported by its presence in big-box retail settings.[38]

In the fiction, the mark of the beast operates as an extension of the capitalist economy—or, more accurately, the key to buying and selling. The marketplace is what true believers must eschew to ensure their salvation. In Left Behind, the Antichrist mobilizes detailed knowledge of consumer preferences to control his subjects and battle his enemies. He circulates customized products that match the particular desires of people, thereby offering them a consumerist version of heaven on Earth.[39] Despite their heterogeneous packaging, these products and media deliver the same homogeneous content of his greatness and the obligation for obedience. Ironically, then, the message for readers of these books is to be suspicious of consumer culture and to vigilantly guard against mind-control through products or information media, especially— it seems—if they appear to be tailored to your desires or beliefs.

Yet, in the nonfictional world of book sales, the authors are quite literally getting rich from their ventures and say that they find it difficult to remind themselves that their goal is to bring God glory, not to make money. The authors of Left Behind, along with Tyndale House and other publishers, readily exploit the mass marketplace to spread their words and increase their profits.

The apocalypse industry advances by fusing with current market logics and systems, norms and forms. The resulting dissonance between messages of consumerist critique and practices of millennial consumerism is left unresolved; it is one of the few acceptable ambiguities within this genre, whereby riches on Earth are both a serendipitous by-product of the larger evangelical enterprise and a validation of the dispensational interpretation of the books. From the vantage point of the late capitalist marketplace, of which this industry is a part, the prophecy must be accurate, or at least worth advancing with fervor, because the products are financially successful.

TECHNOLOGIES OF THE BEAST

Technology plays a crucial role in Left Behind's story and its ongoing contribution to Christian beliefs and fears about the rapture and tribulation. In the story, the most damning of all technologies is the system of surveillance referred to as the mark of the beast, which allows for the ready identification of those who follow the Antichrist. Whereas Revelation posits that the mark of the beast will be inscribed on the forehead or right hand, Left Behind, in this instance, adopts a figurative rather than literal understanding of these verses. The authors single out as the mark of the beast implantable "biochips," which are obviously based upon nonfictional human RFID implants developed by the company VeriChip.[40] In Left Behind, the biochips facilitate unique identification of individuals and the harmonization of databases for the regulation of all travel and participation in the (one-world) economy. According to *The Mark*, which is the eighth book in the series:

> The loyalty mark . . . embedded on a biochip inserted under the skin, will further identify the person to the point where every one shall be unique. . . . Those who neglect to get the mark when it is made available will not be allowed to buy or sell until such time as they receive it. Those who overtly refuse shall be put to death, and every marked citizen shall be deputized with the right and the responsibility to report such a one.[41]

Whereas the mark of the beast signifies voluntary, individual alignment with evil, it performs on multiple levels, many of which correspond with present-day information technology systems: speeding up economic transactions, ascribing trustworthy identifiers to individuals, accurately placing individuals in geographic spaces and limiting mobility outside assigned spaces, and revealing with remarkable accuracy the consumer preferences of individuals, which are data that can be harnessed to manipulate and control, or, in the books, to eliminate people.

The overlaps between advanced technological systems of surveillance in both fictional and nonfictional worlds cleverly help to reinforce the verisimilitude of the novels and lend validity to their interpretation of world events.

Once biblical prophecies are superimposed upon new technologies, the very existence of these technologies can serve as an omen of the events described in the books. Whether with electronic commerce, communication, civic participation, or population control, technology is increasingly regulating and foreclosing human activities, even as it is augmenting and enabling them.[42] Thus, one can observe the effects of "the mark" for regulating populations in current technological systems and public policies: it is ever more difficult to purchase goods without credit cards or bank accounts; it has become incredibly dangerous and in some instances impossible to cross borders without proper national identification, which is increasingly embedded with high-tech biometric identifiers and linked to vast databases; access to public services or resources is being restricted to those who can provide official identification documents verifying citizenship; and many government employees and volunteers (such as teachers and hospital workers) have been "deputized," or more accurately mandated, to report individuals such as illegal immigrants who try to avail themselves of public services without proper identification. Certain technologies of identification and tracking are effectively contaminated, spiritually and socially, by their disproportionate application to marginalized populations. In his discussion of surveillance and the mark of the beast, David Lyon elucidates this point: "Persons on welfare, asylum seekers and refugees, these and similar groups of relatively disadvantaged persons are the first recipients of biometric and DNA measures. It is thus hardly surprising that the stigmas of criminality or poverty are a source of anxiety when similar methods are proposed for bank machines and credit cards."[43] Because the readers of Left Behind books may be more conservative in their political orientation than others, these resonances between prophecy and the exclusion of marginalized members of the community may not cause concern about strangers, but they do cause concern about the salvation of oneself, one's family members, and one's friends.[44]

In support of unambiguous binaries between the saved and the damned, the series introduces an alternative "mark of Christ," which is a novel innovation absent from the book of Revelation. This luminescent mark appears on the foreheads of true believers and can be perceived only by other true believers. In cutthroat times of tribulation, treachery, and terrorism, the attractiveness of such a reliable sign of faithful allies is easy to understand, as are the convergences with nonfictional terrorist threats and religious conflicts. When archenemies can look, and act, and talk like true believers in the novels—or like mainstream Americans, as the case may be, in the nonfictional world—a trustworthy sign system, especially one that is illegible to community outsiders, becomes the most prized possession of the army of the faithful, which is given the militaristic appellation of "Tribulation Force."

The series, however, briefly calls into doubt the authenticity of signs, even the most sacred of ones, thereby refracting uncertainties of modern risk societies and postmodern cultural logics. One of the many characters with enviable computer skills, the teenage hacker named Chang, adopts *both* marks in order to infiltrate the Antichrist's palace and effectively operate as a spy. This renders him disturbingly ambiguous to his fellow Tribulation Force comrades because if the marks operate as absolute, indelible, and irreversible signs, how can one be both/and? In another instance, a spy named Ernie infiltrates Tribulation Force by applying a credible counterfeit mark of Christ upon his forehead. Only after his suspicious behavior calls his faith into question is the smudge rubbed off his head and his traitorous intent revealed. The series' brief flirtation with the deconstruction of static sign systems does not last long, however, but instead folds back into certitudes and clear moral distinctions, which seemingly become all the more stable because of the climate of insecurity within which they operate. As Glenn Shuck writes, "What makes *Left Behind* remarkable, however, is the juxtaposition of doubt and insecurity amid the familiar displays of moral certainty and spiritual chauvinism."[45] Instabilities of modern life and multiplicities of identity invite a reactionary, highly selective, and widely attractive mode of fundamentalism, typified by Left Behind, which clings tightly to clear marks and inflexible boundaries as well as to the desirability of ensuring their existence.[46]

Thus, contradictions occur in the books' messages about the role of technology in the battle between good and evil. The mark of the beast serves as a symbolic portent of future destruction but also as a physical embodiment of the global community—it is social control through technological means. The Tribulation Force resistance movement accordingly shuns centralized technological systems, whether of media consumption or bureaucratic management. Oddly enough, echoing popular discourse of the 1990s, the Internet is presented as a pure medium, somehow democratic in nature and free of the sordid taint of the unholy. Tribulation Force therefore sparks a grassroots resistance movement by harnessing this medium to disseminate inspirational texts and organize like-minded souls against the Antichrist. Crawford Gribben elaborates:

> When secure communication is possible only through the internet, [Tribulation Force member] Chloe begins her resistance to Antichrist's global hegemony by establishing an alternative economy, based on resistance to the "mark of the beast," by developing an international Co-op. . . . Building a worldwide business empire is a peculiarly American method of combating the tyranny and evil of Antichrist. Her Tribulation Force partner, Ben-Judah, likewise disseminates his prophetic teaching through "the most popular Web site in history."[47]

It should be no surprise, then, to discover that the Left Behind franchise strives for the same degree of popularity with its online presence. Its Web site lures viewers with its graphic portrayals of destruction, its highly specialized products (for example, for soldiers and children), its interactive interfaces (for example, to upload one's own testimonials, reviews, or prayer requests), and its range of media, including a PC game based on the series and daily devotional text messages sent to one's cell phone.[48] Because evangelicals have always adopted the latest media technologies to deliver their messages,[49] the authors of Left Behind should be viewed as continuing this tradition, even if the media and the messages have changed. With their explicit embracing of new media, it is not a far stretch to say that the authors fashion themselves as part of the modern-day Tribulation Force leadership, the following of which is vast, even if the threat is vague. Positioned as such leaders, the authors perceive themselves in a strangely supernatural light. Thus, in talking about the possibility of LaHaye and Jenkins being killed in a terrorist attack, Tim LaHaye says, "I believe we're immortal until our work is done and that Jerry [Jenkins] and I've got a lot more work to do."[50]

Whereas the novels posit centralized databases and high-tech systems of management and surveillance as the tools of the Antichrist, decentralized communication networks are presented as inherently enabling—both of profits and of profitable mobilization of resistance. From the books, one can discern the mark of the beast and its support structure in the technologies of the state or in bodies of international governance: with such systems, the UN automates a 0.1 percent tax on all transactions and controls populations with a supercomputer transparently named "the Beast."[51] Such antigovernment overtones resonate strongly with libertarian political sensibilities, encouraging readers to conclude that government bureaucracies and services, which claim to be for the public good, may actually facilitate domination of the world by the forces of evil. Rather than espouse an easy rejection of technology, however, Left Behind introduces implicit selection criteria for decentralized systems over centralized ones, for entrepreneurial programming over public programs. In this way, the books rationalize the systems of production, distribution, and consumption relied upon by the apocalypse industry.

SAVING ONESELF

Perceived as a form of ideology, the dispensational premillennialism espoused by Left Behind may promote a certain egoistical detachment on the part of evangelical Christians, or a theological buffer between them and the problems of the world. If the Second Coming is preordained and those who are "saved" will be raptured before the atrocities of tribulation occur, then the only immediate spiritual concern of Christians is with individual "true belief" for them and their families, not with ongoing wars, genocide, famine, arms proliferation, global warming, economic vulnerability of most of the world's population, and so on.[52] In fact, the rapture standpoint could be seen as encouraging materialism and discouraging progressive social intervention because, paradoxically, all that is needed for salvation is true belief, so those without basic necessities can save themselves without profound structural changes or the economic assistance of others.

Left Behind goes so far as to align those working for social justice with evil incarnate because, in the series, these are exactly the projects engaged upon by the Antichrist to gain public legitimacy and further his dominion. Writing about this problematic, religious scholar Glenn Shuck relates, "To unbelievers [the Antichrist] seems like a saint or even the Messiah. He works to correct economic inequalities, attempts to end poverty and cure dreaded diseases, and leads the world onto a path of total disarmament. Believers, however, see through his ruse."[53] Under the rhetorical cover of social justice and peace, the evil that is brought about by the Antichrist in the books includes the slaughter of one-third of the world's population by phantom horsemen, a devastating nuclear attack on the United States that kills almost everyone and destroys most infrastructure, and the effective—if unknowing— enslavement of those who accept the mark of the beast and succumb to the charisma of the Antichrist.

The fatalism of Left Behind extends as well to the mark of the beast. Those who have accepted the mark of the beast cannot be saved, even if they repent, so this obviates any efforts on the part of believers to save anyone who is already damned. Believers can therefore insulate themselves from others without any moral or spiritual compunction. Remarkably, this popularized form of dispensationalism functions not only to cast doubt and suspicion upon those working toward progressive social change, because these are the tools of the Antichrist, but also to upend bedrock practices of missionizing tradition-ally associated with evangelists.

Alternative interpretations of Revelation focus on *post*millennialism, mean-ing that Christ will not return until after one thousand years of peace have passed. By contrast, this may be a much more activist and liberal position that eschews the separatism of premillenialism by thrusting onto believers the responsibility for bringing about peace—there is no eschatological fast lane for easy escape. The difference between the beliefs of these camps explains, in part, newfound tensions between Catholics and evangelicals over the Left Behind story. Many Catholics, for instance, feel that these books dangerously spread fear by focusing disproportionately and too intently upon Revelation to the neglect of the "good deeds" message of the gospels.[54]

Apparent contradictions, therefore, arise with the traditional evangelical mission of converting nonbelievers and performing good deeds and the books' contemporary articulation of dispensationalism, which encourages and excuses self-interest, isolationism, and jingoism. In Left Behind, working toward sav-ing others or bringing about social justice are not necessary and might even distract believers from their steadfast focus on their own salvation and the salvation of their family, friends, or community. Schadenfreude modulates the apocalypse industry such that proponents take comfort in the salvation of believers and savor the eventual punishment of nonbelievers.

A related dissonance in the evangelical worldview occurs in the presentation of wars and human suffering. Rather than advocate for world peace, the sentiment of the apocalypse industry is that wars, especially those in the Middle East, are necessary preconditions for the Second Coming and should therefore be tolerated or supported.[55] This position manifests in the novels with clear expressions of anti-Semitism and frustration with Jews for not converting to Christianity, which is perceived as a necessary event for the return of Christ.[56] Beyond the novels, this particular exegesis may reinforce the staunch pro-Israel stance of many influential, "Christian right" evangelicals in the United States.[57] In light of these observations, one can conclude that the premillennialist doctrine is mutating mainstream evangelism into a form of Gnosticism:

> It is not repentance or brotherly love that is the defining attribute of Gnostic salvation but freedom—freedom from history, the cosmos, nature, as well as from morality itself. . . . The Gnostic valorization of freedom at the same time articulates an exceedingly vindictive denunciation of the physical world, a condemnation far harsher than any perspective found in Christian orthodoxy.[58]

The interpretation of Revelation propounded by Left Behind deviates starkly from historical Christian beliefs in postmillennialism and traditional practices of evangelism. However, as Max Weber famously observed, strong affinities exist among religious beliefs and economic systems, so one should expect mutations in belief systems alongside the emergence of new forms of capital.[59] The ideology of contemporary rapture fiction harmonizes with millennial capitalism. Rapture fiction performs a drama of extremism, consumerism, isolationism, and social polarization, thereby tolerating—and arguably helping to normalize—the structural conditions and social practices that are at the source of many insecurities today.

CONCLUSION

Left Behind embodies the tensions and complexities of our times, even though the dominant, intended meaning of its story is both straightforward and transparent. On the surface, it expresses an explicit critique of selfish, commodity-driven, or "immoral" behavior in the modern secular world. First, those possessing an insufficient degree of faith or who lived their lives for immediate pleasures instead of for future eternal rewards were punished by *not* being raptured and therefore forced to endure the trials of tribulation. Second, of those who remained on Earth, those who voluntarily aligned themselves with the Antichrist were similarly living for the present and demonstrating extreme hostile intolerance for believers. The story tells readers that these unbelievers, all of whom have taken the mark of the beast, will be punished in the worst possible way when Christ returns to destroy them in the bloody battle of Armageddon.

This didactic storyline betrays striking similarities to long-standing myths about the suffering that must befall those who make bargains with the devil. Cultural instantiations of this narrative device can be found in Michael Taussig's study of sugar plantation workers in Columbia and mine workers in Bolivia.[60] In these settings, the emergence of narratives and practices surrounding deals with the devil occurred in concert with the proletarianization of labor and with the particular economic and social insecurities that grew out of that process. When peasants strike secret bargains with the devil to increase production and wages in the short term, so the mythological explanation goes, those wages harbor a curse that brings bad luck upon the individual, such as barren lands, sterility, and a painful, untimely death. Similarly, Left Behind enacts its own parallel cultural structure whereby those who establish pacts with the devil, whether knowingly or not, eventually suffer the consequence of damnation for all eternity. An interesting and important difference between these two renditions is that lucrative, short-term financial gains are not indicative of a devil bargain with the characters in or authors of Left Behind. Instead, devil profits are presented as being secular in nature, accrued by people with questionable "moral values" through content or products devoid of spiritual purpose. Within this schema, conservative Christian values serve as a mark—visible only to believers—of holy capital accumulation.

Rather than attribute the immense popularity of the series simply to effective marketing, structural shifts in the bookselling industry, and moral panics, one should also attend to the resonances of the books' particular dispensational premillennialist message with contemporary insecurities. Taussig writes, "Magical beliefs are revelatory and fascinating not because they are ill-conceived instruments of utility but because they are poetic echoes of the cadences that guide the innermost course of the world."[61] From a functionalist perspective, all cultures—including today's security cultures—seek to integrate contradictions and dissonances, both in meaning and practice, into a coherent explanatory framework. By investigating those contradictions and dissonances, and theorizing their causes and effects, one may begin to piece together an explanation of the signification of myths such as those in Left Behind. The phenomenon of rapture fiction, in other words, should be taken seriously for the structural crises to which it may be responding and the hegemonic values and social relations it may be reifying and organizing.

The apocalypse industry is inflected by and dependent upon a particular market modality of corporate centralization, niche-market colonization, and mass distribution. The apocalypse industry similarly arises from a dominant conservative religious and political culture that feeds upon fears of instability that characterize the modern world and responds with a standardized message of clear dichotomous symbols—or marks—of good and evil.[62] Figuratively speaking, there are multiple "beasts" being marketed here. The first beast is the character of the Antichrist and his various technologies of identification and domination. The second beast is one of palpable fear of the apocalypse, dismissal of religious difference, and excited anticipation of the imminent suffering of non-Christians. The final beast is that of a millennial capitalist worldview of neoliberal policies, globalized economies, and individual responsibility. The avid consumption of these beasts by readers of these books and by others may indicate something about the desirability of spiritual stability, even at the expense of others, as compensation for pressing social, political, and material insecurities marking societies today.

It is between the messages of rapture media and the mode and context of their transmission that interesting dissonances occur. In Left Behind, the world economy may serve the interests of evil, but the apocalypse industry is thoroughly integrated with the capitalist economy. Media and networking technologies may be the tools of the Antichrist, but they are also the tools of the authors and the novels' heroes. The intent of the authors and of evangelists more generally may be to save souls, but the message of the books is to insulate oneself against nonbelievers and eschew social justice because the damned cannot be saved and the end is near. The result may be a dangerous rationalization of social inequalities that elevates the logics of the neoliberal economy to the level of the sacred.

PART TWO

Surveillance Infrastructures

CHAPTER 6

Residential Fortification

THE QUEST FOR SECURITY ORGANIZES modern life. In a world perceived as increasingly unstable and insecure, the hyper-regulation of boundaries and borders has become a dominant response. Boundary regulation in urban and suburban settings may be seen most clearly with the rise of forti- fied enclaves, such as gated communities, but little attention has been paid to the ways in which technological surveillance contributes to spatial exclusion by means of its integration into urban space and its enforcement of social norms. This chapter illustrates how surveillance technologies and their related discourses communicate a sense of social stability that fails to match the lived experiences of people in both public housing and gated communities. As with gates and walls, electronic surveillance may operate as a less visible but similarly political fortification of urban space. Surveillance can simultaneously demar- cate and police residents as well as outsiders, all the while presenting durable barriers to social inclusion for marginalized groups within cities.

As discussed in chapter 4 on identity theft, responsibility for security is being distributed to individual citizens, or insecurity subjects, to ensure their own safety through consumption. On the level of the home front, this com- pels many home owners to purchase elaborate alarm systems, surveillance cameras, and private security services.[1] Others elect to move into private gated communities where these services come as standard fare, in addition to guarded entry points and high walls, of course. While people who cannot afford or choose not to consume such security products may be thought of as being "on their own," others who depend upon state assistance, such as people living in public housing, are treated as if they are suspect to begin with and in need of paternalistic supervision. Nonetheless, few people living in these settings question these neoliberal trends, and most people seemingly believe in the benefits of privatization and security interventions, even if they do not personally taste the promised fruit of these changes.

This chapter argues that remarkable similarities exist between the experi- ences of residents in low-income public housing and gated communities. Contrary to the popular discourse of surveillance as ensuring protection from external threats, in practice both groups feel subjected to undesired individual scrutiny and policing of their behaviors. One key difference lies in the relative mobility and minimal personal risk of gated community residents compared to those in public housing. For many living in public housing, this is not a "choice" but a necessity. A second difference lies in the underlying logics behind surveillance in these communities: toward the enforcement of disciplinary state laws in public housing (for example, targeting residents who are attempting to "cheat the system" in some way) and toward the enforcement of conformity in appearance and behavior in gated communities. These differences are important because they underline the fact that while security regimes may be proliferating throughout society, the burdens of surveillance are not distributed equally.

FORTIFIED SPACES

The literature on fortified enclaves highlights the ways that built forms and social norms function politically to enforce sociospatial segregation and to send clear symbolic messages about who does and does not belong.[2] While design deterrents to social integration may take the form of gated communities or enclosed malls and office buildings, they can also manifest in the more direct, if less visible, forms of benches that cannot be slept upon, sprinkler systems that keep people away from buildings or parks, or inadequate public transportation systems.[3] The naturalization of urban and suburban designs may simultaneously serve to maintain certain social orders and exclusions while reducing public awareness of social problems.

Fortified enclaves may be interpreted as reactions to the unsettling of social boundaries—whether through demographic shifts, the development of political democracy, or other factors.[4] The privatization of public space allows "new urban morphologies of fear" to acquire durable, material forms that threaten to attenuate democracy and delegitimate public institutions.[5] Although many gated community residents are concerned about security, people also base their decisions on a range of other factors, such as property values, convenience, or the lack of nongated alternatives.[6] This last point is especially salient in cities like Phoenix, where gated communities account for one-third of all new residential construction. Even so, researchers have found that patterns of segregation, attenuated social life, and diminished property rights are enforced by such trends toward privatized gated living.[7]

Many public housing complexes can also be thought of as modern fortified enclaves. Under the rubric of "defensible space," architects and planners have designed such spaces with the goal of deterring crime.[8] The key tenets of defensible space are (1) encouraging territoriality through the use of material and symbolic barriers, and thus catalyzing a sense of ownership by residents, (2) providing clear lines of sight for optimal individual surveillance, (3) creating aesthetically pleasing "images" to symbolically dispel any stigma associated with high-rise or other housing, and (4) situating housing for optimal geographical juxtaposition with areas considered safe.[9]

Since the introduction of the defensible space concept in the early 1970s, there has been significant—and ongoing—controversy about the empirical validity of the findings concerning crime reduction.[10] Beyond these debates over efficacy, some have offered counterevidence suggesting that one should not presume that crime is external to public housing in the first place or that residents will trust police officers, when they might have ample historical reasons not to trust them.[11] Still, planners and urban studies scholars continue to mobilize the defensible space concept, and housing and urban development (HUD) planners have intentionally designed spaces with these tenets in mind, thus obviating any perceived need for electronic surveillance systems in many locations.[12]

Greater residential fortification and social and economic segregation are also coincident with recent developments in security cultures and pressures for people to become insecurity subjects. Rather than being the simple outgrowth of individual fears and demands, fortification and other security efforts become articulations of the simultaneous retreat from the welfare state and growth in the state's policing and security functions. Seen from this perspective, alterations in spatial relations tie back in to broader political economies, state policies, and cultural beliefs; these changes may be grounded in and mediated by local contexts, but they signal shifts in cultural logics and institutional structures that extend beyond any individual city or community under study.

TECHNOLOGY AND SPACE

The integration of information technology (IT) into urban spaces operates within this neoliberal milieu. Modern urban telecommunications networks act to enforce the uneven distribution of goods and services, as do other infrastructures, leading to what Stephen Graham and Simon Marvin have called "splintering urbanism."[13] Under this planning paradigm, those with financial resources obtain privileged access to transportation systems, utilities, communications networks, and secure living spaces. Meanwhile, "public" infrastructures are increasingly restricted, privatized, or dismantled, such that individuals without sufficient resources are cut off from basic necessities and placed at increased risk. The result is a state of social polarization and fragmentation, whereby the affluent become disconnected from place and insulated from the plight of those outside their networks.[14] This represents a form of social sorting, whereby material and technological infrastructures divide populations by social address, meaning in this instance primarily by class and secondarily by ethnicity.

Urban information technologies do not simply regulate access to services or spaces, however; they also facilitate monitoring and control of the public through enhanced data collection. Technological surveillance systems range from the relatively obvious closed circuit television (CCTV) systems to the almost completely undetectable: global positioning systems in mobile phones; radio-frequency identification (RFID) tags embedded in smart cards used to access buildings, garages, or pass through toll stations; chemical agent detectors in public places; and so on. When technological surveillance is incorporated into spaces and infrastructures, it increases the amount of data available both for social control functions and capital accumulation imperatives, as can be seen by police profiling and public/private sector data sharing, respectively.[15]

As with spatial designs, technologies function politically to produce, mediate, and normalize social relations.[16] Architectural designs are intended to "program" spaces for certain uses, and even if the designs fail, which they invariably do to some degree, the spaces are no less programmed because of the designers' inability to predict their effects upon bodies, movements, or interactions. The same holds true for technologies. A useful concept here is that of *underdetermination*. In the field of the philosophy of technology, this concept means "that technical principals alone are insufficient to determine the design [or success] of actual devices."[17] I employ underdetermination slightly differently to acknowledge that technologies do determine social relations, identities, and possibilities to an extent, but that users and social contexts also give meaning and values to the technologies. Put simply, social context matters. To the degree that technologies are underdetermined, they acquire dominant meanings and restrict alternative ones through social practices, rituals, and myths,[18] which is why it is especially important to attend to the meanings that people ascribe to technological systems, such as surveillance, through discourse and practice. This is one path toward understanding the politics of such systems, their larger signification, and their potential for alteration.

Working from this theoretical backdrop, the remainder of this chapter focuses on residents' experiences of surveillance and security systems in low-income public housing and gated communities. The interview data presented here grew out of research that took place in Phoenix, Arizona.[19] Phoenix is the fifth largest city in the United States, is home to heightened class and ethnic polarization, and is proximate to the U.S.–Mexico border, so surveillance and security issues are a clearly identifiable part of the social imaginary in this particular region. As I will show, although residential surveillance may function as a form of electronic fortification that operates upon logics of suspicion and exclusion, it may also have surprisingly similar effects upon the experiences of the poor and the affluent.

"NOTHING TO HIDE" IN PUBLIC HOUSING

Questions about security and surveillance in public housing—as elsewhere—invariably invoke the response that if you are not doing anything wrong you have nothing to hide. Those who do have something to hide, the discourse continues, are almost exclusively "outsiders" looking to commit crimes or otherwise cause trouble in communities. In public housing, one thing follows rapidly in the wake of claims of nothing to hide: detailed stories of invasive, unwarranted monitoring of residents themselves. The holistic evaluation residents give of surveillance, once the platitudes are dispensed with, is that it is ineffective at preventing crime and ensuring safety and that it facilitates unjust particularism by those doing the monitoring.

As I ARRIVE TO INTERVIEW the property manager of the public housing site, she spies me at the glass door. As I fumble with the intercom system, she opens the door for me via a remote control. Her office is situated immediately inside the main entrance to the building, where through the slats of her lowered Venetian blinds she can keep an eye on people coming and going, without herself being all that visible. Upon entering her office, the door to which is also kept locked and is opened via a separate remote control, I see video monitors displaying surveillance feeds from throughout the building and its grounds, including the front door that I just walked through.

The surveillance system at this site consists of approximately half a dozen video cameras trained on hallways and points of entry and egress and a key card system for regulating and remotely tracking building and parking lot entry. At least one of the video cameras has pan–tilt–zoom functionality for following individual movements through hallways. All the cameras are hardwired (as opposed to wireless), and the video feeds are piped into the property manager's office, where they are saved in analog format on VHS videotapes. Unless there is a specific incident worthy of investigation, the tapes are kept for one week before being reused; periodically, the old tapes are replaced with new ones as a way to combat the unavoidable degradation of analog video quality. The key card system, by contrast, is digital, and all data are stored indefinitely on the hard drive of the property manager's computer. These data allow for automated tracking of residents, who are each issued personal cards programmed with unique identification numbers. The data generated by this system include information on who entered the building or parking lot, what time they entered, and how long the door was left open. The property manager, or others, can then run queries on the data to search for "suspicious" activities, such as someone returning every night around 3:30 in the morning. The analog video surveillance and digital key card systems are not synchronized, making it nearly impossible to link what is visible on the tapes with what is readable on the computer screen.

The property manager tells me that the surveillance systems are intended, foremost, to protect residents from external threats. Surveillance is explicitly part of the defensible-space design of the building, which qualifies for classification as a "Phoenix Crime Free Multi-Housing Program" site by demonstrating its compliance with such design criteria as keeping shrubs trimmed below the level of the windows and posting warning signs to potential criminals. The outsiders that the system aims to deter are characterized by the manager as "riffraff" or simply "bad guys" who want to engage in theft, drug use, or prostitution. It is her hope that the surveillance will "push some of the riffraff and stuff a little further beyond our boundaries to kind of safeguard our residents."

Residents echo the property manager's sentiment of surveillance acting as protection from external threats, at least initially, by describing crimes that they have experienced or have heard of. One woman in her early forties related:

> Oh yeah, my car was stolen February last year. I got it back, thank God. But, God, I've had to put oodles and oodles of money into it to get it right. [The video footage showed] that they jumped the fence, broke the box. The one [person] stayed there at the fence, you know, to make sure the gate stayed open, jimmied open. And they had my car out in eighty seconds.

Another woman described how burglars climb up the side of the building, like Spiderman, to steal from the residents' apartments:

> Several years ago, my sons were staying with me, one was a caregiver, and one was just staying for a while. And he went down and they bought brand-new bikes, $400 each. And we got permission to put them on the patio and keep them locked up there, because they weren't gonna be leaving. And we were sitting there watching TV one night and lo and behold my son went outside to smoke, because I won't allow it my apartment, I'm asthmatic. And he come back and "Mom, somebody stole my bike! They came right up on the second floor!" . . . When I first moved in, the lady who was the manager then, she said, "You might want to close your window." "No," I said, "because you have to be pretty much like Superman to be able to come up to burglarize me." She said, "Oh." No. "Spiderman," I said, "you have to be like Spiderman in order to get up there to do any harm." No, you don't. You know what, one of our ladies, Miss [X], lived up on the third floor and they came up, clear up the third floor from the outside and she was in bed. She wasn't asleep. But she was, it scared her, she kept her patio door open like I do, dumb, dumb, but I do. And they came right in her patio door, and they robbed her, they took, they looked in her drawers, and I mean they got some jewelry, they got her money that she had in there, and they took her TV and her stereo. And they walked right out the front doorway.

As one man assessed the purpose of surveillance: "I think the problem is just wanting to keep people out. It's gotta be, because you never hear anything about problems getting out, it's always [problems getting] in."

Although the surveillance system is designed to protect against such intrusions, and residents are periodically informed about security measures that are being taken, residents ultimately place little trust in the deterrence capabilities of surveillance. For instance, when I asked one resident what she thought of the surveillance cameras, she responded, "I think they just got 'em up there for show. To tell you the God's truth, and I think, I'm imagining probably, that they don't even [monitor] them, and sometimes maybe even forget to turn the suckers on." When I followed up by asking about the potential of cameras to deter crime, she asserted, "Don't do no damn good because yeah, it takes a picture of them, and, if no one's monitoring it, you don't know till the next flippin' ass day anyways." Answers of this sort show that residents are acutely aware of the limitations of surveillance systems for providing the kind of security that would be meaningful in their lives. This does not mean, however, that residents are critical of the technologies themselves or of the technologies' ability to facilitate intrusive monitoring of their activities.

Whenever I ventured to ask a question about residents' feelings about being observed, they would reply in a somewhat conflicted way. First, the popular discourse about wrongdoing came quickly to their lips: "I ain't got nothing to hide" or "If I was doing something wrong I would [feel uncomfortable]." The property manager similarly resorted to this formulation:

> Early on there were [complaints about the surveillance system]. I know when I first got here, you know, it's like we're in a prison, [but] clearly if you're not doing anything wrong, what are you worried about? It's only people that are up to something that should be concerned about it. Everybody else should feel better knowing that there's some safeguard measures taken. . . . Every so often somebody will say something, but I find usually they're the ones that I have to be watching anyhow.

This is a remarkable statement: that critics of surveillance are more likely than others to engage in criminal or otherwise unsavory activities and that complaining about surveillance *does* nominate residents to be an increased target of it. This position also highlights the conflict that residents express in their secondary responses to the question of being observed. While surveillance systems are not bad in and of themselves, they say, the secondary examples they provide suggest that surveillance becomes one more element of individualized monitoring and social control in their everyday lives.

When I asked one man about whom he thought the surveillance systems were trying to monitor, he launched into a detailed personal narrative about his very real fears of individualized scrutiny (I quote it here in length to convey the sense of emotional insecurity that such "security" practices can instill in residents):

> Oh, oh, [they're trying to keep out] all kinds of people, who knows, you know? I mean, they even told me today, see, a friend of mine, well see I don't have friends anymore, I just got a couple of acquaintances, and this one guy I know from Value Options [a local discount store], who you know, I've known him for a long time, just about every time I go down there, he's there, and we have the same, you know, psychiatrist and stuff and he asked me the other day, he says, you know, "I'm in a bind. I didn't get my check," he says. "You think I could stay at your place tonight?" And I says, "Well, I tell you what, I'll let you stay at my place tonight, but all you're gonna do is, you're just gonna sleep there, and then in the morning you're gonna have to leave." And the manager [saw him with the surveillance system and] got on me about that this morning. I mean she says, "If I see that guy around again," she goes, "I'm gonna call the cops and you're going [to be thrown out] too." Now I don't see how she could tell me that. See, I get paranoid a lot, and I've been thinking about that all damn day now! That I'm gonna get kicked out if the guy comes back! I mean, he's gonna come back, he's gotta pick up his jacket, and you know!

Do you think she was [just] trying to scare you or intimidate you?
I don't know what her trip is with me, it just, she don't like me for some reason, I don't know why, I'm always being, you know, as nice as I can to her and everything, and still she's got something against me, I don't know what, because I haven't done nothing to her, but she's, you know. . . . Once I walk in the door here, I feel safe. I feel very safe. But then, especially if [the property manager's] on, on shift, I kinda shake in my boots until I get past her office and up the stairs.

Why do you have that reaction?
Like I said, she's threatened me: "I'm gonna call the cops on him and I'm gonna have you thrown out!" I said, "What did I do?"

So have you been shaking in your boots before today?
Every time we have a dispute or something, she scares me. I lived on the streets for two years, and I'll tell you what, I'd kill myself before [living on the streets again]. I'm Christian, and you know, if I ever did it, I would pray to God for about five minutes and tell him why and everything, but I will never live on the streets again. I won't do it.

If she didn't mean it, do you think it was fair [of her] to say that?
She meant it, she like, I don't know, it seems like she likes to do it, I don't know. I don't know what her social life is like, but it must be pretty

shitty, you know, to come into an office where you gotta a little bit of power and then flaunt it over people who are disabled and shit.

Rather than this being an isolated sentiment about surveillance of residents, other interviewees arrived at similar conclusions. One woman said, "It seems to me, they're more concerned of what we're up to, than [with] people coming from the outside in. That's just what it seems like to me. But they're always wanting you to tell on everyone else when you see something suspicious." Finally, the property manager herself confessed to actively spying on residents—using electronic surveillance and other means—to root out the "bad" ones in order to protect the "good" ones:

> For a while there, I had a couple individuals I was trying to evict, and I was using [surveillance] as a means of tracking, dating and all that stuff, and activity of people coming and going, and coming and going. . . . Even out on a criminal way of looking at things, but sometimes fraud, you know, "Oh no, my boyfriend's not living with me." "Well he comes in every day; he leaves every day; he has his own key." "No, no, no, he's not living [here]." So you can put the, you know, the monitor and see every day when he's coming in, say well, if someone's coming in seven days out of seven days, week after week, for all intents and purposes, they're living here, so it [surveillance] has other things that we can document as well.

> *And if someone's living here illegally, do you call in the police?*
> Well, if we have an unauthorized person, you know that's one of the hardest things to prove. Yeah, he has a couple shirts here, but every so often stays the night. Again we'll try tracking their history as far as usage of the card, to see if you know it's being randomly used quickly, boom, boom, boom, if there's some kind of history there. We can say okay, we have reason to believe, I'm coming in to do an inspection. Now I can open up closet doors, I can open up anything that's [owned by the] City. But as far as their dresser drawers, under their bed, things like that I'm not allowed to touch. I'm not allowed to touch their items. I'll open up the vanity mirror and see if there's a men's shaving kit or whatever in there and I'll document those items. I can also ask.

> *It sounds uncomfortable.*
> Pardon?

> *It sounds uncomfortable anyway to—*
> Well it is, it's really, really hard to prove [that someone is living there who should not be].

The property manager's description of her practices confirms that residents' concerns of being scrutinized are not without merit. Tellingly, she simply could not hear my question about being uncomfortable looking through other people's belongings—for her it was an issue of practical difficulty, not ethical ambiguity.

Thus, the "community" climate that technological surveillance is being inserted into in public housing is one already characterized by suspicion. The surveillance system then facilitates and amplifies these internal monitoring practices. Rather than being neutral, the system coproduces unequal power relations by design. Surveillance technologies may possess a valence for constructing subjects who are seen as suspect and therefore worthy of monitoring and control. Beyond this, the invasive uses of surveillance in public housing can be explained further by the underdetermination of the technologies. When surveillance systems are implemented in contexts marked by suspicion and inequality, the systems reproduce those identities and relations. The combinatory effect is one of marginalizing surveillance. The behavior, associations, and possessions of public housing residents are under the microscope (unlike people in most other places of dwelling), and they know it and adapt accordingly. Resistance undoubtedly takes place, such as residents lending out their secure-entry cards to nonresidents, but this does little to alter the marginal identity affixed to them by "the system" and its agents.

The main discursive themes covered in this section were those of surveillance being for external threats, residents having nothing to hide, and residents being exposed to heightened degrees of internal scrutiny. This is not to say that monitoring of residents is necessarily without just cause. Internal crimes exist; many residents told me about drugs and prostitutes being brought into the complex. Nonetheless, these surveillance practices do show that the rhetoric of surveillance shielding residents from external threats is a misleading oversimplification, because the threats are not only external and because insiders are being watched and policed far more than outsiders by housing authority personnel.

"SOMEWHAT PROTECTED, SOMEWHAT VIOLATED" IN GATED COMMUNITIES

As with the examples of surveillance experienced in public housing, a similar tension exists between what residents say are the intended functions and the actual uses of surveillance systems in gated communities. The first discursive move of residents is to explain the surveillance as providing protection from external threats, often with no direct experiences of criminal activity in the neighborhoods. (Although the focus here is on the experiences and perceptions of residents rather than on official crime rates, reported crimes in these communities are quite low, relatively speaking, for the Phoenix metro area.[20]) These phantom threats are perceived as being introduced, more often than not, by the many Latino workers maintaining the grounds, engaging in home repair, or building new houses. Soon after providing this rationale for surveillance, however, residents volunteer a series of complaints about being scrutinized, hassled, or made to feel uncomfortable by the security personnel operating the systems or by the systems themselves. Unlike residents in public housing, though, those in gated communities perceive security personnel as their disgruntled employees, who—it should be noted—could not afford to live in the same communities that they serve. Residents rationalize putting up with feelings of intrusion as part of a conscious trade-off, in exchange for feeling that they and their property are safe and secure.

In this section, quotes from interviewees are used to demonstrate how technological surveillance becomes just one more mechanism, along with homeowners' association (HOA) rules and regulations, for ensuring social conformity. Whether through video cameras, key card tracking, or computerized databases of vehicle license plates and house addresses, technological surveillance intensifies existing practices of social surveillance, even to the extent of serving as a deterrent to active community engagement, including walking around one's neighborhood.

The security systems at the two gated communities studied range from nominal to extreme. The smaller site has two guard-gate entrances, with small guard stations of about ten square feet. Only one person is in each station at a time, and they are staffed only from 6 A.M. to 10 P.M. Residents enter either by means of a clicker or by manually punching a code on a number pad. While it is policy that guests be screened by guards, guests will often simply "tailgate" a resident's car into the community—entering before the guard gate descends; this is a practice ignored by the security personnel. There are surveillance cameras at these gates, as well as next to gates leading into an adjacent community.[21] The larger gated-community site, by contrast, offers four gates, two large guard stations that are staffed by four to five guards at all times, key card entry, guards patrolling on bikes, and roaming checkups by the HOA to ensure compliance with community rules and regulations. This second community takes security seriously, so there is no possibility for entrance without gaining clearance from a guard or being in possession of a community member's key card.

At the first gated community, several instances of property theft motivated the installation of video cameras at the gates to deter future thefts. One resident explains:

> I believe they were installed because—so first of all, my phase of my community, phase two, elected to not have guards on duty from 10 P.M. to 6 A.M., and I believe shortly thereafter there began to be some thefts in people's backyards of . . . pool equipment, backyard stuff, where people were either accessing the property, tailgating through the gates, or they're

coming off the golf course . . . it was expensive pool equipment, like, not a net, but someone's jumping over the fence, taking filters or hardware.

One security guard in the community added that an incident of theft at the internally located country club inn, where guests can stay when visiting the golf course, for instance, was the primary catalyst for the purchase of surveillance cameras. The second gated community, by contrast, had cameras installed as part of the initial development plan, and residents had no knowledge of any thefts in the four years since the community was opened.

The perceived threats to property or human safety in these gated communities are from individuals who are "external" to the community but nonetheless have regular access to it—namely, Latino workers. When asked about the effectiveness of surveillance, one resident responded:

> Well, I think surveillance could be effective in determining potential crime candidates. . . . To maintain the whole community and the golf courses, and you know. I mean, you know those people, can't, I'm sure, you know, they're minimum wage, or close to minimum wage people that you know, I'm certainly sure they [the guards] can't screen them to the extent [necessary], so they don't know who they exactly hire all the time. So I'd say it's not necessarily residents that they're targeting [with surveillance], but outsiders. Whether it be employees that are working the grounds, like I said, or people that are just coming in contracting [doing construction work].

In this passage, the interviewee reveals that he sees manual laborers as marked in advance as "crime candidates" by means of their status as minimum-wage earners and that one alternative response to surveillance might be to "screen" the workers more extensively in advance. The prospect of correcting vast income disparity or of paying workers more is not on the table as a solution to the potential risk to property that these workers pose. Instead, surveillance is conceived of as a more viable response.

Another resident, although obviously uncomfortable with the question of whom the surveillance systems are intended for, responds in an unusually forthright fashion:

> I think probably [surveillance is for] working-class individuals and predators, whether it would be of a sexual nature or a criminal nature. . . . Yeah, I think, just in general, just based on the location, and our geography, I think that there's probably a general stereotype of what we would consider criminal, predators. . . . I would probably say Hispanic.

What is revealed in this type of response is a disturbing stereotype of workers that is indicative of an uneasiness toward those from other class or ethnic backgrounds but also of the general hostility in the region toward anyone who might be an undocumented worker. The surprising grouping of Latino workers with "sexual predators" demonstrates not only the extent of the stigma attached to such workers, but also, perhaps more importantly, the irrational level of fear engendered by the unknown Other.

When the questions turn to interactions that residents have with security personnel, the narrative of external threats quickly subsides into a series of gripes about living under surveillance. Most of these complaints stem from a general climate of surveillance that includes monitoring by neighbors, HOAs, and security personnel to ensure adherence to community rules and regulations.

Technological surveillance, rather than signaling a radical change in living experiences, becomes one more mechanism contributing to this general culture of social control. As with the data from public housing, the point of discussing technological surveillance alongside other forms of social regulation is to draw attention to how social context and practices influence the use of surveillance systems and infuse them with meaning at the same time that the systems introduce subtle alterations in and intensifications of existing cultures of control. Surveillance technologies become part of the social fabric, so it would be misleading and empirically inaccurate to present them as external tools applied to discrete social problems.

There are many cases where surveillance-facilitated social regulation can occur. One resident describes breaking community rules by letting a contractor in on a Sunday (which apparently is an official day of rest in the neighborhood) and the shock of being traced back to his house by means of his license plate number:

> I had a contractor try to come through on a Sunday and didn't know exactly all the rules, and apparently they stopped him and would not allow him to come in, even though I was there in person . . . they did not follow us [when we drove on by], but then later on they showed up at the house, so it's kind of like they do know who you are.

Others describe receiving citations for not conforming to HOA rules for acceptable yard vegetation:

> We knew that there was potentially a rule that there wasn't a certain plant allowed . . . a palm of any sort, whether it [be] low growing or tall growing. And I kinda [said] "Huh?" . . . So I, we, decided that being in the backyard, it's a low-growing one, we have, we don't have an open fence to the golf course or anything, so, it wouldn't be that big of a deal, we even considered putting them in pots, and regardless, we didn't even plant the thing in a pot or in the ground yet, and the landscapers left the gate open and there was a picture taken of the palm sitting on the side

yard, and we were notified that we were in violation and it needed to be corrected.

Other rules prohibit parking on the street:

> [You are] less likely to leave your cars out, you know. It's a rule not to leave your car out on the street, you know. [In] communities that have other associations, you'll still see people parking in the street, because they're not being looked at, they're not being surveilled, you know, surveillanced.

On one level, these cases are simple inconveniences that homeowners must put up with in exchange for living in these privatized communities. Still, adapting one's life to such strict rules and being actively corrected if one does not self-police creates a living experience in tension with American ideals of property ownership and individual expression. As one resident put it, being under surveillance makes him feel "somewhat protected, somewhat violated. Protected from a sense of there's roaming security, there's drive-by security, violated in terms of CC&R [Covenants, Conditions and Restrictions] violations." This is an interesting conflation of the two meanings of violation: of experiencing some kind of personal trespass, on one hand, and of being cited and fined for breaking community rules, on the other. One can interpret this to mean that the condition of living under such strict rules and of having others tell you how to live is experienced as a form of personal violation, especially when these residents are paying so much for the privilege of living in these communities.

Some residents communicated an embodied sense of self-regulation, or what Michel Foucault would call disciplinary power,[22] so that—in this case—the trend toward privatized public space serves to eliminate the concept of "the public" in the social imaginary too. In one telling example, a resident confessed that he refrains from walking around adjacent communities because he feels too observed and worried about being confronted by security personnel:

> I wanted to go walk around the homes under construction, and I got the feeling there that there was a camera on every corner. . . . It made me feel a little uncomfortable . . . it made me think twice because I know they're all centrally monitored and I didn't want to deal with the hassle of someone saying, you know, technically he's trespassing, if that's the issue. So I did not choose to go walk by any of the houses.

This person's concern about walking around the neighborhood is tied to clearly demarcated, yet artificial, boundaries placed between communities. As he expands upon this theme, he says that it leads to a great sense of isolation in his home life, because he lives alone and does not know any of his neighbors.

Surveillance, then, is not necessarily about directed social control; rather, it is about the production of governmentalities (the conduct of conduct) that alter the field for social thought and action.[23]

Finally, when gated community residents begin to discuss surveillance throughout everyday life, not just in their communities, they will say that they have "nothing to hide" but will confess that they are bothered by the conformity that surveillance practices enforce. In the following passage, a young woman introduces some interesting dissonances in her position on what it means to be aware of surveillance cameras:

> Well, I know that if I go into a bank that I'm being watched. I know that there's cameras. I mean you can see them, they're obvious. I think that in some instances people are unaware that they're being watched in a grocery store or a department store. A lot of people don't pay attention to that kind of stuff. I just happen to notice them when I go in, because, you know, you see them. But had I not, if I go through life with blinders on, then yeah, you would never notice that there were cameras there. I think that people who really have nothing to hide . . . they really are unaware of where the cameras are, because it's not a big deal to them.

One tension here is that cameras are "obvious" and impossible to miss, yet many people have "blinders on" and are "unaware" of them. At the same time, the woman concludes by saying that if people have nothing to hide, then they will probably be unaware of surveillance, implying that because she *does* notices cameras then she *might* have something to hide. Judging from her tone of voice in the interview, she definitely did not mean to say that she deserved additional scrutiny. If anything, she felt critical of others who were not as aware as she was. Regardless, she fell back upon the popular, ready-made discourse of surveillance being worrisome only for those with something to hide.

Other conflicts can be seen in articulations of concern over the social dangers of conformity brought about by increased surveillance in the world beyond the gates of the community. As one woman said:

> You pretty much force people into boxes. I think that if you want to create robots, that's exactly what you will do. If you have cameras all over, you will create robots, you know, do this, do that, you know whatever. . . . I think it's inappropriate when it creates an atmosphere where you feel like you're boxed in, into something. I think that if you continue to box people in, I think that eventually what happens is people rebel, and revolt, and I think that's, that's when you have more harm than good, that it's inappropriate to have that.

There are also nuanced status performances inflecting surveillance practices in these gated communities. Seemingly, one of the things that bothers residents the most is that security personnel do not treat them with the degree of respect that they feel like they deserve:

> I don't really know what [training] those guards have. I mean a majority of the time if I ever run into them, I'm not impressed by them personally. . . . I've had a run-in or two with a couple of them just because of their lack of, I guess, of respect . . . Or you know, I didn't have the right tags yet on my car or whatever, and it's like I don't really wanna bother with that, of course, because I know I'm a homeowner, and so as I enter, I just expect them to some degree, to just . . . work with me . . . it's kind of like they take it a little bit [to an] extreme.

Gate guards, on the other hand, see a lack of respect on the part of some residents who are "always complaining" about the money that they are spending in HOA fees for security or about the guards not being diligent enough at screening people out.

When it comes down to it, though, residents willingly adopt the position of insecurity subjects and submit to the additional scrutiny, inconvenience, and conformity in order to gain "peace of mind," especially when they are out of town, which many homeowners are for the summer months when temperatures can exceed 120 degrees Fahrenheit (or 49 degrees Celsius). One resident put the trade-off into perspective by saying, without any hint of irony, that the community was "like the family living place where you know you could be free." He meant by this that the community embodied the ideals and values of "traditional" American neighborhoods, where one need not worry about crime. Technological surveillance is just one more component in the social surveillance apparatus of gated communities, designed to safeguard a restricted form of "freedom" that seems to mean freedom not only from exposure to people from other classes, ethnic groups, or cultural backgrounds, but also freedom from the responsibility of outwardly demonstrating signs of individual difference from one's neighbors.

This section has identified two dominant discursive themes. The first stressed the use of surveillance to protect community members from outsiders, and the second conveyed a sense of heightened demand for conformity by residents in the communities. That residents of gated communities hold both those things to be true, unlike those in public housing who ultimately place little faith in the protective functions of surveillance, could indicate a need on their part to construct a rational "trade-off" to justify living in their highly scripted environments. In gated communities, surveillance may act as another form of fortification that insulates community members from outsiders and possibly increases fear of unknown others, but it also tightens the net of scrutiny, conformity, and social restriction within which community members are already entangled.

CONCLUSION

Whereas much has been written about gated communities of late, the explicit comparison of community types in this chapter calls attention to the troubling dissonances and unexpected resonances in the narratives of individuals operating in radically different social worlds. The embedding of surveillance technologies into residential spaces reinforces neoliberal security cultures. Surveillance is used to intrusively police the poor in public housing and attempt to eliminate those who might be "cheating the system" in some way. Surveillance is also used to guard the fortified enclaves of private gated communities, under the rubric of keeping out—or at least keeping a close eye on—those who cannot afford to live in such spaces but are necessary for maintaining them. Interestingly, surveillance practices also subject the affluent to a type of scrutiny that heretofore has been reserved for the poor,[24] and this scrutiny is justified as a necessary sacrifice of rights associated with living in privatized environments. In these ways, residential surveillance operates within and contributes to a neoliberal environment of reduced social programs and increased social control throughout public and private life. As with architecture, surveillance technologies function as political tools with agential force to shape human practices. The tendency of these surveillance systems is for monitoring internal everyday activities, not external exceptional ones.

In the examples provided in this chapter, both the poor and the affluent say, initially, that surveillance is intended to protect them from outsiders. The personal experiences they describe, however, illustrate that much of the monitoring capabilities and control functions of surveillance systems are directed at the residents themselves, whether in public housing or gated communities. I see this as a revealing dissonance between discourse and practice—or, more accurately, between *popular discourse* about the functions of surveillance and the *discourse of practice* about instances and perceptions of being surveilled. This tension is representative of social instabilities engendered by neoliberal forces that run against the grain of the American dream of equal life chances, for those in public housing, and freedom with property, for those in gated communities.

It is the space between popular discourse and discourse of practice where opportunities for awareness and critique are effaced by the ambiguity and supposed neutrality of community rules, architectures, and technologies. It is also a space where difference resides and is obscured, especially, so it seems, for the affluent. This is probably so because, in a sense, to acknowledge the particularistic uses of surveillance and fortification might also imply a recognition of particularism more generally, or the dominance of ascribed over achieved status in society.

An interesting difference between the narratives of these two community types is that residents in public housing talk about having "nothing to hide" in their communities, while those in gated communities do not. Instead, gated community residents mobilize the discourse of nothing to hide only when discussing surveillance in the world outside the walls—on streets, in banks, in shopping centers, and so on. One explanation for this difference could be that gated community residents believe that they have made a rational choice to live where they do and submit to the rules and enforcement practices of their neighborhoods.

Residents in public housing, by contrast, have no such direct avenues for altering practices of social regulation where they live. Additionally, given the myriad ways that many of these individuals are investigated, evaluated, sorted, and controlled by state apparatuses and agents of public welfare and housing, they may have developed heightened sensitivity to the politics of electronic surveillance systems, as other research has shown.[25] For public housing residents, the discourse of nothing to hide serves a symbolic function of asserting innocence even in the face of individualized scrutiny by state agents with control over residents' ability to meet their basic human needs.

While the data presented here suggest a structural similarity in experiences of being surveilled in public housing and gated communities, clearly this isomorphism does not mean that the life chances, conditions, or concerns of these two groups are comparable. Nor does this similarity imply that the outcomes or emotional effects of surveillance-facilitated interventions can be equated. After all, the ultimate material risks faced by those in gated communities are the inconveniences of fines or of needing to move elsewhere. For those in public housing, as my interviewees confess, the ultimate risks are not risks at all but are instead the dangers of living homeless on the street or the disturbing "alternative" of suicide.

If the hyper-regulation of boundaries and borders is a response to social instabilities, on local and global levels, it is worthwhile to question not only the regulation itself but also the fundamental causes of such instabilities. Rather than being measured responses to threats of crime or terrorism, social regulation may be more about contending with the fallout from economic inequalities, which are compounded by the dismantling of social programs and rise in sociospatial segregation. As with security policies on the national level, it seems that the surveillance and security interventions intended to protect people from external threats require that people in turn subject themselves to greater unwarranted and uninvited scrutiny and control. Thus, it is not surprising that a tension would exist between what people say surveillance is for and how it is actually deployed, because it is, in some senses, a technological fix to a complex social problem that it cannot hope to solve.

CHAPTER 7

Controlling Mobilities

CONCERNS OVER NEW SURVEILLANCE TECHNOLOGIES and security policies tend to focus on the most obvious systems or flagrant breaches of privacy. These can include the spread of closed circuit television (CCTV) systems in urban areas, illegal government wiretapping programs, or liberal data sharing among private industries and government agencies. All the while, the rapid proliferation of digital technologies throughout everyday life creates opportunities for surveillance capabilities that resist critical investigation or public awareness.[1] Transportation infrastructures offer a case in point. Transportation flows are increasingly monitored and controlled with systems of diverse technologies, yet it is difficult to envision the data generated by traveling; how others might be interpreting, sharing, and responding to those data; and how mobilities or experiences might be altered based upon individual or automated responses to those data.[2]

In this chapter, I investigate the surveillance and security dimensions of "intelligent transportation systems" (ITS) in the United States, with a particular focus on the mediation of data by engineers in transportation control centers. Intelligent transportation systems are being—or have been—deployed, in some fashion, in most major cities around the world. A great deal of attention has been given to the rationalizing of transportation and tracking of passengers for purposes of efficiency, security, and commercial marketing.[3] Especially for public transportation, global positioning systems (GPS) and "smart card" systems can be used to track the exact location of—and identity of each person on—trains and buses.[4] Similarly, smart cards embedded with radio-frequency identification (RFID) chips allow for automated electronic toll collection on highways and bridges.[5] License-plate recognition systems are deployed to minimize traffic congestion by limiting entry into cities (such as London) and assessing fines if entry-time restrictions are violated.[6] In-car systems such as black boxes, GPS units, or vehicle-to-vehicle communication technologies also open drivers up to increased scrutiny by insurance companies, marketers, rental car agencies, law enforcement, and, potentially, others.[7] Obviously, significant national and regional variation exists with ITS. It appears likely that the United States is prioritizing ITS for highways, roads, and bridges to maximize the throughput of vehicular traffic instead of—or as a supplement to—building additional roads or lanes, whereas other countries are prioritizing ITS for public transportation systems that have been operational for decades if not longer. The concentration in this chapter will be on publicly operated highway and road-based ITS in the United States, and especially on the human mediation of these systems by transportation engineers in the southwestern United States, where I conducted interviews and observational studies.[8]

ITS OVERVIEW

A heterogeneous network of technologies comprises ITS for highways and roads: video cameras, embedded or mounted traffic sensors, smart cards, smart-card readers, GPS devices, license-plate readers, geographic information systems (GIS), computers, software, communications equipment, fiber-optic networks, wireless networks, electrical supplies, traffic signals, emergency vehicle detection devices, and so on. The most visible public interfaces for ITS are traffic signals, which regulate the flow of motorized vehicles, bicycles, and pedestrians on streets; "dynamic message signs," which can alert drivers to upcoming road conditions; and ramp meters, which regulate the flow of vehicles onto highways. Perhaps the most important ITS interfaces, however, are the ones hidden from public view: traffic control centers, which monitor and respond to traffic conditions through remote manipulation of the system (and its data) as a whole. The hallmarks of these control centers are their impressive and oftentimes massive "video walls," which display road conditions in real time, whether through a graphic representation of roads and signals, CCTV video feeds, or some combination of both (see figure 2).

Typically speaking, departments of transportation for states, as well as for large cities, possess the most advanced ITS. In the United States, a nationwide ITS program was established by the Intermodal Surface Transportation Efficiency Act of 1991,[9] and the government has invested over $1 billion in the systems since then.[10] Although ITS are managed by the U.S. Department of Transportation, states and cities draw upon the ITS mission and protocols to implement their own systems, relying largely upon local resources to keep systems operational. In large metropolitan regions, sensors are embedded every one-third of a mile on highways and are used to measure speed, volume, and density of traffic. Other nonvisual sensing systems include both sonar and radar detectors to fine-tune speed and volume readings. Installed every mile on the highways are high-end CCTV cameras equipped with pan, tilt, and zoom capabilities with a minimum range of half a mile. Local municipalities off the highway system have less-developed but nonetheless impressive systems for their roads. These include sensors mounted at intersections for the detection of flow, speed, and density for each lane; sensors for the

2. Intelligent transportation systems (ITS) video wall for state department of transportation. Photo by Torin Monahan.

detection of emergency vehicle strobe lights, which when triggered will change traffic signals to give emergency vehicles "green" lights; and CCTV cameras at many, but definitely not all, intersections. The local ITS centers also receive information from the traffic signals throughout their cities and can alter signal times remotely and detect (and oftentimes fix) malfunctions. Finally, ITS operators at both the state and local levels routinely spot accidents or verify accident locations reported by others and then convey that information to public safety and emergency personnel. It is important to note, especially for the discussion of surveillance to follow, that almost all these systems are interoperable and interconnected. Thus, not only can local and state ITS operators monitor and control each other's systems, which they do frequently, but so can law enforcement agencies easily tap into these systems and their data.

The key to ITS is the translation of transportation flows into data that can be acted upon, preferably in real time or in advance, through predictive modeling. The systems in the United States are currently geared toward the management of aggregate flows: to time traffic signals for optimal vehicular throughput or to update traffic signs to let drivers know of alternate routes for avoiding congestion or accidents, for example. As with other forms of mobile communication,[11] the technological trajectory, however, is toward the atomization of aggregate flows: to monitor individual vehicles with road sensors, GPS, RFID tags, license-plate readers, and so on.[12]

Although ITS officials draw clear lines of demarcation between the functions of their systems and those of law enforcement, in practice, as this chapter will show, these lines are quite blurred and the functions will probably continue to converge. Mainly, the systems are interlinked and accessible by personnel beyond the specific control center with jurisdiction, whether for traffic control or public safety purposes. Some operators also relate stories of listening to police radios while performing their traffic-management duties and assisting police officers in locating suspects. Finally, many ITS centers have been slated as "emergency operations centers" to manage evacuation procedures or coordinate response teams in the event of terrorist attacks or natural disasters. The systems are always, if latently, oriented toward national security, such that the operators routinely monitor "critical infrastructures" for suspicious activity.[13]

The lines between the functions and interests of private industry and public agencies are much less clear, even in principle. This is so because public-private partnerships are integral to the official ITS mission, whereby private companies are contracted to install and service equipment or to implement and manage entire subsystems, such as electronic toll collection.[14] Increasingly, state governments are selling to private companies the management rights for public highways that since their inception have been seen as essential public goods. Indiana, for instance, recently sold operating rights to all 157 miles of its primary interstate highway (I-90) to a consortium of foreign construction companies for $3.8 billion.[15] The consortium stands to gain $11 billion in toll revenues over the seventy-five-year life of the contract.[16] Many other states and countries are following suit and embracing this neoliberal rationality, which is clearly articulated by Indiana's governor, Mitch Daniels: "Any businessperson will recognize our decision here as the freeing of trapped value from an underperforming asset, to be redeployed into a better use with higher returns."[17] With some of the management duties and individual transportation data in the hands of industry, privacy concerns may be amplified because companies have an interest in using or selling those data for the marketing of products and services.[18] Less obviously, social inequalities may be aggravated as companies restrict access to public highways through tiered toll-payment schemes or build private highways that are inaccessible to the general public, thereby constraining the mobility of the poor who cannot afford the added expense but often need to travel farther to work than do the relatively affluent.[19]

Similarly, the management of abstract flows by ITS operates as a type of surveillance with unequal effects on the ground. Drawing upon the definition of surveillance as practices of identification, tracking, monitoring, or analysis that enforce degrees of social control, ITS are unmistakably a form of surveillance.[20]

The acknowledged goal of ITS operators is to collect and analyze data to manage transportation flows, or to manage the mobilities of others. The privacy of those individuals may not be at risk, as such, but they are nonetheless subjected to surveillance and their actions are influenced by it. This mode of surveillance may be more controlling than others because of its relative invisibility, as it is embedded in infrastructure and managed remotely, increasingly by automated computer software.[21] Furthermore, this surveillance may be more insidious because it is not seen as such by ITS operators; they perceive the systems as neutral even as the systems actively abstract complex social practices into discrete data for impersonal intervention.

Nonetheless, ITS and ITS operators engage in activities of social sorting, valorizing certain mobilities over others, while normalizing unequal experiences of space. The control made possible with ITS should be seen as part of a larger transformation in the regulation of mobilities, spaces, and spatial experiences, from ideals of universal access to experiences of differential access based largely on socioeconomic status.[22] The dominant rationality of "flow" pervades the discourse and practice of ITS operators and infuses the systems with certain politics, which are enforced and felt on the level of bodies and materialities, even if they do not achieve representation in the systems.

CULTURE OF SECRECY

It is more difficult than one might expect to obtain access to ITS control centers. In most cases, operators or administrative personnel would speak with me or my research assistant when we first called but would quickly clam up when they discovered that we wanted to interview them and see the control rooms. Many centers refused to return our phone calls or respond to our e-mails after the initial contact. Several sites agreed to participate in the research and then had a change of heart after talking with their legal departments. The sites to which we did get access strung us along for some time while obtaining approval from their supervisors or legal staff. Given that these are publicly funded programs, the sites are in public buildings, the operators are government employees, and the researcher possessed some cultural credibility as a professor at a large public university, the obstacles to learning about ITS were inordinately high.[23] Part of that may have to do with concerns over having insufficient time for an interview or the general "firewall culture" of government employees trying to avoid unnecessary scrutiny.[24] It soon became apparent, however, that ITS operators knew that their centers had the look of surveillance and that they wanted to distance themselves from that characterization of their work.

UPON MY ARRIVAL at one city department of transportation, an engineer escorted me quickly to a small, drab conference room where another operator met with us for the scheduled interview. While my escort went to check the

3. Intelligent transportation systems (ITS) video wall for Local City. Photo by Torin Monahan.

conference room schedule for any conflicts, I asked the other engineer if we would have time to see the control center as well, the sophistication of which I had heard about from engineers at another nearby city. He nervously vacillated, saying that things were probably too busy today, but that maybe I could view it through the glass of a secure door before I left. Shortly thereafter, the other person returned and informed us that there was a scheduling conflict in the conference room, so we would have to conduct the interview in the control center after all. The vast control center—referred to as the "war room" by the engineers—boasted the largest video wall I had seen apart from those at state-level DOT centers, which can be as large as movie screens. As we sat at the elegant control desk, with its embedded, flip-up monitors, another engineer emerged from a connected back office and joined the interview. Throughout the interview, one portion of the video wall displayed my interviewees and me sitting at the desk, while other portions displayed a map of the city's roads, CCTV feeds, computer video displays, and Fox News (see figure 3). Contrary to the engineer's initial objections that employees in the control center were too busy, they all joined the interview without any apparent interruption of their work.

Before the interview could begin, however, I needed to convince the engineers to sign informed consent forms, which were required for this project by my university's institutional review board for human subjects research. They were reluctant to sign because the forms indicated that I was conducting research on public surveillance systems. Even though government documents on ITS devote pages to describing the sensing and CCTV technologies as "surveillance,"[25] the operators of the systems were loath to see their technical work in that light. For them, surveillance implied the intention to monitor or spy on individuals, whereas all they cared about was rationalizing vehicular throughput in a completely disembodied and impersonal way. They did sign the forms after I explained that I was using surveillance as a generic term. Nonetheless, their objections demonstrated worries about negative public attention. The objections and our discussion of them also revealed assumptions on their part that intentionality is required for "surveillance" to take place and that ITS are purely technical, not political or social in any way, and therefore should certainly not be seen as surveillant.

Because their systems rely upon CCTV cameras, which are conspicuous and increasingly ubiquitous on city streets, ITS engineers anticipate questions about privacy and have prepared software-based responses to them. As an example, when I was concluding the interview described here, one engineer prompted one of the others saying, "You got to show him the little preset thing." It turns out that the "preset thing" was a programmed gray patch that could be applied to individual cameras so that operators could not see into people's houses or apartments. Once the software is running, if an operator zooms in too far, to the point where one might be able to view people in their private spaces, a gray box suddenly appears to block the view. The engineer explained:

> All I care [about] is the traffic there: is it moving, is it not moving, is it backed up, is it not backed up? And one of the issues you have is, you put a camera on an intersection, and invariably people live near intersections. The biggest problem with cameras is a lot of times they'll lose power to them, they'll swing over and go to a preset, a default preset, and a lot of times it'll point right into somebody's house. Yeah, and it's like "Aaaaah I don't wanna see that!" Yeah, the camera just, the camera decided to be silly and got some capability. And a lot of the newer ones [cameras] will allow you to program a preset on them, and our newest ones will allow you to program areas that you can't even view.

It is interesting that by switching the privacy patch off and on at will, just to demonstrate to me what "before" and "after" might look like, the engineers are tipping their hand, revealing that the software is indeed a façade. They have complete control over whether to employ it, implying that its main function is to prove to outsiders that they care about privacy, even if everyone must trust them not to take advantage of the system's privacy-violating capabilities. At the same time, it is fascinating to observe how engineers discursively recognize the unpredictable agency of the systems, whereby a camera "decided to be silly and got some capability." Because the systems have acquired some agency, their surveillance modalities must be mediated by the engineers or the systems must be further automated with corrective software patches. Related to this concern over surveillance is the mantra of all the interviewees: "We do not record any video footage." Yet interviewees confessed that it was technically easy to do, if one so desired. Plus, their digital systems are constantly recording or "capturing" data onto computer hard drives in any event, even if the data are periodically purged.[26] The engineers may have no interest in watching individual people, but the systems possess vast potential for "function creep" to purposes that were not originally intended.

EXCEPTIONS TO THE RULE

As ITS become ubiquitous, the primary rationales for the systems may shift to accommodate secondary purposes of police or security functions, or of commercial marketing. This was a point candidly acknowledged by ITS operators: "I think that what you're seeing here is an infancy of deployment of this type of equipment. I think once the equipment becomes operational and there's a lot of it, then they'll find every kind of use possible for it." Many of these potential uses already exist. In interviews, examples of obvious cases of surveillance accumulated slowly, usually offered as anecdotal asides to the dominant message of traffic management. Although the history of communication technologies and transportation systems illustrates that the control properties of new systems have often been taken advantage of for police purposes,[27] for my informants, these capabilities emerge as serendipitous discoveries. As one traffic engineer recounted:

> I heard on the radio that somebody had assaulted a Circle K [convenience store] manager, and we had a camera at that location where we could see the Circle K. The gentleman came out of the Circle K and walked down the street and fit the description perfectly of what they were saying he was. I watched him come out and go into a bar around the corner, and the whole time I'm on the radio with the officer who responded. And I said "He's here; he's in the bar." And then he came out of the bar and got on the bus. And there was only one bus going westbound at the time. So, [the police] didn't have any problem. They pulled the bus over about a quarter mile down the road and hauled him off.

Here, one of the same traffic engineers who initially objected vociferously to me talking about ITS as "surveillance" described in detail how he tapped into the explicit surveillance functions of the system to assist the police. Whereas this surveillance occurred through real-time processing of information and active coordination of different communication media, other publicized cases of ITS lending themselves to function creep are more retrospective and data-driven, as with Great Britain's recent admission of secretly spying on people by sifting through the data generated by individuals' "smart cards," which they use to access public transportation.[28]

The interoperability and interconnection of systems signal another obvious avenue for function creep. When I asked operators and administrators about the logistics of verifying accident locations for public safety, they admitted that public safety personnel often simply connect to the system and control the cameras without the need for ITS engineers to get involved. In fact, the design preference for all new control centers is to combine ITS and public safety departments within the same building so that access to the systems will be identical. In interviews with police, they admit that they occasionally use ITS for police purposes, even if it is less precise than the surveillance they would set up for specific investigations. One detective viewed ITS video cameras as important inoculation for the American public to become desensitized to public surveillance systems that the police would like to use. Barring any technical or legal safeguards (such as encryption for privacy protection or new laws governing ITS use, respectively), secondary uses of the systems will likely continue to grow without much public awareness or oversight.

National security concerns, especially in the post-9/11 context, provide another strong rationale for secondary ITS functions. In the years following September 11, 2001, many U.S. government agencies have transformed their missions to prioritize national security and have incorporated security responsibilities, as was discussed in chapter 1. Departments of transportation are no exception. As might be expected, the monitoring of "critical infrastructures," such as bridges and tunnels, is part of the responsibility of many ITS control centers. Moreover, many control rooms are slated to become emergency operations centers in the event of terrorist attacks or natural disasters. As emergency operations centers, they could coordinate evacuation procedures and response teams, including police and fire departments, and possibly hazardous materials teams or military units. An engineer for one city-level department of transportation center explained:

Right now the state has its own state emergency operation center [EOC], so, if the governor declares a state of emergency, it is the Division of Emergency Management that handles [the governor's] directives. . . . But actually our IT department and some other parts of our city have identified this facility as being an important facility that needs to keep running in case anything happens, and we're kind of worked into that whole process. Because we do have some of the backup systems and, so there is some recognition in the value of what we do here and keeping it live and

well. We've only been here a year and the EOC is just really kinda getting off the ground, and over the next few years, I can just see a lot of
growth in working out all those [coordination] issues. . . . Yeah, and that
would be, you know, kinda again one of those Homeland Security con-
cepts, you got your police and your fire and if anything unpleasant were
to happen, they've got their secured command center to dispatch the
resources that are needed.

The responsibilities for critical infrastructure monitoring and emergency operations management provide insight into the multidimensional character of
ITS, whereby the analytic distinction between primary and secondary functions is too facile a characterization of the systems, even if it is an accurate
description of the daily practices of engineers. These security functions point
to the inherent, and in this case intentional, surveillance capabilities of ITS.

These examples of function creep highlight the lack of explicit protocols
or collective conversations about the surveillance functions of these systems
or the desirability of harnessing those functions. Instead the surveillance
modalities are exploited because the systems allow them to be. The discourse
of abstract control of flows at a distance illustrates an approach to the systems
that denies the existence of these alternative uses, as well as social context.
Nonetheless these systems, along with their discourses and practices, actively
shape the world and sort bodies in very biased ways, sometimes increasing
vulnerability for certain populations. It is to this social sorting that I next turn.

THROUGHPUT RATIONALITY

Whereas the police and security applications of ITS may be the most visible instantiations of surveillance, the active management of people and their
mobilities should also be considered as such. Both existing ITS and dominant
throughput rationalities are coproductive and hegemonic, oftentimes to the
detriment of other experiences of space or modes of transport. As one engineer put it:

As the *cities mature*, and the right of way is used up, we lack the ability to
add more pavement, add more lanes, add more capacity to the roadway.
But with the ITS Smart Technology, we're moving toward a traffic control system that will make and manage the capacity more efficiently. And
so you know, when you reach build-out, you know, there's nothing else
you can do, save for using the capacity, *using the pipe* way more intelligently [emphasis added].

There are many assumptions embedded in such an articulation. First, "mature"
cities are those that have reached a threshold with the number of vehicles
their roads can carry and with the space available for the construction of new

roads or lanes. The history of a city, its cultures and institutions, are subordinated to the development of its roadways in any evaluation of a city's evolution. Second, rather than question the automobile as the dominant form of transportation or criticize development patterns that lead to increasing distance between places of living and work, the logical solution advanced by ITS is to utilize existing infrastructures more "intelligently," meaning in a more efficient, informatized way. Finally, from this perspective, streets and highways are reduced to metaphorical "pipes," serving as conduits from one place to another, rather than as places in their own right.

Within this discursive framework, and within these "smart" infrastructures, alternative mobilities or experiences of space are often marginalized. The infrastructures themselves, once analytically reduced to "pipes," become intolerant of or actively hostile to difference. Of course, this is true of the history of road development more generally, especially in the United States, but as the roads achieve greater throughput of vehicles, there is a corresponding diminishment of nonvehicular space, or gaps between vehicles.[29] For instance, maximum throughput makes it much more difficult to back out of a driveway on a busy street, turn onto such a street, or cross streets, especially as a pedestrian.

The ways in which ITS traffic engineers speak of pedestrians illustrates the marginalization of difference, which is informed and reproduced by the systems. First, there is a sense of frustration with pedestrians for slowing down the traffic flow—or, more precisely, for forcing engineers to slow down traffic flow to ensure that signals will be "synced"[30] in the eventuality that a pedestrian pushes the "walk" button:

> If you have to accommodate a lot of ped time, it means the intersections are going to take a longer time to get around [that is, for the signal lights to cycle from red to green to red], and the longer it takes an intersection to get around, typically, the slower the drive speed is, so then you end up with intersections where the speed limit's forty-five miles an hour, and there's no way you can time it for that speed so you end up timing it for a lower speed.

This concern with limiting throughput in order to accommodate pedestrians compels some engineers to take shortcuts, timing intersections for a higher vehicle speed in the hope that few pedestrians will cross the streets and that the signals will remain synced. Invariably, this approach fails, traffic gets backed up, and the signal times need to be recalibrated. A second approach is to limit the amount of time allotted for pedestrians to cross the street, forcing them to move quickly or face increased risk of being hit. In the cities I studied, pedestrians were assumed to walk at a rate of four feet per second, and the signals were timed accordingly. Obviously, the handicapped, the elderly, and children may not be able to achieve the necessary speed to make it across streets, some of which can be up to seven lanes wide. This is one very real danger introduced by a transportation system rationalized for vehicles and destinations, rather than people and places.[31]

A final example, this time of a pedestrian getting hit by a car, reveals the tendency of ITS surveillance to objectify people and privilege vehicles as primary units of analysis. A control room operator related:

> Unfortunately I watched a lady get hit by a car one day. . . . A man made a right turn right in front of her, as she was walking across the street [in a marked crosswalk], and she literally walked into the van and got caught by it. I'm like, "how in the hell could that happen," and I was sitting here watching it the whole time, and I couldn't believe what I was watching.

In this instance, the operator who witnessed the accident strangely elects to fault the lady for somehow walking into a moving car, rather than saying that the person in the moving car violated the pedestrian's right of way by cutting across her path and hitting her. While it is common for most people to lend agency to vehicles by saying things such as "the car went through the light," when filtered through the lens of ITS, the operator takes this tendency a step further to blame the pedestrian who was in the right, at least according to the law. The history of U.S. transportation systems is one where engineers and planners have divided neighborhoods, displaced people, and discriminated against nondrivers in extremely racist and classist ways, most egregiously through the use of eminent-domain laws to expand highways through minority communities.[32] The use of ITS builds upon these previous biases rather than replacing them. ITS are control systems and forms of marginalizing surveillance that disproportionately endanger people who are not driving private automobiles. Similarly, the perspective of the engineer relating this story is undoubtedly shaped by the logics of the system he oversees and his professional training. Intelligent transportation systems present themselves, therefore, as a lens for perceiving the rearticulation of throughput rationalities in digital and increasingly automated forms.

In summary, as ITS are integrated into existing transportation infrastructures, they reproduce and modulate a rationality of maximum vehicular throughput at the expense of other experiences or values. They monitor and regulate flows retrospectively, in real time, and prospectively. Currently, this largely invisible and normalized form of social control occurs mostly at the level of aggregate data, but more and more it is individualized, with systems tracking and storing unique identifiers (from smart cards, GPS devices, license plates, and so on) for future scrutiny and intervention. Systems in development include the networking of all vehicles on the road, which is a functional spillover from military research such as that by the U.S. Department of Defense, which plans to have one-third of its vehicles completely "autonomous" by 2015.[33] As the examples in this chapter demonstrate, neither ITS nor the social orders established by them are value-neutral. They carve up the world in very discriminatory ways according to the contexts within which they are applied, with the likelihood of reinforcing inequalities and insecurities that are not represented by the transportation grids, flow diagrams, or software codes that define the parameters of the systems.

CONCLUSION

The prevalence of digital technologies throughout everyday life enables new modalities of surveillance. Whether the technologies are mobile phones, smart cards, GPS units, or video cameras, they tend to create and store data, as a default, thereby lending themselves to surveillance uses. If the key to determining whether surveillance is occurring rests in the criterion of "control," as I have asserted, then one must look to the social practices surrounding such systems and analyze them in spatial context to see how control is or is not manifested. One must also attend to how various assemblages of digital technologies become embedded in infrastructure and hidden from view, to the extent that certain rationalities of movement or spatial experience are normalized, depoliticized, and hidden from view. In this chapter, I have highlighted the surveillance dimensions of ITS, as seen through the discourse and practice of control center operators. While it is apparent that ITS perform at the level of infrastructure to control and sort people in non-neutral ways, much more empirical research needs to be done to better understand the physical and symbolic negotiations of ITS by people in other domains and across multiple mobilities.

The difficulty of obtaining information on the actual work of ITS engineers and the functions of the systems is itself revealing. Engineers understand that what they do can be perceived as surveillance, mostly because of dominant cultural meanings associated with video cameras. As a result, these government workers seek to insulate themselves from scrutiny by preventing access to their spaces. They articulate a pure, technical version of their activities (that is, managing flows) that strips people from the equation entirely. Their implied rhetorical argument is that without people, or even representations of them beyond the unit of the car, surveillance cannot be occurring. This is true, from their viewpoint, because surveillance is perforce a social, intentional, and interested activity; what they do is technical, whereby any attention to individual people is unintentional and disinterested. This, of course, is a highly problematic distinction. Technical operations are always social and embodied practices.[34] Moreover, surveillance can operate on the level of groups—or upon groups of mobilities, as the case may be—without any explicit intention or interestedness on the part of those running the systems.[35] Surveillance does not have to be intended to be felt.

Even if one were to accept engineers' initial description of ITS as rational traffic management, their narratives betray the polyvalence of ITS, which is also the case with all information and communication technologies. They proudly talk of listening to police radios and using the systems to assist police in apprehending criminals. They admit that personnel from public safety control centers access and direct their systems, and while ITS engineers do not record any video footage, they cannot prevent others with access from doing so. Finally, many ITS centers serve a dual function of being emergency operations centers in the event of terrorist attacks or natural disasters. Given the fact that the interstate highway system, which ITS help to regulate, was initially conceived of as a national security infrastructure, these security functions of ITS should not be that surprising—they are part of the historical trajectory of the U.S. highway system. These secondary uses illustrate the function-creep potential of ITS. Still, perhaps the differentiation between primary and secondary uses is dangerous; it may serve to inoculate such systems against criticism because one could always say that any problematic uses are not the primary or intended ones. At the very least, these few examples signify the valence of such systems toward explicit surveillance and security applications.

The social-sorting ramifications of ITS should not be overlooked, even if they are the most difficult to perceive. The dominant rationality of efficient vehicular throughput pervades American culture as a whole, dramatically affecting experiences of mobility, space, and place.[36] When streets are perceived as conduits from one place to another, instead of as places in their own right, the imperative for speed subordinates that of sociality, or of a sense of collective responsibility for social well-being.[37] In this way, ITS can be seen as sustaining ongoing neoliberal development patterns by emphasizing "pipes" over places, maximizing the flow of privately owned vehicles through those pipes, and facilitating the privatization of highways and industry (and state) profits through tiered toll schemes and the abrogation of public rights to access. Control manifests in the governing of mobilities, directing where one can go, by what means, and under what conditions. Control also manifests in the unequal privileging and supporting of certain mobilities over others: private over public transportation, driving over walking or bicycling. This can increase the danger of commuting for people who are failed insecurity subjects, meaning in this context those who cannot or choose not to armor themselves in private automobiles.

CHAPTER 8

Masculine Technologies

GIVEN TODAY'S SECURITY CULTURES, one could say that insecurity subjects and failed insecurity subjects alike are gendered feminine.[1] The former are charged with compensating for the state's neglect of social needs, whereas the latter are deemed as requiring paternalistic monitoring and intervention. Modern surveillance technologies, on the other hand, operate much more on the masculine and controlling end of the gender spectrum. Because surveillance is often touted as safeguarding individual security, including preventing acts of violence against women, it is worth critically examining surveillance from a gender-studies perspective. Rather than being restricted to video cameras, though, everyday surveillance depends upon vast databases of personal information. The current technological milieu requires an expansion of conceptual categories and empirical material to account for the oftentimes post-optic operations of gendered power in these new domains. The term *post-optic* is not meant to imply the decline of visual surveillance, as almost all surveillance has a visual component. Rather, the term shifts attention away from video surveillance and toward the complex integration of surveillance functions into all information and communication technologies.

The research that has been done on video surveillance provides the groundwork for addressing gender issues with other surveillance technologies. The voyeuristic uses of video surveillance are not all that surprising: usually men sit comfortably in control rooms where they monitor unsuspecting women—and others—from afar. Studies find that at least one in ten women are watched by control room operators for voyeuristic reasons alone.[2] One effect is that women in public and private spaces are increasingly scrutinized without necessarily achieving any additional protection from harassment or assault.[3] Indeed, in some cases it seems as if the bundling of cameras into popular devices like cellular phones enables new forms of uninvited scrutiny and objectification of women. One example of such practices occurred at my previous university, where pictures were taken of female students, without their awareness or consent, and then placed on an Internet site for viewers from around the world to "rate" their sex appeal.

The voyeuristic uses of surveillance technologies are clearly troubling, especially as these technologies propagate throughout societies. Nonetheless, the gender implications of surveillance systems extend well beyond voyeurism, manifesting in radical new forms of disembodied social control. To perceive this expanded field of gender and surveillance, however, electronic surveillance must be understood broadly as technological systems that facilitate the control of people. This includes the host of data-generating and data-sorting systems for commercial transactions, communications, transportation, medical records, and so forth. Acknowledging the control potentials of data management expands the field for social analysis to reveal unfolding power relations in seemingly mundane technical activities. There are shifts underway across most public domains to reduce social identities, mobilities, and practices to mere "data" that can be managed and sorted as abstractions without a clear understanding of the embodied power relations and social effects produced by those activities.

This chapter offers an exploration of the gender dimensions of surveillance systems in three public domains: welfare, health care, and transportation.[4] The primary argument is that modern surveillance systems operate upon logics of disembodied control at a distance. As such, they artificially abstract bodies, identities, and interactions from social contexts in ways that both obscure and aggravate gender and other social inequalities and insecurities. By exposing the dominant rationalities of such systems and critiquing the discourses that support them, one can challenge the supposed impartiality of such technologies and question the power relations to which they give rise. Therefore, the goal of this chapter is to introduce a new line of inquiry into gender and surveillance, one that perceives surveillance as operating on the level of abstraction but with embodied effects for women and men.

GENDER AND TECHNOLOGY DESIGN

My approach to surveillance is grounded in three conceptual categories of gender and technology design. I understand technologies to betray their gendered dimensions through (1) body discrimination, (2) context or use discrimination, and (3) discrimination by abstraction. These three areas definitely overlap and bleed together, so I introduce them here merely as heuristics for analysis. What they share in common is attention to issues of power, specifically how unequal power relations are reproduced and reinforced by technological means.

Body discrimination can be understood as technologies that simply are not designed with a full range of bodies in mind. These technologies privilege certain bodies—usually male, young, white, and able ones—over others. One example might include speech-recognition software, which has been very slow to accommodate women's voices, while it has excelled at deciphering male speech. Another example might be automobile air bags, which deploy at a height, velocity, and trajectory that cause more injuries to women than to their typical male counterparts.[5] To varying degrees, many technologies, if not most, are like these: they are products designed better for use by men than by women; or, within their social contexts, they tend to empower men and disempower women. This is, in large part, a product of the frame of reference of technology designers, software developers, and engineers, most of whom are men designing with themselves in mind.[6] The speech-recognition software problem clearly fits into this explanatory framework because the people who happened to "be around" to test and debug the software were men. That the male body is taken as the standard and other bodies as exceptions is, of course, a product of androcentric philosophical traditions,[7] which are then reproduced by the technological artifacts and systems that mark women's bodies as "other."[8] This results in technologies with a certain "valence" against women, where the concept of valence accounts for the force of technologies to trigger certain predictable uses and outcomes.[9]

Inquiry into *context or use discrimination* focuses attention on discrimination that is engendered by existing social contexts and/or institutional relations. Surveillance technologies easily support such discrimination. Because almost all control-room operators of video surveillance are men who are removed from the spaces they are monitoring, they tend to use the technologies in voyeuristic and particularistic ways. As Hille Koskela persuasively argues, this effectively masculinizes the spaces under observation because (1) video surveillance occurs in traditionally feminine spaces (for example, shopping malls or public transportation), (2) it serves as a hidden form of sexual harassment, and (3) unlike the physical presence of security personnel, video surveillance operators fail to detect, document, or deter verbal forms of sexual harassment that may be occurring in those spaces.[10] When social contexts are already marked by sexist relations, then surveillance and other technologies tend to amplify those tensions and inequalities. For example, surveillance is used to control the appearance and behavior of cocktail waitresses in casinos.[11] The intention is to position waitresses, by way of their dress and doting upon gamblers, as objects of desire for customers, and to keep them subordinate to the male bartenders and management.[12] Waitresses do resist, but cautiously and intelligently; otherwise bartenders will slow down waitresses' orders and their tips will suffer. Similar patterns exist with the use of surveillance in strip clubs to enforce control by male managers over female strippers, making certain that they do not cheat the system by taking unreported tips (usually for performing sexual acts).[13] Finally, the construction of women as vulnerable in public places such as outdoor recreational parks can compel them to accept surveillance begrudgingly in exchange for the promise of increased safety.[14]

It should be noted that feminist scholars have fruitfully investigated many other technologies for their context- or use-discrimination encodings. Leslie Weisman argues that architecture and planning tend to codify sex inequalities in a "spatial caste system" of disconnected, sex-inscribed territories (for example, home versus office), leading to less value placed upon work done by women and unequal mobilities between the sexes.[15] In this vein, Ruth Schwartz Cowan and Judy Wajcman have deconstructed myths of domestic technologies and public utility infrastructures, respectively, as clear symbols of progress.[16] They find that although housework labor for women is not reduced, in part because of rising expectations for cleanliness, capitalist and patriarchal relations are reproduced by means of demarcating public and private spheres according to their respective gendered commodities. In a remarkable study of the development of the microwave oven, Cynthia Cockburn and Susan Ormrod reveal how unequal gender relations allow for the de-skilling of cooking and the blaming of women for microwave mishaps, while simultaneously affording a space for male, high-tech expertise in the traditionally feminine domain of the kitchen.[17] Studies of context and use discrimination highlight the valence toward unequal power relations with the introduction of new technologies. Because technologies are underdetermined, existing conditions of inequality inflect technologies and technological systems, reproducing unequal social orders. This conclusion, however, does not discount in any way the many efforts of active appropriation by women (and men) to minimize the discriminatory effects of technologies in social contexts.[18]

Discrimination by abstraction is probably the most controversial reading of technology and gender. By this concept I mean the ways that technological systems, especially those that produce representations of data, strip away social context, leaving a disembodied and highly abstract depiction of the world and of what matters in it. The act of filtering out bodies and social contexts facilitates a kind of control at a distance that is the hallmark of modern surveillance systems.[19] In the process of producing abstract representations that can be monitored and controlled, however, social inequalities and experiences tend to drop out of the equation. Bodies become data. At the same time, while social contexts are abstracted away, inequalities are solidified and aggravated by means of their lack of representational presence. If inequalities, gender-based or otherwise, are not represented in data, it is difficult to address them, but that does not mean they are not present.

Dreams of disembodied, sterile, and heroic control at a distance have deep roots in Western technoscience. Carolyn Merchant argues that the machine metaphor employed to describe the ordering of self, society, and cosmos during the "scientific revolution" led to a mechanized worldview that encouraged the exploitation of the natural world and, by relation, women.[20] Mary Terrall adds that in the eighteenth century science was further masculinized through heroic expeditions, which ensured that women could only partici-pate by being audience members.[21] Finally, Londa Schiebinger observes that by the nineteenth century, gendered representations of science had dropped out altogether, leaving a supposedly pure and apolitical method of inquiry and knowledge accumulation.[22] Given this historical process of the simultaneous subjection of nature and women on one hand and the erasure of gender in representations of science and technology on the other, it makes sense that scientific techniques, instruments, and methods of knowing would appear objective today. To assert otherwise—that technoscience is value-laden, politi-cal, and gendered masculine—rubs against the grain of centuries of institu-tional and cultural assertions to the contrary.

Surveillance technologies operate in this tradition. They still privilege sight, the primary sense of scientific inquiry, whether for the watching of people or for the monitoring and manipulation of databases. Michel Foucault famously introduced the specter of Jeremy Bentham's panopticon, or "all-seeing prison," as a metaphor for how bodies could be disciplined and con-trolled throughout societies by means of the internalization of disciplinary structures.[23] The rationalization and potential control of people and their activities becomes even more powerful, however, as information and com-munication systems become ubiquitous. Instead of everyone being subjected equally to the disciplinary gaze, we are now witnessing advanced social sort-ing made possible by electronic surveillance in all its forms.[24] The case made by this chapter is that the methods of abstraction upon which new surveil-lance systems are predicated are those in the spirit of the scientific revolution and Enlightenment rationality: of masculine control at a distance.

Domains of Everyday Surveillance

The sections that follow analyze how Enlightenment rationalities of dis-embodied abstraction and control at a distance permeate everyday surveillance systems in the domains of welfare, health care, and transportation. I chose these domains because they are primary arenas of public life that are accessed by a diverse range of people and in which surveillance can be difficult to perceive, usually because it operates at the level of abstraction. Surveillance, therefore, includes systems that may not initially—or primarily—be intended as surveil-lant but nonetheless lend themselves to that use or have that effect. Modern systems of technological surveillance have in common an ability to filter out social contexts and reduce social actors and practices to mere data that can be analyzed and sorted according to "objective" criteria. In other words, exercises of power are rendered invisible by nature of the supposed neutrality of tech-nologies, normalizing the sociotechnical sorting of the world.

These surveillance systems and practices are highly masculinized, at least on a theoretical level, because they depend upon disembodied representations of the world and an evacuation of social relations and contexts. Moreover, when the logics of these systems are applied back upon social space and used to govern people and practices, social inequalities are both solidified and obscured. Because social control through surveillance happens at a distance, or as an automated part of the system, these inequalities are more likely to be perceived as individual rather than collective problems.

The masculinization of spaces and practices manifests differently in each of the cases that follow. With welfare systems, recipients are constructed as deviant and in need of paternalistic supervision, the likes of which tend to place undue financial, physical, and emotional burdens upon the poor. With health care systems for tracking inventory and people in hospitals, nursing staff and patients are constructed as unruly and in need of disciplined management by administrators and data systems. With transportation systems, as discussed in chapter 7, imperatives of vehicular flow take priority over all other mobilities or uses of public streets and the social space of the street—or what can be construed as an embodied experience of social space—is transfigured into a representational space of rational vehicular throughput.

Technological surveillance in each of these domains (welfare, health care, transportation) reveals degrees of rational control at a distance. Whereas unequal power relations can and do occur through body discrimination and context or use discrimination, the emphasis of this chapter is upon discrimination by abstraction. The case I am making here is that discrimination by abstraction is a masculine and masculinizing property of these systems, but it is important to clarify that this does not mean the systems discriminate only against women. Instead, they effectively devalue embodied lived experience, social equality, and alternative forms of life. *An easy mistake to make here is to conflate gender with sex.* By arguing that these particular surveillance systems are gendered masculine, I am claiming that they draw upon and reproduce traditionally masculine logics of rational, active, and disembodied control. Whether men or women are the subjects or objects of surveillance is irrelevant for this analysis of discrimination by abstraction, even if the sex of the people involved would be pertinent for an analysis of body, context, or use discrimination.

WELFARE BENEFIT SYSTEMS

Surveillance of the poor is nothing new. Poor women of color, especially, are often the first targets of new surveillance systems. Examples proliferate. State-sponsored video surveillance in public places, for instance, inordinately focuses upon spheres dominated by poor and minority women, such as public transportation systems in the United States.[25] The Medical University of South Carolina infamously instituted a program of involuntarily drug testing of women who presented for obstetrics care at the Medicaid maternity ward and then arresting them if they tested positive for cocaine use; in some cases, women gave birth while handcuffed and were then transported straight to jail.[26] Throughout the United States, welfare "client information systems" construct fine-grained portraits of the income and spending patterns of recipients, the majority of whom are women. These systems are then used to facilitate the scrutiny and control of poor women by caseworkers and others.[27] In his superb study of women's resistance to welfare surveillance systems, John Gilliom demonstrates how the concept of "privacy" is ultimately insufficient for analyzing the concerns of women subjected to forms of "bureaucratic surveillance" such as the examples described here; instead, surveillance is about relations of power, domination, and conflict that are embedded within institutional structures and fueled by dubious cultural assumptions about the criminality of the poor.[28] These are just a few of the many possible examples of marginalizing surveillance geared toward poor women.

The case of "electronic benefit transfer" (EBT) systems for welfare and food stamp recipients demonstrates starkly the impositions of database surveillance on poor women and others. These systems were mandated by the Welfare Reform Act of 1996 with the explicit purpose of minimizing fraud. A secondary goal of such systems is, ostensibly, to reduce the stigma associated with the use of food stamps: now a "card," looking very much like an ATM card, is substituted for the stamps. EBT systems are perceived by policy makers to be effective at cracking down on abuse because they track all spending data (such as times, locations, and items), which can then be scrutinized by caseworkers who can interrogate recipients and penalize them as they (or the automated systems) see fit.

EBT tracking is a form of electronic surveillance that can have serious ramifications for those monitored by it. Welfare recipients' purchases are now scrutinized, with the result that the creative arrangements people implement in order to make ends meet are cracked down upon. For example, if women choose to pay a babysitter with the EBT card, letting the babysitter purchase clothing or the like, then these purchases are flagged for investigation by caseworkers. It should be noted that the EBT cards double for the distribution of food stamps and other welfare benefits, so using them for purchasing clothing is not necessarily a "violation" of the rules anyhow. Nonetheless, these women are made to feel as though it is. Virginia Eubanks highlights this surveillance dynamic by describing a video called *Watching Me*, which was produced by the women she works with at the Young Women's Christian Association (YWCA) in upstate New York:

[This video] opens with women reciting a litany of abuses: "He watches my every move," "He only lets me spend the money the way he says," "She doesn't like my friends," "He threatens to take my children away." Then the hook. "Do you think I'm talking about my boyfriend, my lover, my husband?," they ask. "No. I'm talking about my case worker."[29]

The economic hardships associated with the implementation of EBT systems should not be underestimated. The EBT system has had a profound impact upon the lives of poor minority women. Before the advent of this system, food stamp recipients were able to purchase food from local markets and cooperatives. Now, because many of these venues do not accept the magnetic-strip EBT cards, "benefits" recipients in upstate New York and elsewhere must hire a taxi and travel several miles to the nearest large chain supermarket that accepts the cards.[30] This situation adds burdens of labor, time, and cost to the lives of these women and certainly impedes the larger assumed goals of economic assimilation.

As with many neoliberal policies, these systems combine elements of social control with the privatization of public goods and services. The lucrative contracts for running EBT systems have been awarded to private companies like Citicorp Services Inc., which currently runs the systems in thirty-four states.[31] Meanwhile, EBT cardholders are charged fees for withdrawing cash from ATMs or requesting "cash back" from stores. These fees quickly add up. A *New York Times* article reported, for example, that a mother trying to support a family on $448 a month was charged up to $2.35 for each of her transactions throughout the month.[32] And an audit of the New York EBT system found that these surcharges, which are taken as profits for Citicorp, added up to $700,151 per month for recipients in the state of New York.[33] In a very real sense, the meager public resources allotted for the poor are being expropriated by private corporations, leaving the poor (and even state policy makers) with little recourse for challenging these contractual arrangements once they are in place.

The example of the EBT system illustrates how neoliberal security cultures of privatization and responsibilization are being inscribed in technological systems and institutional arrangements. While corporations may benefit tremendously from such arrangements, the poor—and especially poor women—are subjected to increased scrutiny and control. As Gilliom writes, these emerging forms of bureaucratic surveillance manifest "a way of seeing and knowing the world that excludes much of our true complexity while moving a small cluster of characteristics to the forefront."[34] Surveillance, in other words, is not objective, but it is objectifying in a very restricted and disciplinary sense. Even if women were not the primary targets of such surveillance systems, these systems, by filtering out social context and objectifying others, enforce masculinized representations of social experience and value.

HOSPITALS AND RADIO-FREQUENCY IDENTIFICATION SYSTEMS

As with many other industries, hospitals are embracing advanced personnel- and inventory-tracking systems. The stated goals are to reduce medical errors, save money, and generally increase the efficiency of healthcare delivery.[35] President George W. Bush weighed in on the issue with a mandate in 2004 for the incorporation of health information technology (HIT) systems into all U.S. medical practices.[36] And the Obama administration has pledged to provide $19 billion over the next few years to fund HITs, with a specific focus on electronic health records.[37] The intention of the tracking systems may not be explicitly for surveillance purposes, but the systems nevertheless possess affordances for such uses—especially for tracking nurses, the majority of whom are women.[38] The most interesting of these systems are those that use radio-frequency identification (RFID) chips embedded in name tags, bracelets, or stickers for tracking people and medical equipment. Once a hospital is equipped with an RFID system, people and inventory can be tracked in "real time," and locational databases can be generated to scrutinize the movement (or nonmovement) of people and objects at a later date. As might be expected, when these systems are used to track people, they apply almost exclusively to patients and nurses, and almost never to physicians or hospital management.

In writing about RFID systems in hospitals, Jill Fisher calls attention to the important fact that intentionality is not a necessary condition for surveillance to be taking place. She explains: "Surveillance is about control; if the RFID systems can monitor groups or flows to regulate practices, then social control and thus surveillance are occurring."[39] One of the ways that social control manifests is through the tracking of equipment. Traditionally, nurses hoard scarce equipment in the hospital so that they know where it is and can readily access it when needed. Staff members typically learn to coordinate their activities and share both equipment and knowledge to fulfill their responsibilities in these complex and stressful workplaces. Thus, the cultivation of cooperative social relations among staff is necessary for hospitals to function. RFID systems for equipment are intended to rationalize these social systems so that computers can tell anyone where equipment is at any time. Coincidentally, such systems also strip away some of the power of nursing staff while simultaneously intensifying their workloads: often nurses are the ones charged with maintaining these systems and rounding up equipment—on top of their usual duties. There is some evidence to suggest that nurses, in turn, may sabotage such systems by destroying the RFID tags.[40]

The tracking of people represents a more obvious mechanism of surveillance and social control in hospital settings. This includes the tagging of patients and hospital staff. Patients are tagged with RFIDs not only to give them unique identifiers for the prevention of medical errors but also to track their movements from one ward to the next (from lab work, to surgery, to hospital room, and so on). With some systems, when patients are released from the hospital their RFID bracelets are cut, sending a signal to housekeeping to make up the room and free up the "bed" for another patient.

This function was designed in response to nurses who would postpone reporting the release of a patient so that they could keep the flow of patients under their care more manageable. The RFID system functions as a "technological fix" to monitor the status of patients and increase management's control over nursing staff by disallowing nurses from regulating their own workloads in this manner.

When administrators demand the tagging of nurses themselves, the level of surveillance can become oppressive. Even if the stated intention is "workflow management," the implications for nurses are those of labor intensification, job insecurity, undesired scrutiny, and privacy loss. The social context becomes a "prickly"[41] one that is hostile to worker empowerment and greatly reduces worker satisfaction. To date, such efforts at top-down micromanagement of staff by means of RFIDs have met with resistance. Only when implemented with complete "buy in" and participation from the nursing staff have such systems been embraced.[42] One desired feature for nurses and others is an "off" switch on each RFID badge so that they can take breaks without subjecting themselves to remote tracking.[43]

Nonetheless, RFID systems lend themselves to surveillance by means of their "passive" data collection, their increasing ubiquity, and their abstraction of social space.[44] It is the control-at-a-distance dimension that especially enables the masculinization of work spaces and practices, meaning that individuals in these spaces are governed by paternalistic logics of control that transcend the spaces themselves. There is a discernable rationality at work with these systems. Fisher explains: "By reframing the actions of participants within the system as data, the tracking of those actions is artificially delinked from the politically charged realm of surveillance and the contextually complicated social and material spaces of hospitals."[45] The RFID systems and their supplemental discourses objectify and rationalize space: they rescript what counts and what matters in those spaces, whereby the things that matter most are the things that can be counted. At the same time, the assumption is that this is an apolitical and natural process of technological development and that no "surveillance" can be occurring because only abstract flows are being monitored and managed. The facts of the system are thoroughly socially constructed and value-laden, but the process of their construction is erased, leaving behind a system of social control that is highly reductive.

Another, and more provocative, use of RFIDs for patients involves implanting RFIDs into patients' arms. The FDA approved this use of RFID implants for humans in 2004, giving the company Verichip the green light to cultivate medical markets for these devices. In many ways, the process is similar to the microchipping of pets, such as dogs and cats, so that if they are found somewhere after being lost, they can be scanned at local shelters and veterinarian offices and their owner information determined. For human patients, RFID implants are designed to help medical staff rapidly identify a person and his or her medical history, which might be especially helpful if the person is debilitated in some way and cannot communicate.[46] Outside medical domains, other uses of these technologies are for security clearance in military, intelligence, or technology industry settings,[47] or for the transmission of credit card information in nightclubs, as has been documented in Spain.[48] Theories about the commodification of the body are no longer figurative when credit information is embedded subcutaneously in people's arms.

A feminist critique of RFID implants would attend to the ways in which technologies of abstraction are literally embodied, while the social context is stripped away, reducing the body to data in the eyes of the system. Thus, concern about implants is not a call for bodily purity; we are all already cyborgs to varying degrees.[49] Instead, it is the potential for implants and RFID more generally to realign power relations and circumvent or discredit individual expertise—of patients to speak for themselves of their own bodily experiences, for instance—that is of particular concern. Apart from implants, other implications of hospital RFID systems include the potential loss of control by patients over their own personal information or the diminished ability of nurses to organize and manage their workplaces. The valence of these systems, in other words, is toward decontextualized representations and mechanisms of control.

INTELLIGENT TRANSPORTATION SYSTEMS

As the preceding chapter discussed, in the domain of transportation, electronic systems are being implemented across the United States, United Kingdom, and elsewhere to automate and rationalize transportation control functions.[50] I briefly revisit intelligent transportation systems (ITS) here to provide a gender analysis of them as a masculine form of surveillance. Unlike the electronic surveillance systems being deployed for welfare-benefits distribution or for tracking people and objects in hospitals, ITS utilize video surveillance cameras and have elaborate "control rooms" for traffic engineers to actively monitor transportation flows. In a sense, aspects of ITS look a lot more like what one might traditionally expect of surveillance: people sitting in rooms watching "video walls" displaying the many video feeds from all the cameras distributed throughout the city at intersections or along highways. Nonetheless, recall that ITS engineers object to any intimation that they manage surveillance systems. For them, the term "surveillance" implies people watching people and scrutinizing their behavior, at best, or a Big Brother police state, at worst. Alternatively, they claim not to be interested in people at all, only in efficiently managing data and flows. According to them, the images of—or information about—people captured by the system are only depersonalized data, and in that context people cannot be surveilled, even if their movements are regulated.

ITS control and rationalize the movements of people in very specific ways, and the values and assumptions that undergird the design of these systems enforce certain social orders, perhaps even more effectively because they are invisible to most people. For instance, these systems betray a discernable prejudice against bodies, especially in the form of pedestrians or bicyclists. Because the system prioritizes automobile traffic, other forms of mobility are marginalized and devalued. Thus, transportation engineers say that the primary purpose is to manage "traffic," meaning cars, even though the system itself is presented in government literature as coordinating multiple mobilities.[51] From this dominant lens, pedestrians and bicyclists represent "systems noise" that must be attended to but that ultimately detracts from the primary mission of maximizing vehicular flow.

This bias against bodies is obscured by ITS. In turn, the abstract representational system is imposed back upon social space, upon streets and people, so that the values of its design become part of the background logic of everyday practices. Preferential treatment for certain mobilities over others is reinforced and normalized, along with accompanying inequalities, whereby the poor tend to be subjected to greater transportation burdens than their relatively affluent counterparts.[52] Recall as well that another traffic engineer complained that the task of accommodating difference (in the form of pedestrians) presented a special problem for the overall functionality of the system because traffic lights may get out of sync. Pedestrians are bodies, whereas cars are data objects. Because the system is designed to increase the flow of data objects and to value that outcome, pedestrians are problematic variables in the throughput equation. These bodies not only slow down the drive speed—they also possess the potential to destabilize the whole system and its synchronization of lights.

A case could be made that these transportation systems transform streets into "arteries," making streets hostile to difference, whether different mobilities, different uses of streets and sidewalks, or different priorities for public space. With some possible exceptions of coordinating multiple modes of mass transit,[53] ITS, especially in the United States, appear to augment and automate existing design biases, which prioritize the flow of private automobiles at the expense of all other modes of transportation or alternative uses of streets. For instance, the general absence of bike lanes and crosswalks in U.S. cities reveals a persistent, discriminatory value system embedded in the infrastructure upon which ITS are overlaid.

Feminist scholars have long criticized the rational planning of cities, demonstrating how the idealized Euclidean grid of city planners functions as a "poem of male desires"[54] of spatial control that also tends to artificially dichotomize social space into male and female spheres, with the female sphere forever subordinated to the male one.[55] I propose that intelligent transportation systems be read against this backdrop. The systems are outgrowths of masculine rational planning; they dissect urban and suburban spaces; and they impose a paternalistic kind of order upon what is perceived to be the disorderly world of the street.

CONCLUSION

This chapter has analyzed the gender implications of surveillance in the domains of welfare, health care, and transportation. Each of the technological systems in these domains imposes degrees of social control by means of its automated functions. Although their primary intended purposes may not be surveillance, the effects are those of surveillance. I have made the argument that these systems operate upon ideals of masculine control at a distance and as a result enforce a masculinization of space and practice. They do this by reducing social space and practice to abstract representations or data and then imposing those representations back upon their contexts of derivation. Of course, individuals and groups resist and have agency, but the power relations are vastly asymmetrical and the technological systems have a normalizing effect that masks their inherent politics.[56]

I introduced three conceptual categories for analyzing gender and technology: body discrimination, context or use discrimination, and discrimination by abstraction. Of those categories, scholarly attention to context or use discrimination with surveillance has been the most documented and theorized to date. Because most institutions, workplaces, and public and private spheres are already deeply patriarchal, new technological systems that are introduced into those arenas take on those values and reinforce those relations. This is why the finding of men watching women with surveillance systems is so prevalent. What I have tried to develop here, however, is a line of inquiry into discrimination by abstraction. In the spirit of feminist critiques of the scientific revolution, the Enlightenment project, and the rational planning of cities, I have delved into the potential of new technological systems not only to surveil people but to simultaneously represent and control people in very partial, discriminatory ways.

Rather than simply deconstruct surveillance as a form of masculine control, a valuable next step would be to identify and theorize conditions that lend themselves to power equalization along the lines of gender, as well as race and class. Each of the three cases of discrimination by abstraction discussed in this chapter could be responded to with a reconstructive feminist approach. Such an approach would ground the technologies in social context, embodiment, and place. Donna Haraway's concept of *situated knowledges* captures well this alternative epistemological orientation because it insists on the placement or "marking" of knowledge within its particular political, economic, and cultural contexts.[57] In contrast, the masculine tradition of science typically depends upon "unmarked" knowledges, which "are those character-ized by a presumption of objectivity that usually obfuscates their social embeddedness in white, male, or other dominant cultural perspectives."[58] If situated knowledges were given more voice, value, and influence, it is likely that spaces, systems, and social relations could be reconfigured in more just ways.

Electronic benefit transfer systems for welfare and food stamp distribution could be responded to, for instance, by questioning the foundational, dis-criminatory assumptions of the increasingly privatized welfare system. Social responsibility for the needs of everyone could be addressed through guaran-teed wages, health care, child care, and so on without falling back on an indi-vidualizing system of management and control that presumes deviance. As Virginia Eubanks relates, women on welfare are made to feel isolated and responsible for the failures of the welfare system to meet basic human needs.[59] When they come together as a group to share their experiences in a social context of self-conscious situated knowledge—as opposed to the presumed unmarked and objective knowledge of EBT databases—their experiences are validated and their collective knowledge is expanded. Welfare could be grounded in context to emphasize rights over "benefits," social over individ-ual responsibility, and public over private management of the systems.

RFID tags in hospitals could be implemented, as well, in a way that stressed social context, collective needs, and stakeholder participation. Jill Fisher writes of one example where the decision to adopt an RFID system was made by nursing staff, instead of by hospital administrators; as a result, there was far greater buy in from hospital staff.[60] A focus on embodiment would also highlight and legitimize any feelings of discomfort felt by hospital patients and personnel about potential surveillance or labor intensification, which could lead to solutions that allowed for greater privacy or control over one's workplace. It may be the case, of course, that a situated, contextual approach to hospital technologies could lead to a decision that RFID systems were unacceptable in these environments.

Finally, intelligent transportation systems could be reconfigured to sup-port multimodal transportation and perhaps even introduce degrees of friction for private automobiles so that streets could begin to be reclaimed as social places. The hegemony of the automobile could be disrupted so that trans-portation opportunities were equalized for all members of society, probably through a robust mass transit system and disincentives for automobile use. London offers an example of such productive disincentives by limiting entry into the city by car and then using a surveillance system to assess fines if entry restrictions are violated.[61] Ultimately, reducing and slowing down vehicular throughput on streets could alter experiences of them, from spaces of transit to places of social exchange.[62]

While voyeurism of women by men may be the most obvious point for feminist critique of technological surveillance, the emptying out of social context through abstract representations may be far more damaging in the long run. Technologies of control at a distance exert a surveillant force upon social practices and relations and now extend to almost all spheres of public life. The logics of technological, disembodied control are inscribed in infrastructures and institutions, facilitating the governance of people and the naturalization of inequalities. The reduction of people and social practices to data that can be easily manipulated is an exercise of power that demands feminist critique and intervention.

CHAPTER 9

Countersurveillance

RESISTANCE TO SURVEILLANCE, especially to dominating forms of surveillance, is a vital dimension of power negotiations. As Michel Foucault observes, "Where there is power, there is resistance, and yet, or rather consequently, this resistance is never in a position of exteriority in relation to power."[1] Put differently, resistance is not reactive or in dialectical relationship to power; rather, it is co-constitutive of it. There are clearly many forms that resistance to surveillance can take; they range from civil society organizations like the American Civil Liberties Union challenging government spying programs in courts, on one end of the spectrum, to individuals not complying with marketers' requests for personal information like zip codes and e-mail addresses, on the other. People are not simply passive subjects compliantly succumbing to demands for their behaviors, preferences, and beliefs to become more transparent to and controllable by others.

Nevertheless, when the field for social action and identity construction is radically constricted, opportunities for effective resistance—at least effective resistance without great personal risk—are diminished. One dominant argument of this book, for instance, is that neoliberal policies and practices have transformed public spaces and rights into private ones and have individualized what might be thought of as collective problems. Demands for people to become insecurity subjects fit neatly within this neoliberal framework because these demands push responsibility onto individuals to meet security needs through consumption, regardless of the veracity of security threats or their probability of actualizing. Resistance to surveillance can also function within and therefore unintentionally reinforce these security cultures if it does not also challenge the rules that govern possibilities for resistance. To make this case, this chapter analyzes practices of countersurveillance by activists and media artists—particularly against video and closed circuit television (CCTV) systems in urban areas—and theorizes their political implications.

Countersurveillance activism can include disabling or destroying surveillance cameras, mapping paths of least surveillance and disseminating that information over the Internet, employing video cameras to monitor sanctioned surveillance systems and their personnel, or staging public plays to draw attention to the prevalence of surveillance in society. In some cases, marginal groups selectively appropriate technologies that they might otherwise oppose when used by those with institutional power.[2] These examples illustrate the underdetermination of technologies and suggest further avenues for political intervention through countersurveillance. However, because surveillance systems evolve through social conflict, countersurveillance practices may implicate opposition groups in the further development of global systems of control.

Countersurveillance operates within and in reaction to ongoing global transformations of public spaces and resources. According to social theorists, a crisis in capital accumulation in the 1970s precipitated a shift from mass production to flexible production regimes, catalyzing organizational decentralization, labor outsourcing, computerized automation, just-in-time production, and, increasingly, the privatization of that which has historically been considered "public."[3] These structural transformations aggravated conditions of social inequality, leading to the development of new mechanisms of social control to regulate bodies in this unstable terrain. Some of the most effective forms of social control are those that naturalize the exclusion of economically or culturally marginalized groups through architecture or infrastructure. Mass incarceration of over 2.3 million individuals in the United States alone is one extreme measure of such postindustrial exclusion.[4] Less dramatically, but perhaps more pervasively, fortified enclaves such as gated communities, shopping malls, and business centers have multiplied exponentially over the past decade and seem to be as prevalent in "developing" as in "developed" countries.[5] Additionally, privatized streets, parks, and security services effectively sacrifice civic accountability and civil rights while increasing affordances for the monitoring of public life.[6] Finally, telecommunications and other infrastructures unevenly distribute access to the goods and services necessary for modern life while facilitating data collection on and control of the public.[7] Against this backdrop, the embedding of technological surveillance into spaces and infrastructures serves to augment not only existing social control functions but also capital accumulation imperatives, which are readily seen with the sharing of surveillance operations and data between public and private sectors.[8]

Through a range of interventions into the logic and institutions of global capitalism, countersurveillance tacticians seek to disrupt these trends in the privatization, sanitation, and elimination of public spaces, resources, and rights. While the ideologies and intentions of those engaging in countersurveillance are manifold and disparate, they are unified in the mission of safeguarding—or creating—the necessary spaces for meaningful participation in determining the social, environmental, and economic conditions of life. Because of this orientation, the term *countersurveillance* will be used here to indicate intentional, tactical uses or disruptions of surveillance technologies to challenge power asymmetries.

In this chapter I review several countersurveillance practices and analyze the power relations simultaneously revealed and reproduced by resistance to institutionalized surveillance. The emphasis here is upon the *framing* of surveillance problems and responses by activists, or on points of symbolic conflict rather than physical confrontation. Thus, it is assumed that while countersurveillance practitioners may have immediate practical goals, such as circumventing or destroying video cameras, that they are foremost engaged in acts of symbolic resistance with the intention of raising public awareness about modern surveillance regimes. I analyze two categories of countersurveillance efforts—interventions into the technical and social faces of public surveillance—and then theorize the efficacy and implications of countersurveillance more generally. The data are drawn primarily from Web sites, video productions, and publications, but I conducted several interviews with activists in the United States to corroborate the critical readings offered here. The main argument is that activists tend to individualize both surveillance problems and methods of resistance, leaving the institutions, policies, and cultural assumptions that support public surveillance relatively insulated from attack. Furthermore, while the oppositional framing presented by activists (that is, countersurveillance versus surveillance) may challenge the status quo and raise public awareness, it also introduces the danger of unintentionally reinforcing the systems of social control that activists seek to undermine.

TECHNICAL INTERVENTIONS

Surveillance circumvention and destruction are two activist interventions that concentrate on the technical side of modern surveillance. Of course the technical and social dimensions of all technologies are thoroughly intertwined, as science and technology studies scholars have well demonstrated,[9] so the point in separating them out here is to draw attention to the specific sites of intervention as defined by countersurveillance tacticians.

Institute for Applied Autonomy

The first example is offered by the Institute for Applied Autonomy (IAA), which is a collective of technicians, artists, and activists engaged in projects of productive disruption and collective empowerment.[10] According to its Web site, "[IAA] was founded in 1998 as a technological research and development organization concerned with individual and collective self-determination. Our mission is to study the forces and structures which effect self-determination; to create cultural artifacts which address these forces; and to develop technologies which serve social and human needs."[11] Some of these projects include automated graffiti-writing robots, a propaganda-distributing robot called "Little Brother," and a Web-based application called "iSee" that allows users to map paths of least surveillance in urban areas.

The surveillance-mapping iSee application offers a provocative entry point into countersurveillance territory. The opening flash display on the Web site depicts a blue robotlike icon of a person who has a cannonball bomb with a lit fuse for a head. Next, the lens of the viewing area pulls back, revealing that the person is squarely placed underneath a large microscope with a red video surveillance camera as its lens. The red cameras then multiply, triangulating on the person, who begins a passage, represented by yellow dash marks, along city streets. The graphic rotates and pulls back one last time to reveal that the name of the application ("iSee") has been traced by the route taken by the robotlike figure. In the upper left corner, in a mock allusion to numbering conventions for software development, the Web site overtly references the tense political climate of surveillance in places like New York City: "iSEE v.911: 'Now more than ever.'"

Once past the opening scene, the application presents the user with a street map of Manhattan with a dramatic black background and abundant red boxes indicating areas under video surveillance. The map is engaged by clicking first on a starting point and second on a destination point. After a few seconds of calculation, a yellow route is indicated for a person to travel the path of least surveillance to his or her destination. As with other online mapping programs, the user can zoom in or out, scroll up, down, or sideways, or "reset" to begin the mapping process anew. Finally, the bottom right corner displays the travel distance and the number of cameras that one will be exposed to along the route specified.

This Web site offers rich symbolic referents that extend well beyond the utility of a route-generating application. The figure of a person as robot communicates both the dehumanizing threat of individual conformity (or self-regulation) in the face of ubiquitous surveillance and the construction of individuals as social machinery, data points, or risk potentialities from the point of view of those doing the monitoring. That this iconographic robot-person has a cannonball bomb with a lit fuse for a head represents the explosive volatility of the situation: viewing people as threats to be monitored and controlled, rather than as citizens with civil liberties, may destroy civil society and may lead to violent opposition. Finally, the placement of this solitary figure underneath its own scrutinizing microscope(s) stresses the atomization of individuals as suspect bodies strangely decontextualized and divorced from political, social, or economic realities. The tacit critique here is that once atomized as such, surveillance regimes view individuals from a universalistic perspective and are therefore unable to perceive particularistic conditions, such as racism or economic inequality, which inscribe all social relations. If such particulars fall outside the sterilizing camera frame, then they cease to exist as mitigating circumstances or—perhaps more importantly—as social problems worthy of attention and correction.

Such iSee applications are now available for the cities of New York, Amsterdam, and Ljubljana. The aim of these Web sites is neither to directly interfere with the surveillance apparatus in these cities nor to allow individuals to effectively circumvent monitoring, although that is the immediate and practical outcome. Instead, the goal is to raise public awareness and foster public debate over the prevalence of surveillance cameras and their effects on public life. Because technological infrastructures become invisible when they are functional,[12] and the political effects of technologies, more generally, are off the radar screen of most people,[13] the intervention of iSee renders visible the larger pattern of surveillance proliferation and calls into question its purpose, agenda, and effects. The iSee intervention jolts viewers and users into awareness; it invites inquiry into surveillance devices distributed throughout our lives; it opens up a space for discussion about what kinds of surveillance are acceptable and what kinds are not.

RTMark

If the Institute for Applied Autonomy's iSee application offers an intervention for circumventing video surveillance in public spaces, the group RTMark advocates a more radical and direct approach: destroying the cameras. RTMark, or ®™ark, is well known in activist and culture-jamming circles for its high-profile projects. One of its more famous ventures was "The Barbie Liberation Organization," which swapped voice boxes between Barbie and GI Joe dolls so that Barbie would say things like "Vengeance is mine!" and GI Joe would declare things like "Math is hard!"[14] More recently, RTMark's "The Yes Men" gained international attention by pretending to be spokespersons for Dow Chemical (which is now the parent company of Union Carbide) and promising on BBC World Television to provide reparations for gas victims in Bhopal, India.[15] RTMark's guide to surveillance-camera destruction is an engaging and deliberately messy Web site (vis-à-vis its other pages) that celebrates low-tech, decentralized, populist, and "fun" approaches to these activities.[16]

The "Guide to Closed Circuit Television (CCTV) destruction" is a nut-and-bolts document that supports this humble orientation through its stark design and formulaic style. After the document's title, a provocative black-and-white picture of a CCTV tower, and other prolegomenon (for example, contact e-mail for suggestions), the page presents an itemized and hyperlinked table of contents for quick reference. The main sections include "WHY DESTROY CCTV CAMERAS," "TYPES OF CCTV CAMERA," "METHODS OF ATTACK," and "TRAINING."[17] Each section remains structurally true to the "guide" genre by parsimoniously explaining exactly what one needs to do and what one needs to know, without much other information to distract from the countersurveillance task(s) at hand.

The section on methods of attack is the most provocative. The methods described are placing plastic bags filled with glue around cameras, affixing stickers or tape over camera lenses, shooting cameras with children's high-powered water gun toys filled with paint, temporarily disabling lenses with laser pointers, cutting CCTV cables with axes or garden tools, and dropping concrete blocks on cameras from rooftops. Rather than simply describing methods for disabling video surveillance cameras, however, the instructions reveal a pattern of values and an engaging subtext about camera destruction as an embodied social practice. Thus, methods that draw public attention to the surveillance systems or that reveal cameras as inoperable (such as shooting them with paint guns) are preferred to those that do not heighten public awareness (such as disabling cameras with a laser pointer). Along these lines, regarding the method of bagging cameras, the site says: "To Bag a camera theres a high chance that you can reach it with ease. If this is the case dont hesitate to smash the glass, lens and any other components. Dont bag it afterwards, people need to see the units smashed" (spelling errors and abbreviations are accurate to the Web site and serve to reinforce the rough aesthetic).

Other values communicated by the guide are those of fun, efficiency, and permanence. The paint gun method is celebrated as being "Fast, fun and easy," and therefore "Highly recommended," and, similarly, cutting camera cables emits "Satisfying sparks." The paint gun method is also touted for its relative efficiency ("one hour action can easily take out 10 cameras"), compared to the laser pointer, which has questionable efficacy and is therefore not recommended. Finally, permanently destroying equipment is valued more highly than temporarily disabling it: cutting cables "Requires complete costly rewiring" and block drops on cameras will "totally" destroy them "in a shower of sparks." With the paint gun method, by contrast, the camera is "easily cleaned," so the intervention is "only effective for short time only."

These countersurveillance activities are intended to be social and to raise social awareness. A section on "working together" highlights the importance of trusting those you work with and getting to know their strengths and weaknesses. And clearly disabled cameras, much like the Web site itself, are intended to alert people to the prevalence of unregulated surveillance. One might even say that camera destruction by activists is not a goal of the Web site at all but that it instead seeks to provoke the public to insist that controls be placed on surveillance proliferation. The subtext of the site is one of overcoming both conformity and compliant adaptation to the surveillance society. This message can be read in passages on physical training ("Dont go to the gym—you need to be deconditioned not conditioned") or on learning one's territory ("Don't use paths or streets [only cross them at right angles]"). In this document, embodied social practice and acts of reflexive subversion serve as responses to surveillance technologies that are seen as socially sterilizing.

ON THE SURFACE, the Institute for Applied Autonomy's iSee project and RTMark's guide to surveillance camera destruction may seem like radically different responses to public surveillance. iSee is a high-tech application facilitating circumvention of video surveillance through its generation of paths of least surveillance. The guide to camera destruction, on the other hand, encourages resistance against public surveillance through low-tech, neo-Luddite attacks. Both forms of countersurveillance, however, focus their attention and critique on the *technologies of surveillance*, which act as material representations of large-scale monitoring regimes. Neither of them directly targets the public and private institutions that are mobilizing surveillance or the individuals within these institutions.[18]

The few glimpses these groups offer of their social or political adversaries reveal them as individual police officers or private security guards who are emboldened by the technologies. Both groups note the propensity of video surveillance to amplify existing conditions of discrimination or abuse while obscuring the actors behind the scenes. IAA's information page for iSee mobilizes social science research on surveillance, complete with academic citations, to thoroughly document trends toward increased abuse of marginalized groups with video surveillance, most notably of minorities, women, youth, outsiders (such as the homeless), and activists. Part of the reason that the technologies lend themselves to these uses, the site explains, is that policies for surveillance oversight, access, or data retention are either purposely opaque or nonexistent; this is especially true in the United States because so much public surveillance in that country is conducted by private companies, so the equipment and footage is privately owned. Of course, it should be pointed out that regardless of regulation or oversight, the technologies themselves insulate the operators from immediate, if not all, scrutiny, thereby encouraging widespread voyeurism of women and profiling of racial and other minorities.[19] The RTMark site echoes these sentiments with quotes from well-known "surveillance studies" scholars such as Clive Norris, Gary Armstrong, and Jason Ditton, but otherwise answers the question of "Why destroy CCTV cameras" with the simple response of "Trust your instincts."

Because in the eyes of these groups surveillance technologies catalyze abuse by individuals, the answer is to draw attention to the cameras through provocative Web sites or, more overtly, to circumvent and/or destroy them. The interventions of these activist groups concentrate on the technical side of modern surveillance, and while they are explicitly critical of social or institutional structures, the tendency is to individualize the problems by individualizing the abusive actors—who are identified either as police or security guards. Still, it must be noted that attention to police officers or other agents of surveillance is marginal in their presentations. As the next section will show, countersurveillance can also be targeted at the institutional agents enmeshed within corporate or law-enforcement systems and/or located behind the cameras.

SOCIAL INTERVENTIONS

While some countersurveillance activities, such as those described in the previous section, direct criticism at the technologies themselves, other modes of intervention seek to engage with specific agents of surveillance, such as camera operators, police, and security personnel. This section will investigate two of these social interventions: Steve Mann's Shooting Back project and performances by the Surveillance Camera Players. As with the Institute for Applied Autonomy and RTMark, these interventions represent two ends of the spectrum from high-tech to low-tech (see table 1); as I will argue, they have similar difficulty in moving critiques of surveillance beyond the level of the individual to their larger institutional and political origins.

Shooting Back

Drawing directly upon military metaphors, Steve Mann's Shooting Back project utilizes wearable, high-tech surveillance devices to take video footage "shots" of security personnel and other workers in privately owned stores. Mann or his collaborators are equipped with two sets of recording technologies for this project: a covert wearable camera, implanted either in sunglasses or a baseball cap, and a handheld video recorder that is kept concealed in a bag until needed as a prop. For the intervention, Mann first walks into a store that has a fairly obvious surveillance system, with tinted glass domes in the ceiling, for example. He then asks clerks, managers, and/or guards what the glass domes are for and receives a variety of responses along the lines of "I don't know" or "They're light fixtures" or "They're for security, but you don't need to worry about them if you're not doing anything wrong." All of these interactions are recorded with Mann's hidden, wearable camera. Next, Mann removes the handheld video recorder from his bag and points it in the

TABLE I

Countersurveillance Interventions

	Mode of intervention	
Arena of intervention	High-tech	Low-tech
Technical	Institute for Applied Autonomy	RTMark
Social	Shooting Back	Surveillance Camera Players

faces of his interlocutors. As might be expected, they promptly shy away from
the recorder, tell him that pictures or other recordings are disallowed in the
store, and ask him to leave. Mann responds by parroting their earlier words
about not needing to worry about recordings if one is not doing anything
wrong and asking them why they are so uncomfortable. Then he leaves. The
footage from these interactions is placed on Web sites for public viewing, and
Mann has also created a documentary film from this material.[20]

This countersurveillance intervention is explicitly conceived of as an art
project that appropriates surveillance technologies to challenge their dominant meanings and uses. Mann mobilizes a tactic he calls "reflectionism," or
reflecting experiences of being surveilled back on the surveillers, with the
goal of destabilizing store employees to make them realize that they are
merely "totalitarianist officials" involved in acts of blind obedience and conformity.[21] Mann writes: "It is my hope that the department store attendant/
representative sees himself/herself in the bureaucratic "mirror" that I have
created . . . [and that this helps them] to realize or admit for a brief instant that
they are puppets and to confront the reality of what their blind obedience
leads to."[22] Beyond this somewhat dubious educational goal, the Shooting
Back project further aspires to explode the rhetoric behind systematic public
surveillance in places of commerce. For example, the project raises the question: if surveillance is intended for public safety, then would not more cameras increase the potential for such safety? The answer is an obvious no,
because the primary intended function of cameras in stores is theft prevention, and they are as often trained on employees as on customers.[23]

Shooting Back is a provocative project because it calls attention to the
embodied experiences of watching and being watched, of recording and
being recorded. Usual uses of video surveillance, in contradistinction, tend to
erase all sense of embodied action and interaction through their ambiguity
(you do not know who is watching or when), through their integration into
infrastructure (they become the taken-for-granted backdrop to social life), and
through their mediation of experience (camera operators may feel a disconnect
from those they are watching, and vice versa). Shooting Back disrupts the illu-
sion of detached, objective, impersonal, disembodied monitoring—a camera
in one's face personalizes the experience of being recorded in a very direct
and uncomfortable way. One can speculate that the project is especially destabilizing and annoying for employees, because for them store surveillance systems and monitoring practices are institutional projections that they are
relatively powerless to alter.

Mann's rather unforgiving denouncement of individuals working in
stores, however, reveals certain assumptions about the problems of modern
surveillance. First, by criticizing employees as being "puppets" who blindly
accept their companies' explanations for surveillance and comply with

company policies, Mann implies that all individuals are rational actors with equal social and economic footing. Thus, if low-income employees elect not to fight the system as he does, then they must be either ignorant or weak-willed, or both. Second, by calling store clerks and security guards representatives of totalitarian surveillance regimes, Mann conflates individuals with the institutions they are a part of, effectively sidestepping the important but more difficult problem of changing institutional relations, structures, or logics. Both these assumptions lead to the conclusion that one can contend with the problem of rampant surveillance by intervening on the level of the individual and by educating people about their complicity with the systems. Unfortunately, the fact that people have very real dependencies upon their jobs or that vast power differentials separate workers from the systems they work within (and perhaps from activists and academics as well) become unimportant issues once the critique of surveillance is abstracted and individualized in this way.

Surveillance Camera Players

The Surveillance Camera Players (SCP) is a New York–based ad hoc acting troupe that stages performances in front of surveillance cameras in public places.[24] Founded in 1996 with a performance of Alfred Jarry's *Ubu Roi* in front of a subway station, it has since performed numerous play adaptations of famous (and not-so-famous) works of cautionary fiction or troubling non-fiction, ranging from George Orwell's *1984* to Wilhelm Reich's *The Mass Psychology of Fascism*.[25] Because most surveillance cameras are not sound-equipped, the troupe members narrate their performances with large white placard signs, which they hold up for remotely located camera operators to read. A performance of *1984*, for instance, uses placards describing scene locations (for example, "ROOM 101") or key lines from the book (for example, "WE ARE THE DEAD").[26] When possible, fellow troupe members document the plays with video cameras and distribute information brochures to curious spectators. The players are routinely confronted by security guards or New York City police and asked to disperse, often before the conclusion of their performances.

Up close, it appears as if SCP is directing its messages at camera operators, police, or security guards. The troupe's determination to notice and respond to video surveillance, rather than let it fade uninterrogated into the urban landscape, places it in confrontation with institutional representatives. By speaking to cameras (and their representatives), the actors become perceived as threats to the political and economic systems that support and indeed demand public surveillance, so institutional agents move in to contend with the perceived threat. As with Steve Mann's concentration on individuals, SCP performances force interactions with others, and, because of this, they draw attention to the always present embodiment of surveillance technologies and the social relations they engender.

If one takes a step back, however, the Surveillance Camera Players are really performing for the public: they enroll the unwitting police and security personnel into their play so that the public can witness the spectacle and perhaps the absurdity of modern surveillant relations. The troupe acknowledges this staging explicitly: "The SCP no longer consider their primary audience to be the police officers and security guards who monitor the surveillance cameras installed in public places. Today, the SCP concentrate on the people who happen to walk by and see one of their performances."[27] In a mode true to its "situationist" theoretical orientation, SCP affirms that the revolutionary potential of art thoroughly infuses everyday life because everyday life is a complex artistic performance. In this vein, SCP seeks to repoliticize the everyday by inviting the public to participate in its performances, by inviting all of us to recognize that we are already enmeshed in political performances and that we are required to act—and act well.

The primary adversary for SCP is the state. SCP is concerned about the erosion of public space and personal privacy brought about by the state's support of police surveillance and its permissive non-regulation of private surveillance. Its members write:

> The SCP is firmly convinced that the use of video surveillance in public places for the purposes of law enforcement is unconstitutional, and that each image captured by police surveillance cameras is an unreasonable search. We also believe that it is irresponsible of the government to allow unlicensed private companies to install as many surveillance cameras as they please, and to install them wherever they please.[28]

The implication is that the state is not living up to its responsibility to safeguard civil liberties through improved regulation of public surveillance. Thus, SCP performances confront individual agents of public and private sector security, but the troupe's primary audience is the general public, whom it hopes to cast as transformative actors who can collectively agitate for social change, especially on the level of public policy.

BOTH STEVE MANN'S SHOOTING BACK PROJECT and the Surveillance Camera Players' performances intervene on an overtly social level by challenging institutional agents of surveillance. Mann draws upon relatively sophisticated technical apparatuses to place store representatives in uncomfortable positions. By doing so, he aims to reflect back to them the hypocritical logics and empty rhetoric that they impose upon others and to raise their awareness about their complicity with the surveillance society. SCP, on the other hand, employs decidedly low-tech countersurveillance props such as signs and costumes to address police and security guards with the aim of creating a public spectacle—and to raise public awareness about the everyday surveillance spectacle of which we are all already a part.

These two interventions share in common their focus on individual representatives of institutionalized surveillance. By engaging with store employees or speaking to those behind the cameras, Mann and SCP seek to reveal and challenge the larger structures and rationalities that those individuals represent. A key difference is that SCP overtly enrolls members of the public in activist performances, whereas Mann's project invites public involvement only through the technical mediation of Web sites. Because of this difference, SCP seems more successful at moving beyond its initial site of intervention (the individual) to critique institutions for their dominance over the public, which is a relationship betrayed by the ironic juxtaposition of police removing SCP performers from public streets while private companies remain free to monitor the public at will.

While each of the four countersurveillance interventions discussed in this chapter so far seeks to raise public awareness and to mobilize for social change, none is completely successful at moving its critique from the individual to the institutional plane. SCP comes closest to doing this, but so far its plays remain too isolated and discrete to effect long-term change. This deficiency may be in part because activists construct surveillance problems in individualized and abstracted terms in order to make them somewhat tractable and receptive to intervention. The challenge lies in ratcheting up the unit of analysis to the institutional level so that lasting change can be achieved. The desired outcomes might take the form of better regulation and oversight of surveillance and/or meaningful democratic participation in the process of setting surveillance policies, for instance. In the long run, as I will argue in the next section, the oppositional framing of surveillance versus countersurveillance may be counterproductive for meeting these goals.

Countersurveillance and Global Systems of Control

When viewed from a distance, surveillance and countersurveillance appear to be engaged in a complicated dance, with the larger, cumbersome partner pushing and pulling while the smaller, defter dancer negotiates her- or himself—and others—out of harm's way. The oafish leader is, of course, the state and corporate apparatus surveilling the public, and the partner is the collective of activist adversaries circumventing or destabilizing surveillance systems. Drawing upon Michel Foucault's insights about the disciplinary potential of modern bureaucratic regimes, one could read surveillance societies as bringing about disciplinary or panoptic relationships.[29] But Foucault was also insistent upon the *productive* capacity of power to generate and sustain social relations apart from any property of control that might be possessed by individuals. As Gilles Deleuze expresses it: "Power has no essence; it is simply operational. It is not an attribute but a relation: the power-relation is the set of possible relations between forces, which passes through the dominated forces no less than through the dominating."[30] Therefore, the metaphor of the panopticon is not a static or transcendent statement of disciplinary power but is instead a contingent and situated articulation of modernity in a fluid field of production regimes.[31]

In specific response to Foucault's work, Michel de Certeau's book *The Practice of Everyday Life* provides a point of departure for thinking about the agency of individuals and groups within disciplinary power structures.[32] For de Certeau, the practices of the dominant dancer clearly would be *strategic* ones of building control structures to regulate the activities of those in the field of power, whereas the practices of the defter dancer would be much more *tactical*, poaching off the existing structures to create new meanings and possibilities. The two dancers may be in opposition, but that does not change the fact that they are engaged in a reciprocal relationship and collective activity—although without comparable degrees of influence or control. It is this tense connection that is worth probing, even if there is never an embrace or a union, because after all the exchanges of strategic structuring and tactical appropriation, the dance has moved somewhere across the floor and created a pattern, or a logic, or a world that was not there before.[33]

Examples of this problematic, if not dialectical, relationship between surveillance and countersurveillance practitioners abound. The capture on videotape of the beating of Rodney King in Los Angeles in 1991 did not necessarily catalyze correctives to actions of police brutality, nor did it motivate greater police engagement with urban communities. Instead, police have seemingly used this event to further distance themselves from and maintain antagonistic relationships with communities,[34] while learning from the blowup that they must exert greater control over the conditions where brutality occurs. This enhanced and learned control can be seen in the torture case of Haitian immigrant Abner Louima by the New York City police in 1997. Louima was beaten in a vehicle on the way to the 70th Precinct stationhouse and was then sodomized with the stick from a toilet plunger in the police restrooms.[35] Regardless of the fact that the story did finally emerge, the police officers obviously exercised extreme caution in regulating the places of abuse (a police vehicle and a police restroom), and one can speculate that this level of control was a response to their fear of being surveilled and thus held accountable for their actions.

Another example of the dance of surveillance and countersurveillance can be witnessed in the confrontations occurring at antiglobalization protests throughout the world. Activists have been quite savvy in videotaping and photographing police and security forces as a technique not only for deterring abuse but also for documenting and disseminating any instances of excessive force. According to accounts by protesters of the World Trade Organization (WTO), the police, in turn, now zero in on individuals with video recorders and arrest them or confiscate their equipment as a first line of defense in what has become a war over the control of media representations.[36] Similarly, vibrant Independent Media Centers (IMCs) are now routinely set up at protest locations, allowing activists to produce and edit video, audio, photographic, and textual news stories and then disseminate them over the Internet, which serves as an outlet for alternative interpretations of the issues under protest.[37] As was witnessed in the beating of independent media personnel and destruction of an Indymedia center by police during the 2001 G8 protests in Genoa, Italy,[38] those with institutional interests and power are learning to infiltrate "subversive" countersurveillance collectives and vitiate their potential for destabilizing the dominant system.

A final telling example of the learning potential of institutions was the subsequent 2002 G8 meeting held in Kananaskis, which is a remote and difficult-to-access mountain resort in Alberta, Canada. Rather than contend with widespread public protests and a potential repeat of the police violence in Genoa (marked by the close-range shooting and death of a protester), the organizers of the mountain meeting exerted the most extreme control over the limited avenues available for public participation: both reporters and members of the public were excluded, and a no-fly-zone was enforced around the resort.

It could be that grassroots publicizing of protests (through Indymedia, for example) is ultimately more effective than individualized countersurveillance because such protests are collective activities geared toward institutional change. While the removal of the 2002 G8 meetings to a publicly inaccessible location was a response to previous experiences with protesters and their publicity machines, this choice of location served a symbolic function of revealing the exclusionary elitism of these organizations, thereby calling into question their legitimacy. So, whereas mainstream news outlets seldom lend any sympathetic ink or air time to antiglobalization movements, many of them did comment on the overt mechanisms of public exclusion displayed by the 2002 G8 meeting.[39]

Michael Hardt and Antonio Negri would describe these ongoing exchanges between dominant and subordinate groups as a mutual and perhaps unwitting advancement of Empire—the larger system of global capitalism and its colonization of lifeworlds.[40] They note, for instance, how humanitarian efforts by Western countries first establish discursive universal orders—such as "human rights"—as justification for intervention, and how these universals are then capitalized upon by military and economic institutions as rationales for imperialistic invasions. Similarly, activist struggles appear to teach the system of global capitalism, or those manning its operations, how to increase strategic efficiency by controlling spaces available for political opposition. From this perspective, the flexible ideologies of the 1960s counterculture movements may have disturbed the capitalist system, but in doing so they also described a new territory (the self) and a new mode of operation for the growth of capitalism:

> Capital did not need to invent a new paradigm (even if it were capable of doing so) because the truly creative moment had already taken place. Capital's problem was rather to dominate a new composition that had already been produced autonomously and defined within a new relationship to nature and labor, a relationship of autonomous production.[41]

The postindustrial colonizations of public spaces and resources today are outgrowths of an earlier colonization of "flexibility" as a viable and successful challenge to the rigidities of technocratic bureaucracies.

I would build upon these observations to say that the conflicts between surveillance and countersurveillance practices today represent a larger struggle over the control of spaces and bodies. It is doubtful that most police or security forces are manipulating spaces and bodies with surveillance and other strategies because they intentionally wish to neutralize democratic opportunities; in fact, they probably believe that their actions of social control are preserving democracy by protecting the public and safeguarding the status quo. Be that as it may, such activities advance neoliberal agendas by eliminating spaces for political action and debate, spaces where effective alternatives to economic globalization could emerge and gain legitimacy if they were not disciplined by police and corporate actions. Therefore, it should not be seen as a coincidence that the demise of public spaces is occurring at the same time that spatial and temporal boundaries are being erased to facilitate the expansion of global capital. The two go hand in hand.

Whereas one can readily critique Hardt and Negri for their attribution of agency to capitalism or to the amorphous force of Empire, their systemic viewpoint is worth preserving in what has become a contemporary landscape of social fragmentation, polarization, and privatization. Dominant and subordinate groups serve as asymmetrical refractions of each other in emerging global regimes. Surveillance and countersurveillance are two sets of overlapping practices selectively mobilized by many parties in this conflict, but the overall effect is unknown.

Perhaps non-governmental organizations are the best place to look for effective countersurveillance movements on the institutional level. There are a host of remarkable groups tackling surveillance abuses in societies and lobbying for accountability and policy reform. Some of the best-known organizations are the American Civil Liberties Union, Privacy International, Electronic Privacy Information Center, Statewatch, and the Electronic Frontier Foundation. Other organizations represent niche issues of concern to specific audiences, such as Katherine Albrecht's fundamentalist Christian organization Caspian, which opposes RFID technologies on the grounds that they are the "mark of the beast" (see chapter 5). According to surveillance-studies scholar Colin Bennett,[42] who has done extensive research on civil society groups, their narrow focus on particular issues, especially on privacy, hinders coalition building for widespread policy changes or lasting social movements. In fact, focusing on privacy alone may hamstring such organizations at the outset because privacy is a highly individualized rather than collective concept, and it cannot meaningfully account for issues of power or domination.[43] This does not mean that such groups or similar ones do not attempt to challenge surveillance from a collective standpoint, but in an individualistic political, legal, and cultural climate, such an approach meets with serious difficulties in generating support, especially financial support, for their efforts.

CONCLUSION

Are countersurveillance activities political interventions? Yes, they are clearly political. The central question remains, however, which countersurveillance configurations provide productive critiques and interventions. Because countersurveillance movements, in my definition of them, seek to correct unequal distributions of power, they do destabilize status quo politics on a case-by-case basis—on the ground, at specific, temporally bounded sites of contestation. If our vantage point is once removed, however, individualized countersurveillance efforts may either obscure possibilities for collective action or provide the necessary provocations for those with institutional power to diagnose and correct inefficiencies in their mechanisms of control.[44]

Even if this second conclusion is persuasive, however, it should not imply that activists and countersurveillance practitioners should dispense with their interventionist projects, but instead that they should diligently avoid reproducing the exclusionary logics and reactionary stances of those whom they critique. For instance, high-tech interventions may attract public attention because of their innovative use of technologies, but they can defy replication by others without comparable technical capabilities or resources. Furthermore, focusing on individual agents of surveillance (such as store clerks, security guards, camera operators, or police) artificially reduces the complexity of the problem: many of these individuals are underpaid yet completely dependent upon their jobs, so they might be easy targets, but not necessarily the best ones. The strength of social movements lies in their inclusiveness and in their participatory structures.[45] So while these attributes might signify areas of vulnerability for activists, they remain the magnets that draw people into movements and mobilize them behind causes—they are the qualities that need to be nourished for less individualistic and more effective activism to take root.

Conclusion

MANY MEANINGS CAN BE GLEANED from the host of insecurities that confront societies today. Threats of terrorism, natural disaster, identity theft, job loss, illegal immigration, and even biblical apocalypse command the attention of people. Although there may be a factual basis for many of these fears, they do not simply represent objective conditions. Feelings of insecurity are actively cultivated by politicians and the media, on one hand, and sustained by urban fortification, technological surveillance, and economic vulnerability on the other. The construction of insecurity offers a window into the distinctive problems of modern life in the twenty-first century.

Two unifying threads tie together the myriad insecurities of contemporary American society in particular. First, people are instructed to mitigate insecurity in their daily lives, instead of depending on the state to do so. This can include things like stockpiling water and food, installing alarm systems, shredding bank records, hiring child care providers, or purchasing health insurance. In these ways, the task of social reproduction falls upon individuals and communities to counteract the state's failure to provide social welfare. Second, people are told that they should endorse the most extreme measures—such as torture or domestic spying—taken by the state in its attempt to safeguard national security. The emerging requirement, therefore, is for individuals to take responsibility, largely through consumption, for their own well-being, while granting the state sweeping authority to act in the capacity of national defense, whether at home (through surveillance) or abroad (through warfare).

Insecurities acquire the status of social truth through repetition, and there is no dearth of crises circulating in the media. The types of insecurities typically raised, however, betray the dominant binary logic of individual responsibility and state prerogatives. This framing occludes in the public imaginary persistent social inequalities, especially awareness of and responsibility for the plight of others. It also allows the state to abdicate its responsibility for the provision of human security. Thus, when Hurricane Katrina devastated New Orleans, government agencies such as FEMA were burdened with incompetent leadership and too tightly coupled with the national security machine to provide prompt, effective, and safe assistance for people. Similarly, when warnings of rampant home foreclosures and predatory subprime lending practices were raised in 2006,[1] the U.S. federal government did little to correct the problem until a full-blown crisis had hit in 2008, and then it moved to bail out financial institutions, not assist people who were losing—or had lost—their homes.[2]

In the face of frightful projections about individual and collective danger, cultural and ideological barriers often hinder recognition and mitigation of insecurity. According to sociologist Karen Cerulo, people—generally speaking—are simply predisposed to believe that the best will happen and incapable of imaging that the worst might happen. Cerulo writes, "When sociocultural practices focus our sights on excellence, they can simultaneously divert our gaze from the imperfect, the deficient, and the flawed. In this way, the notion of quality—of the way things are—takes on an asymmetrical character, as reality is evaluated using an 'unbalanced' conceptual continuum."[3] Although Cerulo is referring primarily to our inability to see specific things that are "flawed" in our everyday lives, such as our relationships not being as healthy as we would like to believe, this analysis could be expanded to think about the ways in which entire groups of people might be considered "flawed" because of their lack of success in the neoliberal economy. Failed insecurity subjects, those who cannot manage their own insecurity through consumption, may encounter many forms of averted gazes. Whether they are homeless people sleeping on the streets, sick people who cannot afford health insurance, or disenfranchised people in need of public welfare assistance, the tendency is for most people, government agencies, and private industries to look the other way. Exclusionary material infrastructures (such as fortified enclaves) and public policies (such as city ordinances that target homeless people) assist with this process by literally keeping the marginalized from sight and keeping a sense of collective responsibility at bay. These are some of the ways that social sorting occurs and takes on the appearance of being natural; the process itself is delegated to infrastructure and policy, and therefore largely hidden from public view.

In other ways, however, the gaze is not averted at all but is instead focused on people considered "flawed." This is chiefly the case with the surveillant gaze directed at marginalized populations. As described in the preceding chapters, an intrusive mode of surveillance is directed at poor women of color and others accessing welfare benefits, and at residents in public housing complexes. Other forms of harsh scrutiny and punishment are reserved for undocumented workers guilty of the "identity theft" of fabricating social security numbers in order to work. Still others are singled out as so-called enemy combatants in the "war on terror" and are detained, tortured, and sometimes killed without any legal protections or serious punishment of their assailants. And this is not nearly a comprehensive list of the manifestations of marginalizing surveillance and dehumanizing treatment reserved for people deemed flawed or dangerous to society. One could add to this, for example, the surveillance of students and teachers in public education through punitive testing and accountability mechanisms,[4] the surveillance and removal of homeless people in increasingly privatized public spaces such as train or bus stations,[5] or the advanced monitoring and control technologies used on prisoners in correctional facilities.[6] These are all forms of marginalizing surveillance in that they are applied in their most invasive forms almost exclusively to populations considered suspect or dangerous in some way. In the process, the systems contribute to the construction of marginal identities for target populations.

Thus, one needs to look both at security cultures and surveillance infrastructures, in concert, to understand insecurity today. I have used the term *security cultures* to describe prevailing understandings of threats and appropriate responses to them. Media representations and political discourses, especially, offer a rich terrain for documenting security cultures and analyzing their power to shape public beliefs. In the first section of this book, therefore, I delved into a sampling of widely circulating representations of—and discourses about—threats to individual and collective well-being. Popular entertainment media, such as the television show *24* or the rapture fiction series Left Behind, normalize particular logics of insecurity that extend beyond the pleasurable experiences one might have in consuming those media. In other words, both have pedagogical effects. That is, *24* teaches viewers, perhaps even those at the highest levels of government, the false lesson that torture works and is necessary; Left Behind teaches readers that the apocalypse is upon us, that non-Christians will suffer and that they deserve to do so, and that performing good deeds and striving for world peace are unnecessary tasks because individual true belief is all that is required for salvation.

Similarly, more "serious" discourses about torture, identity theft, and disaster preparedness each convey messages that follow a similar pattern. Policy discourses about torture, for instance, have revolved primarily around semantic debates over what constitutes torture, and secondarily around appropriate oversight; in keeping with neoliberal ideology, collective responsibility and culpability, either for torture or for terrorist attacks, have not been within the realm of conversation. With the moral panic of identity theft or the scares surrounding potential disasters, people are led to believe that the threats are dire and widespread and that managing these threats requires individual responsibility and consumption—in other words, becoming insecurity subjects. This pattern can even extend to representatives of local governments and first responders, such as firefighters, who are advised at security conferences and elsewhere to purchase security equipment in lieu of meeting other needs.

Surveillance infrastructures can embody the values and enforce the norms of security cultures. Throughout the book, I have employed the term *surveillance infrastructures* to account for the many technological systems used to mitigate risks and regulate populations. Public spaces have been idealized as important sites for social exchange, community development, and civic opportunity.[7] Therefore, surveillance systems in public places represent a provocative starting point for inquiry into the ramifications of neoliberal forms of risk management. Accordingly, the second section of the book began by analyzing surveillance in places of residence. In public housing and gated communities I found that surveillance operates much as gates and walls do to regulate belonging and minimize exposure to people occupying different socioeconomic positions. Moreover, surveillance functions as one more mechanism to police residents, whether spying on people requiring public assistance or enforcing conformity of relatively affluent residents in gated communities. Such surveillance practices reify the presumed dangerousness of others, particularly those of lower economic status, and solidify beliefs about the obligation to safeguard oneself through the purchase of private security.

Although police-operated video surveillance on city streets is not as widespread in the United States as it is in other places such as the United Kingdom, transportation departments in the United States are increasingly turning to such systems, along with road sensors and other technologies, to regulate the movement of people. These "intelligent transportation systems" sort populations in unequal but almost completely invisible ways, through things like the timing of pedestrian crossing lights or the charging of tolls for road use. Not only do these systems prioritize transportation by private automobiles, as opposed to more "public" modes of transport like buses or trains, but they also lend themselves to national security and police functions. Thus, they support the security cultures of privatization and securitization while subtly attenuating public spaces, such as streets, which become conduits from one place to another rather than places in their own right. For these reasons, I have argued that technological systems predicated on decontextualized abstractions and rational control at a distance are uniquely "masculine" systems that contribute to social inequalities. Finally, activist and other modes of resistance to surveillance are necessary parts of the process by which security cultures and surveillance infrastructures interact and obtain meaning. It may be the case that individualized forms of resistance, such as the countersurveillance interventions against video surveillance discussed in chapter 9, unwittingly buttress today's security cultures by failing to challenge surveillance practices on the institutional level. Without attending to the interplay of security cultures and surveillance infrastructures, however, much of the politics of surveillance systems would escape notice or be artificially reduced to the restricted (and restricting) concept of privacy.

One emerging bridge connecting these two categories is the privatization of security, or the development of public-private partnerships for security provision and surveillance activities. Many examples of this trend have emerged from the chapters in this book. For instance, private security companies are receiving generous contracts from the U.S. government to police war zones in Iraq and Afghanistan and disaster zones in the United States. Other private contractors are hired to interrogate and torture "enemy combatants" in detention facilities overseas, and, according to some records, these contractors are much more guilty of systematic abuse of detainees than are their official counterparts in the military or Central Intelligence Agency.[8] The Department of Homeland Security (DHS) perceives its role as being an avid "customer" of and cheerleader for industry-supplied surveillance and security products and services. And whether in the form of DHS "Fusion Centers," DHS partnerships with Google, or other instantiations, the sharing of potentially sensitive data between the public and private sectors is reaching an all-time high. In other domains, citizens are compelled to draw upon the private sector for security services not offered by the state, such as private security patrols, fortified gated communities, or credit-alert services.

There are good reasons to be concerned about the ongoing privatization of surveillance and security. Whereas the public sector maintains a commitment to the social good, at least in principle, private companies have no such obligations. The rights of individuals or groups easily fall by the wayside when profit is the primary objective. Thus, we can witness security guards surveilling people in semiprivatized public streets, shopping centers, and transportation hubs and forcibly removing people who are not consuming or who are exercising their free speech rights.[9] Because policies and laws are often ambiguous about what constitute appropriate procedures for and accountability of private security contractors, especially compared to "public" police or military personnel, abuses proliferate. These infractions have to do not only with physical abuse of people, however; they also include flagrant mismanagement and loss of sensitive public data or outright fraud at taxpayers' expense.[10] It stands to reason that when security companies care primarily about profit, safeguards for the protection of people's rights or data would receive little attention, unless a negative image hurt companies' potential for future profits, which—surprisingly—does not often seem to be the case. Societies priding themselves on democratic practices, civil liberties, and the rule of law should be apprehensive about so-called public-private partnerships for security provision. Unfortunately, the mainstream media, politicians, and academics have paid little attention to these developments.[11]

This book has delved into the complexity of insecurity in contemporary American society, although people from other countries will likely find that many of the themes covered here resonate with their experiences as well. The objective was to provide a sampling of cases and a critique of dominant trends, rather than any sort of all-inclusive treatment. Nonetheless, issues of fear, inequality, and insecurity obviously transcend the U.S. context and in other settings often take on far more disturbing incarnations, such as forced migration or genocide. A unifying thread is fear of the Other. In the United States, a host of fears is associated with people considered different or threatening in some way, ranging from suspected terrorists, non-Christians, undocumented workers, or welfare recipients. As Arjun Appadurai provocatively frames it, minorities—of all sorts—are metaphors of the failed Enlightenment project.[12] And, as such, a base instinct is for people to attempt to purge difference, to purge evidence of inequalities, to purge confirmation of the failures of the American dream—or dreams of an inclusive and equal society in other countries.

Barring this, heightened surveillance and regulation of marginalized populations operate as surrogates for more direct forms of exclusion. In addition to the forms of marginalizing surveillance summarized in the preceding paragraphs, the screening and containment of suspect populations at border zones is probably the most troubling instantiation of national efforts to restrict the mobility of the subaltern and ensure nation-state integrity. Biometric surveillance systems and elaborate screening databases are being deployed at many borders to register and sort people according to risk categories, whereby individuals deemed "low risk" are fast-tracked, while individuals considered "high risk" are searched and possibly detained.[13] International airports now house their own detention centers, and many Western countries have established detention facilities to contain people considered risky—whether they are people lacking appropriate travel or identification documents or people seeking asylum—in "camps" existing in a state of legal limbo.[14]

These are some of the ways that surveillance is mobilized in the name of security. Unfortunately, security cultures often aggravate conditions of social inequality rather than correct them. Security cultures tend to increase the vulnerability of marginalized groups who must contend with indifference at best and hostility at worst, often perpetrated in the guise of neutral architectural forms, concerned state or corporate agents, and objective surveillance apparatuses. Insecurity is both socially constructed and social shaping. Moral panics about insecurity and dominant responses to it may be manufactured, but they are no less real or influential for their questionable grounding in empirical fact. Mitigating insecurity in any meaningful and lasting way, however, will require that people confront the mythic dimensions of insecurity, the politics inherent in new configurations of security provision, and the structural obstacles to achieving equality in societies.

Notes

Introduction

1. Economic insecurity is nothing new, of course, but it is intensifying and receiving more attention at the moment. As I write this in October 2008, the U.S. Congress just days ago passed into law a $700 billion bailout package for failing financial firms. Nonetheless, the effects of economic globalization and neoliberal policies have been crippling local economies and aggravating social inequalities for decades worldwide, including in the United States.
2. Wendy Brown, "American Nightmare: Neoliberalism, Neoconservatism, and De-Democratization," *Political Theory* 34, no. 6 (2006): 690–714.
3. David Mechanic, *The Truth about Health Care: Why Reform Is Not Working in America* (New Brunswick, NJ: Rutgers University Press, 2006); Jill A. Fisher, *Medical Research for Hire: The Political Economy of Pharmaceutical Clinical Trials* (New Brunswick, NJ: Rutgers University Press, 2009).
4. Pierre Bourdieu, "The Essence of Neoliberalism," *Le Monde Diplomatique*, December 1998, http://mondediplo.com/1998/12/08bourdieu (accessed July 3, 2009); David Garland, *The Culture of Control: Crime and Social Order in Contemporary Society* (Chicago: University of Chicago Press, 2001).
5. Virginia Eubanks, "Technologies of Citizenship: Surveillance and Political Learning in the Welfare System," in *Surveillance and Security: Technological Politics and Power in Everyday Life*, ed. T. Monahan (New York: Routledge, 2006); John Gilliom, *Overseers of the Poor: Surveillance, Resistance, and the Limits of Privacy* (Chicago: University of Chicago Press, 2001).
6. Ulrich Beck, "From Industrial Society to the Risk Society: Questions of Survival, Social Structure and Ecological Enlightenment," *Theory, Culture & Society* 9 (1992): 97–123; Richard V. Ericson, *Crime in an Insecure World* (Cambridge, UK: Polity, 2007); Cindi Katz, "Banal Terrorism," in *Violent Geographies: Fear, Terror and Political Violence*, ed. D. Gregory and A. Pred (New York: Routledge, 2007); Paul R. Kimmel and Chris E. Stout, *Collateral Damage: The Psychological Consequences of America's War on Terrorism* (Westport, CT: Praeger, 2006).
7. David Altheide, *Terrorism and the Politics of Fear* (Lanham, MD: Altamira Press, 2006), x.
8. Timothy Druckrey, "Secreted Agents, Security Leaks, Immune Systems, Spore Wars," in *CTRL [Space]: Rhetorics of Surveillance from Bentham to Big Brother*, ed. T. Y. Levin, U. Frohne and P. Weibel (Cambridge, MA: MIT Press, 2002); Cindi Katz, "The State Goes Home: Local Hypervigilance of Children and the Global Retreat from Social Reproduction," in *Surveillance and Security: Technological Politics and Power in Everyday Life*, ed. T. Monahan (New York: Routledge, 2006).
9. Kimmel and Stout, *Collateral Damage*; Mark Schaller, Jason Faulkner, H. Justin Park, L. Steven Neuberg, and T. Douglas Kenrick, "Impressions of Danger Influence Impressions of People: An Evolutionary Perspective on Individual and Collective

Cognition," *Journal of Cultural and Evolutionary Psychology* 2, no. 3–4 (2004): 231–247.

10. Murray Edelman, *Constructing the Political Spectacle* (Chicago: University of Chicago Press, 1988); Maria Jarymowicz and Daniel Bar-Tal, "The Dominance of Fear over Hope in the Life of Individuals and Collectives," *European Journal of Social Psychology* 36, no. 3 (2006): 367–392; Benjamin Sylvester Bradley and John R. Morss, "Social Construction in a World at Risk," *Theory & Psychology* 12, no. 4 (2002): 509–531.

11. Jutta Weldes, Mark Laffey, Hugh Gusterson, and Raymond Duvall, *Cultures of Insecurity: States, Communities, and the Production of Danger* (Minneapolis: University of Minnesota Press, 1999), 16.

12. I draw upon the work of Stephen J. Collier and Andrew Lakoff for this typology but use the more common and inclusive term "civil defense" for what they refer to as "vital systems security." Collier and Lakoff, "Vital Systems Security" (manuscript, 2006), http://anthropos-lab.net/wp/publications/2007/01/collier_vital -systems.pdf (accessed June 13, 2007). See also Michel Foucault, *"Society Must Be Defended": Lectures at the College de France, 1975–76*, trans. D. Macey (New York: Picador, 2003).

13. David Wood, Eli Konvitz, and Kirstie Ball correctly identify this as an opportunistic "surveillance surge" that takes place at moments of perceived crisis. Wood, Konvitz, and Ball, "The Constant State of Emergency?: Surveillance after 9/11," in *The Intensification of Surveillance: Crime, Terrorism and Warfare in the Information Age*, ed. K. Ball and F. Webster (London: Pluto Press, 2003), 137–150. See also Torin Monahan, ed., *Surveillance and Security: Technological Politics and Power in Everyday Life* (New York: Routledge, 2006); David Lyon, *Surveillance after September 11* (Malden, MA: Polity Press, 2003).

14. James Ellis, David Fisher, Thomas Longstaff, Linda Pesante, and Richard Pethia, "Report to the President's Commission on Critical Infrastructure Protection" (Pittsburgh: Carnegie Mellon University, 1997); Andrew Lakoff, "Techniques of Preparedness," in *Surveillance and Security: Technological Politics and Power in Everyday Life*, ed. T. Monahan (New York: Routledge, 2006); Erwann Michel-Kerjan, "New Challenges in Critical Infrastructures: A US Perspective," *Journal of Contingencies and Crisis Management* 11, no. 3 (2003): 132–141.

15. Elsewhere, I have developed the concept of *fragmented centralization* to describe this emergent organizational pattern. Torin Monahan, *Globalization, Technological Change, and Public Education* (New York: Routledge, 2005). See also James Hay and Mark Andrejevic, "Introduction: Toward an Analytic of Governmental Experiments in these Times: Homeland Security as the New Social Security," *Cultural Studies* 20, no. 4–5 (2006): 331–348; Michael Welch, *Scapegoats of September 11th: Hate Crimes & State Crimes in the War on Terror* (New Brunswick, NJ: Rutgers University Press, 2006), 33.

16. I am grateful to Tyler Wall for these insights. See also Tyler Wall, "The Fronts of War: Military Geographies, Local Logics, and the Rural Hoosier Heartland" (Ph.D. diss., Arizona State University, Tempe, 2009).

17. George W. Bush, "President Bush Delivers Remarks at West Point," *CNN.com*, June 1, 2002, http://transcripts.cnn.com/TRANSCRIPTS/0206/01/se.01.html (accessed July 3, 2009).

18. Tom Engelhardt, "What 'Progress' in Iraq Really Means," *The Nation* (online), August 13, 2007, http://www.thenation.com/doc/20070827/engelhardt (accessed August 20, 2008).

19. Timothy Lenoir, "Programming Theaters of War: Gamemakers as Soldiers," in *Bombs and Bandwidth: The Emerging Relationship Between Information Technology and Security*, ed. R. Latham (New York: New Press, 2003).

20. For instance, the company Halliburton and its subsidiaries received $22 billion in contacts for work in Iraq, and some of those were no-bid contracts, which are in violation of U.S. law. It also must be noted that Halliburton is the company of which former of Vice President Dick Cheney was once chief executive officer, so the instrumentalism and favoritism behind such transfers of public funds are not difficult to detect. See Robert Scheer, "Taxpayers Lose, Halliburton Gains," *The Nation*, June 27, 2007; John Solomon, "FBI Investigates Halliburton's No-Bid Contracts," Associated Press, October 28, 2004, http://www.globalpolicy.org/security/issues/iraq/contract/2004/1028greenhouse.htm (accessed March 3, 2009).

21. David Cole and Jules Lobel, *Less Safe, Less Free: Why America Is Losing the War on Terror* (New York: New Press, 2007); Welch, *Scapegoats*.

22. For instance, in January 2009, soon after his inauguration, President Obama signed executive orders to begin the process of closing the Guantánamo Bay prison camp, as well as CIA "black site" detention centers in other countries. It may take years for this to actually occur, however. BBC News, "Obama Orders Guantanamo Closure," BBC News, January 22, 2009, http://news.bbc.co.uk/2/hi/americas/ 7845585.stm (accessed March 3, 2009).

23. Beck, "From Industrial Society"; Ulrich Beck, "The Terrorist Threat: World Risk Society Revisited," *Theory, Culture & Society* 19, no. 4 (2002): 39–55.

24. See chapter 5 of this book for further analysis of the conflation of undocumented workers and identity theft with terrorism. For a critique of public protest being characterized as terrorism, see Luis Fernandez, *Policing Dissent: Social Control and the Anti-Globalization Movement* (New Brunswick, NJ: Rutgers University Press, 2008).

25. David J. Hess, *Alternative Pathways in Science and Industry: Activism, Innovation, and the Environment in an Era of Globalization* (Cambridge, MA: MIT Press, 2007), 13.

26. Irma van der Ploeg, *The Machine-Readable Body: Essays on Biometrics and the Informatization of the Body* (Maastricht, Netherlands: Shaker, 2005); Miriam Ticktin, "Policing and Humanitarianism in France: Immigration and the Turn to Law as State of Exception," *Interventions* 7, no. 3 (2005): 347–368.

27. Barbara Ehrenreich, *Nickel and Dimed: On (Not) Getting by in America*, 1st ed. (New York: Metropolitan Books, 2001); Jonathan Xavier Inda and Renato Rosaldo, *The Anthropology of Globalization: A Reader* (Malden, MA: Blackwell, 2002).

28. Arjun Appadurai, *Fear of Small Numbers: An Essay on the Geography of Anger* (Durham, NC: Duke University Press, 2006), 43.

29. Stephen Castles, "Towards a Sociology of Forced Migration and Social Transformation," *Sociology* 37, no. 1 (2003) :13–34; Björn Hettne, "The Fate of Citizenship in Post-Westphalia," *Citizenship Studies* 4, no. 1 (2000): 35–46; Anthony H. Richmond, "Globalization: Implications for Immigrants and Refugees," *Ethnic and Racial Studies* 25, no. 5 (2002): 707–727.

30. Tyler Wall makes a compelling argument that the nation-state has always been defined by modalities of war. He asserts that we selectively ignore the ever-present impact of militarism upon the home front in times of both "peace" and "war." Wall, "The Fronts of War."

31. David Von Drehle, "World War, Cold War Won. Now, the Gray War," *Washington Post*, September 12, 2001, A09.

32. Against this backdrop, *human security* represents a form of security that includes population security's concerns for the provision of social welfare but also stresses human rights—or freedom from fear and want. United Nations Development Programme, *Human Development Report 1994* (New York: Oxford University Press, 1994). As an ideal, human security is meritorious but ultimately insufficient for changing the political and conceptual structures of security. Concerning such humanist approaches to security, Anthony Burke cautions that "they leave in place (and possibly strengthen) a key structural feature of the elite [national security] strategy

they oppose: its claim to embody truth and to fix the contours of the real . . . security's broader function as a defining condition of human experience and modern political life remains invisible and unexamined." Burke, *Beyond Security, Ethics and Violence: War against the Other* (New York: Routledge, 2007), 31. Although it is tempting to fall back on Enlightenment rationalities of autonomous, emancipated individuals, the need is for a deep problematization of the security concept and for a reflexive ethics to attend to mutual needs, persistent conflicts, and the ongoing *process* of achieving security and respect. Otherwise, one may risk reproducing universalist approaches to national security in the desire for something different.

33. Madeleine Akrich, "The De-Scription of Technological Objects," in *Shaping Technology/Building Society: Studies in Sociotechnical Change*, ed. W. E. Bijker and John Law (Cambridge, MA: MIT Press, 1992); Lawrence Lessig, *Code: And Other Laws of Cyberspace* (New York: Basic Books, 1999); Langdon Winner, *The Whale and the Reactor: A Search for Limits in an Age of High Technology* (Chicago: University of Chicago Press, 1986).

34. David Lyon, ed., *Surveillance as Social Sorting: Privacy, Risk, and Digital Discrimination* (New York: Routledge, 2003).

35. Stephen Graham and David Wood, "Digitizing Surveillance: Categorization, Space, Inequality," *Critical Social Policy* 23, no. 2 (2003): 227–248; Michalis Lianos and Mary Douglas, "Dangerization and the End of Deviance," *British Journal of Criminology* 40, no. 2 (2000): 261–278; Nigel Thrift and Shaun French, "The Automatic Production of Space," *Transactions of the Institute of British Geographers* 27, no. 4 (2002): 309–335.

36. Geoffrey C. Bowker and Susan Leigh Star, *Sorting Things Out: Classification and Its Consequences* (Cambridge, MA: MIT Press, 1999).

37. Gilliom, *Overseers of the Poor.*

38. Torin Monahan, "Questioning Surveillance and Security," in *Surveillance and Security: Technological Politics and Power in Everyday Life*, ed. T. Monahan (New York: Routledge, 2006).

39. Ibid.

40. Hille Koskela, "Video Surveillance, Gender, and the Safety of Public Urban Space: 'Peeping Tom' goes High Tech?" *Urban Geography* 23, no. 3 (2002): 257–278; Torin Monahan, "The Surveillance Curriculum: Risk Management and Social Control in the Neoliberal School," in *Surveillance and Security: Technological Politics and Power in Everyday Life*, ed. T. Monahan. (New York: Routledge, 2006).

41. Hay and Andrejevic, "Introduction: Toward an Analytic."

42. As mentioned earlier, these trends in the growth of security industries predate the attacks of 9/11. The attacks did serve as a catalyst, however, for the intensification of surveillance practices. See Ball and Webster, *The Intensification of Surveillance*; Lyon, *Surveillance after September 11.*

43. Torin Monahan and Rodolfo D. Torres, eds., *Schools under Surveillance: Cultures of Control in Public Education* (New Brunswick, NJ: Rutgers University Press, 2010); Aaron Kupchik and Torin Monahan, "The New American School: Preparation for Post-Industrial Discipline," *British Journal of Sociology of Education* 27, no. 5 (2006): 617–631; Monahan, "The Surveillance Curriculum."

CHAPTER 1   SECURING THE HOMELAND

1. Welch, *Scapegoats*, 116.

2. David Cole, "Intolerable Cruelty," *The Nation*, November 21, 2005, 5–6.

3. Giorgio Agamben, *Homo Sacer: Sovereign Power and Bare Life* (Stanford, CA: Stanford University Press, 1998); Elaine Scarry, *The Body in Pain: The Making and Unmaking of the World* (New York: Oxford University Press, 1985).

4. Pierre Bourdieu, *Outline of a Theory of Practice*, trans. R. Nice (Cambridge, MA: Cambridge University Press, 1977).

5. Philip B. Heymann and Juliette N. Kayyem, *Protecting Liberty in an Age of Terror* (Cambridge, MA: MIT Press, 2005).

6. Ibid., 7.

7. Ibid., 11–30.

8. Ibid., 176–176.

9. Lisa Hajjar, "Torture and the Future," *Middle East Report Online*, May 2004, http://www.merip.org/mero/interventions/hajjar_interv.html (accessed October 11, 2008).

10. Ibid; Stanley Cohen, *States of Denial: Knowing about Atrocities and Suffering* (Cambridge, UK: Polity Press, 2001), 103.

11. Heymann and Kayyem, *Protecting Liberty*, 31.

12. Thomas Lue, "Torture and Coercive Interrogations," in *Protecting Liberty in an Age of Terror*, ed. P. B. Heymann and J. N. Kayyem (Cambridge, MA: MIT Press, 2005), 162–163.

13. Monahan, *Surveillance and Security*; C. Katz, "The State Goes Home."

14. David Osborne and Ted Gaebler, *Reinventing Government: How the Entrepreneurial Spirit Is Transforming the Public Sector* (New York: Plume, 1992).

15. Donald Kerwin, "The Use and Misuse of 'National Security' Rationale in Crafting U.S. Refugee and Immigration Policies," *International Journal of Refugee Law* 17, no. 4 (2005): 749–763; Derek Lutterbeck, "Between Police and Military: The New Security Agenda and the Rise of Gendarmeries," *Cooperation and Conflict* 39, no. 1 (2004): 45–68.

16. Lakoff, "Techniques of Preparedness."

17. Ibid.

18. Peter Andreas, "Redrawing the Line: Borders and Security in the Twenty-first Century," *International Security* 28, no. 2 (2003): 78–111.

19. Mike Davis, "Who Is Killing New Orleans?" *The Nation*, April 10, 2006, http://www.thenation.com/doc/20060410/davis (accessed July 3, 2009).

20. This trend toward individual responsibility for social needs is assisted by the discourse of patriotism. Enlisted as patriotic citizens, people willingly engage in civic activities that have been neglected by government, even when the administration's call for volunteers is largely a symbolic one in the service of politics. For instance, with lip service paid to community service needs, the George W. Bush administrations still failed to create or fund the social infrastructure necessary for managing interested volunteers. Thus, after 9/11 and Hurricane Katrina, many people seeking to help were simply turned away. See Scott L. McLean, "The War on Terrorism and the New Patriotism," in *The Politics of Terror: The U.S. Responds to 9/11*, ed. W. Crotty (Boston: Northeastern University Press, 2004).

21. Homeland Security Council, "National Strategy for Pandemic Influenza: Implementation Plan" (Washington, DC: Department of Homeland Security, 2006), 116.

22. Richard Cowan, "Congress Passes New Iraq War Funds," Reuters, June 27, 2008, http://www.reuters.com/article/topNews/idUSN2648734820080627 (accessed July 3, 2009).

23. Joseph E. Stiglitz and Linda Bilmes, *The Three Trillion Dollar War: The True Cost of the Iraq Conflict*, 1st ed. (New York: W. W. Norton, 2008).

24. Carl Hulse, "Senate Approves Avian Flu Aid," *New York Times*, October 28, 2005, http://query.nytimes.com/gst/fullpage.html?sec=health&res=9A00E0DD1E3FF9 3BA15753C1A9639C8B63 (accessed July 3, 2009).

25. Richard Harris, "U.S. Plan to Stockpile Bird-Flu Vaccine a Big Gamble," *All Things Considered*, National Public Radio, January 6, 2006, http://www.npr.org/templates/ story/story.php?storyId=5133306 (accessed July 3, 2009).

26. U.S. Department of Health and Human Services, "Pandemic Influenza Planning: A Guide for Individuals and Families" (Washington, DC: U.S. Department of Health and Human Services, 2006), 4, http://www.redcrossnrv.org/PandemicDocs/Guide%20for%20Individuals%20and%20Families.pdf (accessed August 26, 2009).
27. Marc Siegel, "The False Bird Flu Scare," *The Nation*, June 5, 2006, 5–6.
28. U.S. Department of Health and Human Services, "Pandemic Influenza Planning," 2.
29. Tom Ridge, "Secretary Ridge Addresses American Red Cross in St. Louis," May 27, 2004, http://www.dhs.gov/dhspublic/interapp/speech/speech_0175.xml (accessed June 16, 2008).
30. Michael Chertoff, DHS Homepage, Department of Homeland Security, 2006, http://www.dhs.gov/dhspublic (accessed May 25, 2006).
31. U.S. Department of Health and Human Services, "Pandemic Influenza Planning," 14.
32. Ibid., 7.
33. Ibid., 8.
34. Lakoff, "Techniques of Preparedness."
35. Foucault, *"Society Must Be Defended,"* 247.
36. Ibid., 256.
37. This type of organizational arrangement can be thought of as a form of "fragmented centralization." See Monahan, *Globalization*.

CHAPTER 2   TWENTY-FOUR-HOUR EXCEPTIONS

1. Following from Bülent Diken and Carsten Bagge Laustsen, this "should be read in a non-etatist manner: We [I] do not begin with the sovereign who decides on the state of exception; on the contrary, the one who can declare a state of exception *is* sovereign." Etatism—or statism—in this sense indicates authority granted to an individual figurehead of a government that is centrally overseeing the needs of society; in the postindustrial, neoliberal milieu, the "sovereign" is increasingly divorced from such an aura of governmental legitimacy. Nonetheless, the symbolism of authority is captured and rearticulated through the exercise of raw power. It should also be noted that in the first season of the show, Palmer is in a liminal state, transitioning from presidential candidate to president. By the forth season, he is no longer president but is nonetheless called back in to assume the role of sovereign with regard to national security matters. Diken and Laustsen, "Zones of Indistinction," *Space & Culture* 5, no. 3 (2002): 290–307.
2. Giorgio Agamben, *State of Exception* (Chicago: University of Chicago Press, 2005), 4.
3. Agamben, *Homo Sacer*.
4. Cecilia Menjívar and Néstor Rodriguez, "State Terror in the U.S.-Latin American Interstate Regime," in *When States Kill: Latin America, the U.S., and Technologies of Terror*, ed. C. Menjívar and N. Rodriguez (Austin: University of Texas Press, 2005).
5. Paolo Virno, *A Grammar of the Multitude: For an Analysis of Contemporary Forms of Life* (Cambridge, MA: Semiotext[e], 2004), 32.
6. The structure of the show reinforces this message. The seasons are meant to encapsulate exceptional twenty-four-hour periods in the lives of counterterrorism agents. Because all "routine" or "normal" days are not depicted, they effectively cease to exist.
7. Michelle Hunter, "Deaths of Evacuees Push Toll to 1,577," *Times-Picayune*, May 19, 2006, http://www.nola.com/news/t-p/frontpage/index.ssf?/base/news-5/1148020620117480.xml&coll=1 (accessed August 23, 2009).
8. Lakoff, "Techniques of Preparedness."

9. Saul Landau, *The Business of America: How Consumers Have Replaced Citizens and How We Can Reverse the Trend* (New York: Routledge, 2004).
10. Mark Andrejevic, *iSpy: Surveillance and Power in the Interactive Era* (Lawrence: University Press of Kansas, 2007).
11. Tyler Wall, "'School Ownership Is the Goal': Military Recruiting, Public Schools, and Fronts of War," in *Schools under Surveillance: Cultures of Control in Public Education*, ed. T. Monahan and R. D. Torres (New Brunswick, NJ: Rutgers University Press, 2010).
12. Jeremy Scahill, *Blackwater: The Rise of the World's Most Powerful Mercenary Army* (New York: Nation Books, 2007).
13. MSNBC, "The Democratic Presidential Debate on MSNBC," *New York Times*, September 26, 2007, http://www.nytimes.com/2007/09/26/us/politics/26DEBATE-TRANSCRIPT.html?_r=2&pagewanted=1&oref=slogin (accessed October 11, 2008).
14. Ibid.
15. Ibid.
16. Ibid.
17. Jane Mayer, "Whatever It Takes: The Politics of the Man Behind '24,'" *The New Yorker*, February 19, 2007, http://www.newyorker.com/reporting/2007/02/19/070219fa_fact_mayer (accessed October 11, 2008).
18. Council on Foreign Relations, "Republican Debate Transcript, South Carolina," 15 May 2007, http://www.cfr.org/publication/13338/ (accessed October 11, 2008).
19. Jane Mayer, "Whatever It Takes."
20. Mark Costanzo, Ellen Gerrity, and M. Brinton Lykes, "Psychologists and the Use of Torture in Interrogations," *Analyses of Social Issues and Public Policy* 7, no. 1 (2007): 7–20; Ronnie Janoff-Bulman, "Erroneous Assumptions: Popular Belief in the Effectiveness of Torture Interrogation," *Peace and Conflict: Journal of Peace Psychology* 13, no. 4 (2007): 429–435; Marcy Strauss, "The Lessons of Abu Ghraib," *Ohio State Law Journal* 66 (2005): 1269–1310.
21. Jane Mayer, "Whatever It Takes."
22. Ibid; Justine Sharrock, "Am I a Torturer?" *Mother Jones* 33, no. 2 (2008): 43–49.
23. Jane Mayer, "Whatever It Takes."
24. Ibid.
25. Ibid.
26. Ibid.
27. Paul Virilio, *Speed and Politics: An Essay on Dromology* (Cambridge, MA: Semiotext[e], 1986); Paul Virilio, *Negative Horizon: An Essay in Dromoscopy*, trans. M. Degener (New York: Continuum, 2005).
28. Avital Ronell, *The Telephone Book: Technology—Schizophrenia—Electric Speech* (Lincoln: University of Nebraska Press, 1989), 16.

CHAPTER 3   SITUATIONAL AWARENESS OF THE SECURITY INDUSTRY

1. Scahill, *Blackwater*; Matthew Rothschild, "FBI Deputizes Private Contractors with Extraordinary Powers, Including 'Shoot to Kill,'" *The Progressive*, February 8, 2008, http://www.alternet.org/story/76388/ (accessed August 20, 2008).
2. Naomi Klein, "China Unveils Frightening Futuristic Police State at Olympics," *Huffington Post*, August 8, 2008, http://www.alternet.org/story/94278 (accessed August 20, 2008); Minas Samatas, *Surveillance in Greece: From Anticommunist to Consumer Surveillance* (New York: Pella Publishing, 2004).
3. Torin Monahan and Tyler Wall, "Somatic Surveillance: Corporeal Control through Information Networks," *Surveillance & Society* 4, no. 3 (2007): 154–173.

4. Vida Bajc, "Introduction: Debating Surveillance in the Age of Security," *American Behavioral Scientist* 50, no. 12 (2007): 1567–1591; Torin Monahan, "Naked Security," Surveillance Studies Blog, July 1, 2007, http://www.surveillance-studies.org/blog/2007/07/03/naked-security-by-torin-monahan/ (accessed August 20, 2008); Robert Pallitto and Josiah Heyman, "Theorizing Cross-Border Mobility: Surveillance, Security and Identity," *Surveillance & Society* 5, no. 3 (2008): 315–333; Irma van der Ploeg, "Borderline Identities: The Enrollment of Bodies in the Technological Reconstruction of Borders," in *Surveillance and Security: Technological Politics and Power in Everyday Life*, ed. T. Monahan (New York: Routledge, 2006). The commonplace assumption that nation-states have monopolies on violence or on national security is clearly fallacious given these and other changes in contemporary security-scapes. State security operations have been—and continue to be—privatized and/or conducted in partnership with private industry, often with radical changes in applications, policies, and legal guidelines.

5. Nikolas S. Rose, *Powers of Freedom: Reframing Political Thought* (New York: Cambridge University Press, 1999), 87.

6. Jay M. Cohen, "DHS (Video) Welcome," (video presented at 9th Annual Technologies for Critical Incident Preparedness Conference and Exposition, San Francisco, 2007).

7. Official DHS brochures echo this sentiment with authoritative but overly simplistic statements that "Terrorists do not think like we do." U.S. Department of Homeland Security, "Homeland Security: Science and Technology" (brochure) (Washington, DC: U.S. Department of Homeland Security, 2007), 1.

8. Mark Wickham, "Weapons Technical Intelligence IED Lexicon and Information Sharing Using Metadata Standards[0][0]" (presented at 9th Annual Technologies for Critical Incident Preparedness Conference and Exposition, San Francisco, 2007).

9. Naomi Klein, *The Shock Doctrine: The Rise of Disaster Capitalism* (New York: Metropolitan Books, 2007).

10. Monahan, *Globalization*; Sanford F. Schram, *Welfare Discipline: Discourse, Governance and Globalization* (Philadelphia: Temple University Press, 2006); W. Richard Scott, Carol A. Caronna, Martin Ruef, and Peter J. Mendel, *Institutional Change and Healthcare Organizations: From Professional Dominance to Managed Care* (Chicago: University of Chicago Press, 2000).

11. J. Cohen, "DHS (Video) Welcome."

12. Ibid.

13. Pictometry Visual Intelligence, "Homeland Security" (brochure), 2007.

14. ICx brochure, 2007.

15. Screenshots and video files from this simulation, "Advanced Use-of-Force Training System," can be found at http://www.diguy.com/diguy/serious_games.html (accessed August 18, 2008).

16. http://www.incidentcommander.net/ (accessed August 18, 2008).

17. Aaron Kupchik and Nicole Bracy, "To Protect, Serve, and Mentor? Police Officers in Public Schools," in *Schools under Surveillance: Cultures of Control in Public Education*, ed. T. Monahan and R. D. Torres (New Brunswick, NJ: Rutgers University Press, 2010).

18. U.S. Department of Homeland Security, "DHS Strengthens Intel Sharing at State and Local Fusion Centers" (Washington, DC: U.S. Department of Homeland Security, 2006), http://www.dhs.gov/xnews/releases/press_release_0967.shtm (accessed August 20, 2008).

19. U.S. Department of Homeland Security, "State and Local Fusion Centers" (Washington, DC: U.S. Department of Homeland Security, 2008), http://www.dhs.gov/xinfoshare/programs/gc_1156877184684.shtm (accessed August 18, 2008).

20. Robert O'Harrow, "Centers Tap Into Personal Databases," *Washington Post*, April 2, 2008, http://www.washingtonpost.com/wp-dyn/content/article/2008/04/01/AR2008040103049.html (accessed August 18, 2008).

21. Because this was a "public" security conference open to journalists, academics, and others, I use actual names of individuals who were presenting on panels—that is, of people who knew they were speaking publicly to an audience. I asked my questions of Skonovd as a member of such an audience.

22. *Congressional Record*, "Conference Report on H.R. 1, Implementing Recommendations of the 9/11 Commission Act of 2007," U.S. House of Representatives, 2007, http://www.fas.org/irp/congress/2007_cr/hr1-info.html (accessed August 20, 2008).

23. Jeremy Scahill, "Blackwater's Private Spies," *The Nation*, June 5, 2008, http://www.thenation.com/doc/20080623/scahill (accessed August 20, 2008).

24. James Bamford, "How to Fix It: Stop Outsourcing the CIA," *Mother Jones* 33, no. 5 (2008): 70.

25. James M. Walker Jr., "Virtual Alabama: Alabama Homeland Security's 3-D Visualization of State Geographic Data, Leveraging Existing State Asset Imagery and Infrastructure Data onto a State-wide Application" (presented at 9th Annual Technologies for Critical Incident Preparedness Conference and Exposition, San Francisco, 2007); information about the "Virtual Alabama" project can be found at http://dhs.alabama.gov/virtual_alabama/home.aspx?sm=g_a (accessed August 18, 2008).

26. Walker, "Virtual Alabama."

27. Jesse McKinley, "On the Fire Lines, a Shift to Private Contractors," *New York Times*, August 17, 2008, http://www.nytimes.com/2008/08/18/us/18firefighters.html?_r=1&th&emc=th&oref=slogin (accessed August 20, 2008).

28. Monahan, *Surveillance and Security.*

29. Robert O'Harrow, *No Place to Hide* (New York: Free Press, 2005).

CHAPTER 4   VULNERABLE IDENTITIES

1. Federal Trade Commission, "About Identity Theft," Federal Trade Commission, 2008, http://www.ftc.gov/bcp/edu/microsites/idtheft/consumers/about-identity-theft.html (accessed October 19, 2008).

2. Simon A. Cole and Henry N. Pontell, "'Don't Be Low Hanging Fruit': Identity Theft as Moral Panic," in *Surveillance and Security: Technological Politics and Power in Everyday Life*, ed. T. Monahan (New York: Routledge, 2006); Michael Levi and David S. Wall, "Technologies, Security, and Privacy in the Post-9/11 European Information Society," *Journal of Law and Society* 31, no. 2 (2004): 194–220.

3. S. Cole and Pontell, "Don't Be Low Hanging Fruit."

4. Stuart F. H. Allison, Amie M. Schuck, and Kim Michelle Lersch, "Exploring the Crime of Identity Theft: Prevalence, Clearance Rates, and Victim/Offender Characteristics," *Journal of Criminal Justice* 33 (2005): 19–29.

5. S. Cole and Pontell, "Don't Be Low Hanging Fruit," 128.

6. Erich Goode and Nachman Ben-Yehuda, *Moral Panics: The Social Construction of Deviance* (Cambridge, MA: Blackwell, 1994).

7. Mark Poster, *Information Please: Culture and Politics in the Age of Digital Machines* (Durham, NC: Duke University Press, 2006), 114.

8. It should be pointed out, however, that Mark Poster's articulation elides emotional affect, power relations, and the persistent materiality of such informatized zones.

9. I am indebted to Simon Cole for this insight.

10. Poster, *Information Please.*

11. S. Cole and Pontell, "Don't Be Low Hanging Fruit."

Notes to Pages 53–58

12. Ibid.
13. Robert Vamosi, "Of ID Theft, Paris Hilton, and Methamphetamines," *CNET Reviews*, May 27, 2005, http://reviews.cnet.com/4520-3513_7-6231353-1 .html.
14. Phoenix Police Department, "Identity Theft: Learn to Protect Yourself," Phoenix Police Department, 2006, http://www.ci.phoenix.az.us/POLICE/idthef1.html (accessed June 5, 2006).
15. Stopijacking.com, "Stopijacking.com" (2006), Stopijacking.com (accessed June 30, 2006).
16. Federal Trade Commission, "Federal Trade Commission: Your National Resource about ID Theft," Federal Trade Commission, 2006, http://www.consumer.gov/ idtheft (accessed June 5, 2006).
17. Ibid.
18. Phoenix Police Department, "Identity Theft."
19. Bob Sullivan, "The Meth Connection to Identity Theft: Drug Addiction Plays a Part in Many Crime Rings, Cops Say," MSNBC, March 10, 2004, http:// www.msnbc.msn.com/id/4460349/ (accessed June 5, 2006).
20. Marc Cooper, "Lockdown in Greeley: How Immigration Raids Terrorized a Colorado Town," *The Nation*, February 26, 2007, 11–16; Julia Preston, "270 Illegal Immigrants Sent to Prison in Federal Push," *New York Times*, May 24, 2008; Susan Saulny, "Hundreds Are Arrested in U.S. Sweep of Meat Plant," *New York Times*, May 13, 2008.
21. Cooper, "Lockdown in Greeley"; Saulny, "Hundreds Are Arrested."
22. U.S. Department of Homeland Security, "Remarks by Secretary of Homeland Security Michael Chertoff, Immigration and Customs Enforcement Assistant Secretary Julie Myers, and Federal Trade Commission Chairman Deborah Platt Majoras at a Press Conference on Operation Wagon Train," December 13, 2006, http://www.dhs.gov/xnews/releases/pr_1166047951514.shtm (accessed July 3, 2009). This generation of fear about potential terrorist attacks by illegal residents conveniently ignores the fact that all of the 9/11 terrorists entered the United States legally with the requisite visas. See Monahan, "Questioning Surveillance and Security."
23. Gray Cavender, "Media and Crime Policy: A Reconsideration of David Garland's The Culture of Control," *Punishment & Society* 6, no. 3 (2004): 335–348.
24. See, for example, Donna Leinwand, "Immigration Raid Linked to ID Theft, Chertoff Says," *USAToday.com*, December 13, 2006, http://www.usatoday.com/ news/nation/2006-12-13-immigration_x.htm (accessed July 3, 2009).
25. W. Brown, "American Nightmare."
26. U.S. General Accounting Office, "Identity Theft: Greater Awareness and Use of Existing Data Are Needed" (Washington, DC, 2002), http://www.gao.gov/ new.items/d02766.pdf (accessed July 3, 2009).
27. Loïc Wacquant, "Deadly Symbiosis: When Ghetto and Prison Meet and Mesh," *Punishment & Society* 3, no. 1 (2001): 95–134; Loïc J. D. Wacquant, *Punishing the Poor: The Neoliberal Government of Social Insecurity* (Durham, NC: Duke University Press, 2009).
28. Garland, *The Culture of Control*, 18.
29. See also Ericson, *Crime in an Insecure World*; Kevin D. Haggerty, "Displaced Expertise: Three Constraints on the Policy-Relevance of Criminological Thought," *Theoretical Criminology* 8, no. 2 (2004): 211–231.
30. S. Cole and Pontell, "Don't Be Low Hanging Fruit"; Sullivan, "The Meth Connection."
31. Nancy D. Campbell, *Using Women: Gender, Drug Policy, and Social Justice* (New York: Routledge, 2000), 3.

32. Jon Bonné, "Scourge of the Heartland: Meth Takes Root in Surprising Places," MSNBC, February 2001, http://www.msnbc.msn.com/id/3071773 (accessed June 5, 2006); Jon Bonné, "Lab-Busting in the Northwest: Stalking an Elusive Foe," MSNBC, February 2001, http://www.msnbc.msn.com/id/3071775 (accessed June 5, 2006).

33. Federal Trade Commission, "FTC Releases Top 10 Consumer Fraud Complaint Categories," Federal Trade Commission, 2006, http://www.ftc.gov/opa/2006/01/topten.htm (accessed June 5, 2006).

34. Kupchik and Monahan, "The New American School."

35. Manuel Castells, *The Rise of the Network Society* (Cambridge, MA: Blackwell, 1996).

36. Michael Hardt and Antonio Negri, *Empire* (Cambridge, MA: Harvard University Press, 2000); David Harvey, *The Condition of Postmodernity: An Enquiry into the Origins of Cultural Change* (Cambridge, MA: Blackwell, 1990).

37. Lisa Duggan, *The Twilight of Equality?: Neoliberalism, Cultural Politics, and the Attack on Democracy* (Boston: Beacon Press, 2003); Henry A. Giroux, *The Terror of Neoliberalism: Authoritarianism and the Eclipse of Democracy* (Boulder, CO: Paradigm, 2004); Monahan, *Globalization.*

38. Stephan Graham and Simon Marvin, *Splintering Urbanism: Networked Infrastructures, Technological Mobilities and the Urban Condition* (New York: Routledge, 2001).

39. Fredric Jameson, "Postmodernism, or the Cultural Logic of Late Capitalism," *New Left Review* 146 (1984): 53–92.

40. Emily Martin, "Flexible Survivors," *Cultural Values* 4, no. 4 (2000): 512–517; Emily Martin, *Bipolar Expeditions: Mania and Depression in American Culture* (Princeton, NJ: Princeton University Press, 2007).

41. Martin, "Flexible Survivors," 515.

42. Jean Comaroff and John L. Comaroff, "Millennial Capitalism: First Thoughts on a Second Coming," *Public Culture* 12, no. 2 (2000): 291–343.

43. Jennifer Whitson and Kevin D. Haggerty, "Stolen Identities," *Criminal Justice Matters* 68 (2007): 39–40; Jennifer Robin Whitson, "Assumed Identities: Responses to Identity Theft in an Era of Information Capitalism" (M.S. thesis, Department of Sociology, University of Alberta, Edmonton, 2006).

44. Federal Trade Commission, "FTC Releases Top 10."

45. Jonathan Krim and Michael Barbaro, "40 Million Credit Card Numbers Hacked: Data Breached at Processing Center," *Washington Post,* June 18, 2005, A01.

46. Dawn Kawamoto, "ChoicePoint to Pay $15 Million Over Data Leak," CNET News.com, January 26, 2006, http://news.cnet.com/ChoicePoint-to-pay-15-million-over-data-leak/2100-7350_3-6031629.html (accessed August 25, 2009).

47. Reuters, "Data on 26.5 Million Veterans Stolen from Home," *CNN.com,* May 22, 2006, http://www.cnn.com/2006/US/05/22/vets.data.reut/index.html (accessed June 30, 2006).

48. Rachel Konrad, "Gap Job Applicants' Data Stolen," Associated Press, September 28, 2007, http://www.foxnews.com/printer_friendly_wires/2007Sep28/0,4675,Gap SecurityBreach,00.html (accessed August 25, 2009).

49. Ibid.

50. David Murakami Wood, "I'm Back but Things Are Much the Same" 2008, http://blogs.ncl.ac.uk/blogs/index.php/d.f.j.wood/2008/10/13/i_m_back_but_things_are_much_the_same (accessed October 19, 2008).

51. According to Jeff Ferrell's ethnographic study of dumpster divers, they are seldom interested in the credit information of others anyway, and they throw personal documents back in the trash when they stumble across them. Jeff Ferrell, "Notes from the Trash Heaps of America" (lecture delivered at School of Justice and Social Inquiry, Arizona State University, March 23, 2006).

52. John Leland and Tom Zeller Jr., "Technology and Easy Credit Give Identity Thieves an Edge," *New York Times*, May 30, 2006.
53. Kawamoto, "ChoicePoint to Pay."
54. Jean-François Blanchette and Deborah G. Johnson, "Data Retention and the Panoptic Society: The Social Benefits of Forgetfulness," *The Information Society* 18, no. 1 (2002): 33–45.
55. Jennifer R. Whitson and Kevin D. Haggerty, "Identity Theft and the Care of the Virtual Self," *Economy and Society* 37, no. 4 (2008): 572–594.
56. One can witness the same trend with the demonization of antiglobalization protesters who utilize flexible tactics for organizing and demonstrating. Fernandez, *Policing Dissent*; Jeffrey S. Juris, *Networking Futures: The Movements Against Corporate Globalization* (Durham, NC: Duke University Press, 2008).

Chapter 5 Leaving Others Behind

1. Comaroff and Comaroff, "Millennial Capitalism," 315.
2. "The Fashion of the Christ," *BusinessWeek Online*, May 23, 2005, http://www.businessweek.com/magazine/content/05_21/b3934018_mz001.htm (accessed July 3, 2009).
3. Tim F. LaHaye and Jerry B. Jenkins, *Left Behind: A Novel of the Earth's Last Days* (Wheaton, IL: Tyndale House, 2000).
4. Gene Edward Veith, "When Truth Gets Left Behind," *Christian Research Journal* 24, no. 4 (2002): 11–19.
5. Paul S. Boyer, *When Time Shall Be No More: Prophecy Belief in Modern American Culture* (Cambridge, MA: Belknap Press of Harvard University Press, 1992); Amy Johnson Frykholm, *Rapture Culture: Left Behind in Evangelical America* (New York: Oxford University Press, 2004).
6. David Morgan, *Protestants and Pictures: Religion, Visual Culture and the Age of American Mass Production* (New York: Oxford University Press, 1999).
7. Veith, "When Truth."
8. Susan Harding, "Imagining the Last Days: The Politics of Apocalyptic Language," in *Accounting for Fundamentalisms: The Dynamic Character of Movements*, ed. M. E. Marty and R. S. Appleby (Chicago: University of Chicago Press, 1994).
9. Boyer, *When Time Shall.*
10. Crawford Gribben, "Rapture Fictions and the Changing Evangelical Condition," *Literature and Theology* 18, no. 1 (2004): 77–94.
11. Ibid.
12. The "Jewish problem" also returns with the narrative necessity of converting 144,000 Jews to Christianity as a precondition for the Second Coming of Christ, lending the novels a decidedly anti-Semitic overtone, which has been interpreted as intolerance for religious pluralism more generally. Frykholm, *Rapture Culture*; Sherryll Mleynek, "The Rhetoric of the 'Jewish Problem' in the Left Behind Novels," *Literature and Theology* 19, no. 4 (2005): 367–383.
13. Lynn Schofield Clark, *From Angels to Aliens: Teenagers, the Media, and the Supernatural* (New York: Oxford University Press, 2003).
14. John Agnew, "Religion and Geopolitics," *Geopolitics* 11 (2006):183–191; Carl Davidson and Jerry Harris, "Globalisation, Theocracy and the New Fascism: The US Right's Rise to Power," *Race & Class* 47, no. 3 (2006): 47–67; Didi Herman, "The New Roman Empire: European Envisionings and American Premillennialists," *Journal of American Studies* 34, no. 1 (2000): 23–40.
15. Harding, "Imagining the Last Days."
16. David B. Barrett, "A Century of Growth," *Christianity Today,* November 1998, 50–51.

17. Allan Fisher, "Five Surprising Years for Evangelical-Christian Publishing: 1998 to 2002," *Publishing Research Quarterly* Summer (2003): 20–36.

18. Heather Hendershot, *Shaking the World for Jesus: Media and Conservative Evangelical Culture* (Chicago: University of Chicago Press, 2004).

19. This staggering sales figure includes children's books, graphic novels, and audio books. LeftBehind.com, "The Facts," 2006, http://www.leftbehind.com (accessed September 22, 2006); Gribben, "Rapture Fictions."

20. Fisher, "Five Surprising Years," 25.

21. Larry Eskridge, "And the Most Influential American Evangelical of the Last 25 Years Is . . . ," *Evangelical Studies Bulletin* 17 (2001): 1–4.

22. Carl E. Olson, "Will Catholics Be 'Left Behind'?: The 'Rapture' and the Left Behind Books," *Catholic Scripture Study, International* 1 (2005): 5.

23. Charles B. Strozier, *Apocalypse: On the Psychology of Fundamentalism in America* (Boston: Beacon Press, 1994).

24. Gribben, "Rapture Fictions," 91.

25. Greg Hernandez, "Proving the Market in Faith-Based Films," *San Diego Union-Tribune*, October 18, 2002, E4.

26. Gribben, "Rapture Fictions."

27. LeftBehind.com, "Frequently Asked Questions," 2006, http://www.leftbehind.com (accessed September 22, 2006).

28. "The Fashion of the Christ."

29. Hendershot, *Shaking the World*, 8.

30. Richard Bartholomew, "Religious Mission and Business Reality: Trends in the Contemporary British Christian Book Industry," *Journal of Contemporary Religion* 20, no. 1 (2005): 41–54.

31. Fisher, "Five Surprising Years."

32. Ibid., 29.

33. Ibid.

34. Ibid., 33.

35. For instance, when I assigned the book *The Spychips Threat: Why Christians Should Resist RFID and Electronic Surveillance* for a class of mine, I was surprised to receive a phone call from the publisher telling me that because my university was not "Christian" that the publisher would sell only the hardcover version of the book to students, even though the paperback was easily available at Christian stores and—paradoxically—from online venues like Amazon.com.

36. Bartholomew, "Religious Mission."

37. John Drane, *The McDonaldization of the Church* (London: Darton, Longman, and Todd, 2000).

38. Clark, *From Angels to Aliens*; Frykholm, *Rapture Culture*.

39. Glenn W. Shuck, "Marks of the Beast: The Left Behind Novels, Identity, and the Internationalization of Evil," *Nova Religio: The Journal of Alternative and Emergent Religions* 8, no. 2 (2004): 48–63.

40. Monahan and T. Wall, "Somatic Surveillance"; Jill A. Fisher, "Indoor Positioning and Digital Management: Emerging Surveillance Regimes in Hospitals," in *Surveillance and Security: Technological Politics and Power in Everyday Life*, ed. T. Monahan (New York: Routledge, 2006).

41. Tim F. LaHaye and Jerry B. Jenkins, *The Mark: The Beast Rules the World* (Wheaton, IL: Tyndale House, 2000), 85.

42. Monahan, *Surveillance and Security*.

43. David Lyon, *Surveillance Society: Monitoring Everyday Life* (Buckingham, UK: Open University Press, 2001), 86.

44. Frykholm, *Rapture Culture*.

45. Shuck, "Marks of the Beast," 54.

46. Lee Quinby, *Anti-Apocalypse: Exercises in Genealogical Criticism* (Minneapolis: University of Minnesota Press, 1994).
47. Gribben, "Rapture Fictions," 91.
48. www.leftbehind.com (accessed December 14, 2006).
49. Hendershot, *Shaking the World*.
50. Tim F. LaHaye and Jerry B. Jenkins, "Planned Television Arts Teleprint Conference: Interview with Tim LaHaye and Jerry Jenkins," JSOnline, 2001, http://www2 .jsonline.com:80/lifestyle/religion/oct01/endtrans102301.asp?format=print (accessed December 14, 2006).
51. Gribben, "Rapture Fictions," 88.
52. This position may represent a departure from the sermons of 1980s televangelists such as Billy Graham, who did argue for overt political engagement in matters extending beyond "moral values" to include nuclear disarmament, among other things. Harding, "Imagining the Last Days."
53. Shuck, "Marks of the Beast," 52.
54. Veith, "When Truth"; Olson, "Will Catholics Be 'Left Behind'?"
55. Agnew, "Religion and Geopolitics"; Peter Yoonsuk Paik, "Smart Bombs, Serial Killing, and the Rapture," *Postmodern Culture* 14, no. 1 (2003): 1–17; Hugh B. Urban, "America, Left Behind: Bush, the Neoconservatives, and Evangelical Christian Fiction," *Journal of Religion & Society* 8 (2006): 1–15.
56. Davidson and Harris, "Globalisation, Theocracy and the New Fascism."
57. Herman, "The New Roman Empire"; Jeremy D. Mayer, "Christian Fundamentalists and Public Opinion toward the Middle East: Israel's New Best Friends?" *Social Science Quarterly* 85, no. 3 (2004): 695–712.
58. Paik, "Smart Bombs," 7–8.
59. Max Weber, *The Protestant Ethic and the Spirit of Capitalism* (New York: Routledge, 2000).
60. Michael T. Taussig, *The Devil and Commodity Fetishism in South America* (Chapel Hill: University of North Carolina Press, 1980).
61. Ibid., 15.
62. Urban, "America, Left Behind."

Chapter 6   Residential Fortification

1. C. Katz, "The State Goes Home."
2. Edward James Blakely and Mary Gail Snyder, *Fortress America: Gated Communities in the United States* (Washington, DC: Brookings Institution Press, 1997); Karina Landman, "Gated Communities in South Africa: Building Bridges or Barriers" (paper read at International Conference on the Privatisation of Urban Governance, at Mainz, Germany, June 6–9, 2002); Michelle Mycoo, "The Retreat of the Upper and Middle Classes to Gated Communities in the Poststructural Adjustment Era: The Case of Trinidad," *Environment and Planning A* 38, no. 1 (2006): 131–148.
3. Mike Davis, *City of Quartz: Excavating the Future in Los Angeles* (New York: Vintage Books, 1990); Michael Dear, *The Postmodern Urban Condition* (Oxford: Blackwell, 2000); Steven Flusty, *Building Paranoia: The Proliferation of Interdictory Spaces and the Erosion of Spatial Justice* (West Hollywood, CA: Los Angeles Forum for Architecture and Urban Design, 1994); Torin Monahan, "Los Angeles Studies: The Emergence of a Specialty Field," *City & Society* 14, no. 2 (2002): 155–184.
4. Teresa P. R. Caldeira, *City of Walls: Crime, Segregation, and Citizenship in São Paulo* (Berkeley: University of California Press, 2000).
5. See also Mitchell for an investigation into the relationship between security and exclusion in urban public spaces. Don Mitchell, *The Right to the City: Social Justice and the Fight for Public Space* (New York: Guilford Press, 2003).

6. Setha M. Low, *Behind the Gates: Life, Security and the Pursuit of Happiness in Fortress America* (New York: Routledge, 2003).

7. Ibid.; Kevin Romig, "The Upper Sonoran Lifestyle: Gated Communities in Scottsdale, Arizona," *City & Community* 4, no. 1 (2005): 67–86.

8. Oscar Newman, *Defensible Space* (New York: Macmillan, 1972).

9. It is highly likely, as Mawby claims, that many of Newman's ideas were borrowed from Jacobs. R. I. Mawby, "Defensible Space: A Theoretical and Empirical Appraisal," *Urban Studies* 14 (1977):169–179; Jane Jacobs, *The Death and Life of Great American Cities* (New York: Random House, 1961).

10. Simon Chih-Feng Shu, "Housing Layout and Crime Vulnerability," *Urban Design International* 5, no. 3/4 (2000): 177–188; Alice Coleman, *Utopia on Trial: Vision and Reality in Planned Housing* (London: H. Shipman, 1985); B. Hillier, "City of Alice's Dreams," *Architects Journal* 184, no. 28 (1986): 39–41; T. Hope, "Crime Community and Environment," *Journal of Environmental Psychology* 6 (1986): 65–78; Graham Steventon, "Defensible Space: A Critical Review of the Theory and Practice of a Crime Prevention Strategy," *Urban Design International* 1, no. 3 (1996): 235–245.

11. Michael C. Musheno, James P. Levine, and Denis J. Palumbo, "Television Surveillance and Crime Prevention: Evaluating an Attempt to Create Defensible Space in Public Housing," *Social Science Quarterly* 58, no. 4 (1978): 647–656.

12. Nicholas Blomley, "Un-real Estate: Proprietary Space and Public Gardening," *Antipode* 36, no. 4 (2004): 614–641; Paul Cozens, David Hillier, and Gwyn Prescott, "The Sustainable and the Criminogenic: The Case of New-Build Housing Projects in Britain," *Property Management* 17, no. 3 (1999): 252–261; B. Hillier, "Can Streets be Made Safe?" *Urban Design International* 9, no. 1 (2004): 31–45.

13. Graham and Marvin, *Splintering Urbanism*.

14. Zygmunt Bauman, *Globalization: The Human Consequences* (New York: Columbia University Press, 1998); Zygmunt Bauman, *Community: Seeking Safety in an Insecure World* (Cambridge, UK: Polity Press, 2001).

15. Jay Stanley, "The Surveillance-Industrial Complex" (New York: American Civil Liberties Union, 2004), http://www.aclu.org/FilesPDFs/surveillance_report.pdf (accessed July 3, 2009); Oscar H. Gandy, "Data Mining and Surveillance in the Post-9/11 Environment," in *The Intensification of Surveillance: Crime, Terrorism and Warfare in the Information Age*, ed. K. Ball and F. Webster (Sterling, VA: Pluto Press, 2003); Lyon, *Surveillance Society*; O'Harrow, *No Place to Hide*.

16. Langdon Winner, *Autonomous Technology: Technics-Out-of-Control as a Theme in Political Thought* (Cambridge, MA: MIT Press, 1977); Winner, *The Whale and the Reactor*.

17. Andrew Feenberg, *Questioning Technology* (New York: Routledge, 1999), 79.

18. Bryan Pfaffenberger, "Technological Dramas," *Science, Technology, and Human Values* 17, no. 3 (1992): 282–312.

19. Methods: The research sites included one low-income public housing complex of 136 units in downtown Phoenix, one somewhat porous gated community within the Phoenix metropolitan area, and one highly fortified gated community about thirty miles distant from the city. The sites were chosen primarily based on the criterion of their actively employing video surveillance, and secondarily on the communities' receptivity to participating in the research. Additionally, the gated community sites were chosen to represent two ends of the spectrum of gated community types in terms of exclusivity and security. The qualitative methods combined observation and semistructured interviews. In addition to many informal conversations during fieldwork, a total of twenty-one semistructured interviews, lasting approximately forty-five minutes each, were conducted with residents and employees at the three sites. The interview questions were scripted to elicit residents' impressions of who the surveillance was intended for and what their experiences

were of being under surveillance themselves. In this way, data were gathered both on the popular discourses of security and safety and on the actual practices of living under the scrutiny of such systems. For more details on methods, see Torin Monahan, "Electronic Fortification in Phoenix: Surveillance Technologies and Social Regulation in Residential Communities," *Urban Affairs Review* 42, no. 2 (2006): 169–192.

20. As a point of reference, in 2004, Phoenix reported 9,465 violent crimes and 94,406 property crimes; the corresponding crime rates adjusted for population are 6.62 per 1,000 and 66.07 per 1,000, respectively. The public housing site written about in this chapter is located in Phoenix. The two gated communities are not in cities large enough to have separate listings in the FBI's annual report of crime statistics, but the closest city that is large enough to be listed reported 468 violent crimes and 8,998 property crimes during the same time period; the corresponding crime rates adjusted for population are 2.09 per 1,000 and 40.12 per 1,000, respectively. Federal Bureau of Investigation, "Crime in the United States 2004" (Washington, DC: U.S. Department of Justice, 2005), http://www.fbi.gov/ucr/cius_04/documents/CIUS2004.pdf (accessed July 3, 2009). Of course, many crimes, such as domestic violence, go unreported and are therefore difficult to evaluate objectively. Alesha Durfee and Karen Rosenberg, "Domestic Violence in the United States: Current Research, New Directions," in *Agenda for Social Justice, Solutions 2004*, ed. R. Perrucci, K. Ferraro, J. Miller and P. C. R. Rust (Knoxville, TN: Society for the Study of Social Problems, 2004).

21. During the course of the field research, the surveillance cameras at the main guard gates were dismantled because they were unreliable for identifying license plate numbers, which was their primary intended function.

22. Michel Foucault, *Discipline and Punish: The Birth of the Prison* (New York: Vintage Books, Random House, 1977).

23. Michel Foucault, "Governmentality," in *The Foucault Effect: Studies in Governmentality*, ed. G. Burchell, C. Gordon and P. Miller (Chicago: University of Chicago Press, 1991).

24. Nancy D. Campbell, "Suspect Technologies: Scrutinizing the Intersection of Science, Technology, and Policy," *Science, Technology, and Human Values* 30, no. 3 (2005): 374–402; Gilliom, *Overseers of the Poor*.

25. Eubanks, "Technologies of Citizenship"; Gilliom, *Overseers of the Poor*.

CHAPTER 7   CONTROLLING MOBILITIES

1. Andrejevic, *iSpy*; Oscar Gandy Jr., "Data Mining, Surveillance, and Discrimination in the Post-9/11 Environment," in *The New Politics of Surveillance and Visibility*, ed. K. D. Haggerty and R. V. Ericson (Toronto: University of Toronto Press, 2006); David Lyon, *Surveillance Studies: An Overview* (Cambridge, UK: Polity Press, 2007); Monahan, *Surveillance and Security*; David J. Phillips, "From Privacy to Visibility: Context, Identity, and Power in Ubiquitous Computing Environments," *Social Text* 23, no. 2 (2005): 95–108.

2. For a collection of essays on how these technological politics are unfolding at airports around the world, see Mark B. Salter, ed., *Politics at the Airport* (Minneapolis: University of Minnesota Press, 2008).

3. Accent Marketing and Research, "Town Centres Survey 2003–4: Summary Report," London, 2004; BBC News, "Oyster Data Is 'New Police Tool,'" BBC News, March 13, 2006, http://news.bbc.co.uk/1/hi/england/london/4800490.stm (accessed July 3, 2009); U.S. Department of Transportation, "Developing Traffic Signal Control Systems Using the National ITS Architecture" (Washington, DC: U.S. Department of Transportation, 1998).

4. Heather Cameron, "Using Intelligent Transport Systems to Track Buses and Passengers," in *Surveillance and Security: Technological Politics and Power in Everyday Life*, ed. T. Monahan (New York: Routledge, 2006).

5. Colin Bennett, Charles Raab, and Priscilla Regan, "People and Place: Patterns of Individual Identification within Intelligent Transportation Systems," in *Surveillance as Social Sorting: Privacy, Risk, and Digital Discrimination*, ed. D. Lyon (New York: Routledge, 2003); Jeffrey H. Reiman, "Driving to the Panopticon: Philosophical Exploration of the Risks to Privacy Posed by the Highway Technology of the Future," *Santa Clara Computer and High Technology Law Journal* 11, no. 1 (1995): 27–44.

6. Martin Dodge and Rob Kitchin, "Code, Vehicles and Governmentality: The Automatic Production of Driving Spaces" (NIRSA [National Institute for Regional and Spatial Analysis] Working Papers Series, Maynooth, Ireland, no. 29, March 2006); Dorothy J. Glancy, "Whereabouts Privacy," *STS Nexus*, Spring 2004, http://www.scu.edu/sts/nexus/spring2004/privacy.cfm (accessed July 3, 2009).

7. James Hay and Jeremy Packer, "Crossing the Media(-n): Auto-mobility, the Transported Self and Technologies of Freedom," in *Mediaspace: Place, Scale and Culture in a Media Age*, ed. N. Couldry and A. McCarthy (New York: Routledge, 2004); A. Vahidi and A. Eskandarian, "Research Advances in Intelligent Collision Avoidance and Adaptive Cruise Control," *IEEE Transactions on Intelligent Transportation Systems* 4, no. 3 (2003): 143–153.

8. Methods: This research was conducted from 2004 to 2005 in the southwestern United States. In addition to observational site visits and eighteen semistructured interviews, I reviewed government documents and industry reports on ITS goals and effectiveness. For the observational component, I made four site visits to city and state departments of transportation, where I observed demonstrations of street monitoring systems designed for the optimization of traffic flows. Traffic engineers or administrators walked me through the functions of their systems, showing me the systems' capabilities and limitations and relating to me their own—and others'—involvement in the monitoring processes. For more information about methods, see Torin Monahan, "'War Rooms' of the Street: Surveillance Practices in Transportation Control Centers," *The Communication Review* 10, no. 4 (2007): 367–389.

9. U.S. Department of Transportation, "Frequently Asked Questions: Intelligent Transportation Systems," November 7, 2006, http://www.its.dot.gov/faqs.htm (accessed January 9, 2007).

10. Hay and Packer, "Crossing the Media(-n)."

11. David Lyon, "Why Where You are Matters: Mundane Mobilities, Transparent Technologies, and Digital Discrimination," in *Surveillance and Security: Technological Politics and Power in Everyday Life*, ed. T. Monahan (New York: Routledge, 2006).

12. Cameron, "Using Intelligent Transport Systems"; Dodge and Kitchin, "Code, Vehicles and Governmentality."

13. White House, "National Strategy for the Physical Protection of Critical Infrastructures and Key Assets," February 2003, http://www.dhs.gov/xlibrary/assets/Physical_Strategy.pdf (accessed August 25, 2009).

14. Bennett, Raab, and Regan, "People and Place."

15. Daniel Schulman and James Ridgeway, "The Highwaymen," *Mother Jones* 32, no. 1 (2007): 48–55, 84.

16. Ibid., 50.

17. Ibid., 52.

18. Priscilla M. Regan, *Legislating Privacy: Technology, Social Values, and Public Policy* (Chapel Hill: University of North Carolina Press, 1995); Michael Zimmer, "The Quest for the Perfect Search Engine: Values, Technical Design, and the Flow of

Personal Information in Spheres of Mobility" (Ph.D. diss., Department of Culture and Communication, New York University, 2007).

19. Graham and Marvin, *Splintering Urbanism*; Jason W. Patton, "Transportation Worlds: Designing Infrastructure and Forms of Urban Life" (Ph.D. diss., Science and Technology Studies, Rensselaer Polytechnic Institute, 2004); Julie E. Press, "Spatial Mismatch or More of a Mishmash? Multiple Jeopardy and the Journey to Work," in *Prismatic Metropolis: Inequality in Los Angeles*, ed. L. D. Bobo, Melvin L. Oliver, James H. Johnson Jr., and Abel Valenzuela (New York: Russell Sage Foundation, 2000).

20. It is important to note that not all surveillance should be viewed as negative. As David Lyon has argued, the control dimensions of surveillance can be interpreted as "care" or watching out for those in need, such as children, the elderly, or stranded motorists (Lyon, *Surveillance Society*). Obviously, classifying surveillance practices along the control-care continuum is a highly subjective exercise, whereby even the most obvious examples of care-based surveillance can be viewed as paternalistic and controlling from the perspective of those scrutinized, or from the perspective of scholars studying the scrutiny, as the case may be.

21. Lianos and Douglas, "Dangerization and the End of Deviance"; Thrift and French, "The Automatic Production of Space"; David Murakami Wood and Stephen Graham, "Permeable Boundaries in the Software-sorted Society: Surveillance and Differentiations of Mobility," in *Mobile Technologies of the City*, ed. Mimi Sheller and John Urry (New York: Routledge, 2006).

22. Peter Adey, "'Divided We Move': The Dromologics of Airport Security and Surveillance," in *Surveillance and Security: Technological Politics and Power in Everyday Life*, ed. T. Monahan (New York: Routledge, 2006); Caldeira, *City of Walls*; Low, *Behind the Gates*; Monahan, "Electronic Fortification in Phoenix"; Mimi Sheller and John Urry, *Mobile Technologies of the City* (New York: Routledge, 2006).

23. At the time, I was located at Arizona State University in Tempe, Arizona.

24. Monahan, *Globalization*, 151–154.

25. For instance, see U.S. Department of Transportation, "Developing Traffic Signal Control Systems Using the National ITS Architecture" (Washington, DC: U.S. Department of Transportation, 1998).

26. The term *capture* is a loaded one that I use here in accordance with how the systems are described by my informants. Although it is common to refer to information systems as oriented toward data "capture" (Philip E. Agre, "Surveillance and Capture: Two Models of Privacy," *The Information Society* 10 [1994]: 101–127), it would be more accurate to focus on the act of data "creation" that occurs with such systems. These systems restructure social practices and categories in an active way that is elided by the somewhat positivistic term *capture*.

27. Hay and Packer, "Crossing the Media(-n)," 220.

28. BBC News, "Oyster Data Is 'New Police Tool.'"

29. Patton, "Transportation Worlds."

30. Similarly, the system for emergency vehicle preemption (where green lights are triggered for emergency vehicles) is perceived as a threat to the synchronization of traffic signals.

31. Sarah S. Jain, "'Dangerous Instrumentality': The Bystander as Subject in Automobility," *Cultural Anthropology* 19, no. 1 (2004): 61–94.

32. Robert D. Bullard, Glenn S. Johnson, and Angel O. Torres, *Highway Robbery: Transportation Racism & New Routes to Equity* (Cambridge, MA: South End Press, 2004); Tom Lewis, *Divided Highways: Building the Interstate Highways, Transforming American Life* (New York: Viking, 1997); Patton, "Transportation Worlds."

33. CATA Alliance, "The Game Changer" (2008), http://www.cata.ca/Media_and_Events/Press_Releases/cata_pr10070802.html (accessed October 22, 2008); Defense Advanced Research Projects Agency, "DARPA Urban Challenge"

(2008), http://www.darpa.mil/GRANDCHALLENGE/ (accessed October 22, 2008); ViaMichelin, "Rescue, Assistance and Tracking with Volvo on Call" (2008), http://www.viamichelin.com/viamichelin/gbr/tpl/mag4/art20060115/htm/tech-volvo-on-call.htm (accessed October 22, 2008). I thank David Lyon, Stephen Graham, and Kirstie Ball for bringing these developments to my attention.

34. Donna J. Haraway, *Modest_Witness@Second_Millennium.FemaleMan_Meets_Onco-Mouse: Feminism and Technoscience* (New York: Routledge, 1997); Monahan and T. Wall, "Somatic Surveillance"; Jennifer Daryl Slack and J. Macgregor Wise, *Culture + Technology: A Primer* (New York: Peter Lang, 2005).

35. Fisher, "Indoor Positioning"; Jill A. Fisher and Torin Monahan, "Tracking the Social Dimensions of RFID Systems in Hospitals," *International Journal of Medical Informatics* 77, no. 3 (2008): 176–183.

36. Sarah S. Jain, "Urban Violence: Luxury in Made Space," in *Mobile Technologies of the City*, ed. M. Sheller and J. Urry (New York: Routledge, 2006); Patton, "Transportation Worlds."

37. Loren Demerath and David Levinger, "The Social Qualities of Being on Foot: A Theoretical Analysis of Pedestrian Activity, Community, and Culture," *City and Community* 2, no. 3 (2003): 217–237.

CHAPTER 8   MASCULINE TECHNOLOGIES

1. Of course, relationally, insecurity subjects often occupy a much more masculine role than failed insecurity subjects. Insecurity subjects take charge, through consumption, for meeting perceived needs, whereas those who do not live up to these expectations can be either symbolically emasculated or constructed as dangerous.

2. Clive Norris and Gary Armstrong, "The Unforgiving Eye: CCTV Surveillance in Public Space" (Centre for Criminology and Criminal Justice, Hull University, 1997).

3. Hille Koskela, "'The Gaze without Eyes': Video-Surveillance and the Changing Nature of Urban Space," *Progress in Human Geography* 24, no. 2 (2000): 243–265.

4. The focus on surveillance in these domains is complemented by ongoing research on surveillance in other public institutions, most notably in public education. See for example Monahan and Torres, *Schools under Surveillance.*

5. Sarah S. Jain, "The Prosthetic Imagination: Enabling and Disabling the Prosthesis Trope," *Science, Technology, and Human Values* 24, no. 1 (1999): 31–54.

6. Madeleine Akrich, "User Representations: Practices, Methods and Sociology," in *Managing Technology in Society: The Approach of Constructive Technology Assessment*, ed. A. Rip, T. J. Misa and J. Schot (London: Pinter, 1995); Nelly Oudshoorn, Els Rommes, and Marcelle Stienstra, "Configuring the User as Everybody: Gender and Design Cultures in Information and Communication Technologies," *Science, Technology, and Human Values* 29, no. 1 (2004): 30–63.

7. Elizabeth Grosz, *Volatile Bodies: Toward a Corporeal Feminism* (Bloomington: Indiana University Press, 1994).

8. Anne Balsamo, *Technologies of the Gendered Body* (Durham, NC: Duke University Press, 1996); Nelly Oudshoorn, "On Masculinities, Technologies, and Pain: The Testing of Male Contraceptives in the Clinic and the Media," *Science, Technology, and Human Values* 24, no. 2 (1999): 265–289.

9. Corlann Gee Bush, "Women and the Assessment of Technology," in *Technology and the Future*, ed. A. H. Teich (New York: St. Martin's Press, 1997).

10. Koskela, "'The Gaze without Eyes'"; Koskela, "Video Surveillance."

11. Lorraine Bayard de Volo, "Service and Surveillance: Infrapolitics at Work among Casino Cocktail Waitresses," *Social Politics* 10, no. 3 (2003): 347–376.

12. All casino workers and patrons are under intense surveillance, of course. Terry Austrin and Jackie West, "Skills and Surveillance in Casino Gaming: Work, Consumption and Regulation," *Work, Employment & Society* 19, no. 2 (2005): 305–326; Kurt Borchard, "Las Vegas Mon Amour," *Cultural Studies* <=> *Critical Methodologies* 7, no. 1 (2007): 74–96; Jeffrey J. Sallaz, "The House Rules: Autonomy and Interests Among Service Workers in the Contemporary Casino Industry," *Work and Occupations* 29, no. 4 (2007): 394–427. The point of this example is to illustrate how sexist contexts can reproduce uniquely sexist uses of technologies, allowing for the reinforcement of those social relations.

13. R. Danielle Egan, "Eyeing the Scene: The Uses and (RE)uses of Surveillance Cameras in an Exotic Dance Club," *Critical Sociology* 30, no. 2 (2004): 299–319.

14. Jennifer Wesely and Emily Gaardner, "The Gendered 'Nature' of the Urban Outdoors: Women Negotiating Fear of Violence," *Gender & Society* 18, no. 5 (2004): 645–663.

15. Leslie Kanes Weisman, *Discrimination by Design: A Feminist Critique of the Man-Made Environment* (Chicago: University of Illinois Press, 1992).

16. Ruth Schwartz Cowan, *More Work for Mother: The Ironies of Household Technology from the Open Hearth to the Microwave* (New York: Basic Books, 1983); Judy Wajcman, *Feminism Confronts Technology* (Cambridge, UK: Polity Press, 1991).

17. Cynthia Cockburn and Susan Ormrod, *Gender and Technology in the Making* (Thousand Oaks, CA: Sage, 1993).

18. Francesca Bray, *Technology and Gender: Fabrics of Power in Late Imperial China* (Berkeley: University of California Press, 1997); Susan Markens, C. H. Browner, and H. Mabel Preloran, "'I'm Not the One They're Sticking the Needle Into': Latino Couples, Fetal Diagnosis, and the Discourse of Reproductive Rights," *Gender & Society* 17, no. 3 (2003): 462–481; Aihwa Ong, "The Gender and Labor Politics of Postmodernity," *Annual Review of Anthropology* 20 (1991): 279–309.

19. Lynsey Dubbeld, "Observing Bodies: Camera Surveillance and the Significance of the Body," *Ethics and Information Technology* 5 (2003): 151–162; Wayne D. Woodward, "Technologized Communications as Artifact/Discourse/Relation: The Case of the Technological City," *Cultural Studies* <=> *Critical Methodologies* 3, no. 3 (2003): 330–354.

20. Carolyn Merchant, *The Death of Nature: Women, Ecology, and the Scientific Revolution* (New York: HarperCollins, 1980).

21. Mary Terrall, "Gendered Spaces, Gendered Audiences: Inside and Outside the Paris Academy of Sciences," *Configurations* 2 (1995): 207–232.

22. Londa Schiebinger, *The Mind Has No Sex?: Women in the Origins of the Scientific Revolution* (Cambridge, MA: Harvard University Press, 1989).

23. Foucault, *Discipline and Punish*.

24. Oscar H. Gandy, *The Panoptic Sort: A Political Economy of Personal Information* (Boulder, CO: Westview, 1993); Lyon, *Surveillance as Social Sorting*.

25. Marcus Nieto, Kimberly Johnston-Dodds, and Charlene Wear Simmons, "Public and Private Applications of Video Surveillance and Biometric Technologies" (Sacramento: California Research Bureau, 2002), http://www.library.ca.gov/crb/02/06/02–006.pdf (accessed July 3, 2009).

26. Nancy D. Campbell, "Everyday Insecurities: The Micro-behavioral Politics of Intrusive Surveillance," in *Surveillance and Security: Technological Politics and Power in Everyday Life*, ed. T. Monahan (New York: Routledge, 2006).

27. Eubanks, "Technologies of Citizenship."

28. Gilliom, *Overseers of the Poor*.

29. Eubanks, "Technologies of Citizenship," 106.

30. Monahan, "Questioning Surveillance and Security."

31. Michael A. Stegman, Jennifer S. Lobenhofer, and John Quinterno, "The State of Electronic Benefit Transfer (EBT)" (Chapel Hill: Center for Community Capitalism, University of North Carolina at Chapel Hill, 2003), 14.

32. David Barstow, "A.T.M. Cards Fail to Live Up to Promises to Poor," *New York Times*, August 16, 1999, http://www.nytimes.com/library/politics/081699ny-welfare-atm.html (accessed July 3, 2009).

33. Bruce E. Feig, "Audit of Office of Temporary and Disability Assistance Electronic Benefit Transfer System" (New York: Office of the State Comptroller, 2001), 13, http://www.osc.state.ny.us/audits/allaudits/093001/99s51.pdf (accessed July 3, 2009).

34. Gilliom, *Overseers of the Poor*, 9.

35. Fisher and Monahan, "Tracking the Social Dimensions."

36. George W. Bush, "Executive Order 13335" (2004), http://www.whitehouse.gov/news/releases/2004/04/20040427–4.html (accessed May 20, 2005).

37. Steve Lohr, "Wal-Mart Plans to Market Digital Health Records System," *New York Times*, March 11, 2009.

38. Stephen Timmons, "A Failed Panopticon: Surveillance of Nursing Practice via New Technology," *New Technology, Work and Employment* 18, no. 2 (2003): 143–153.

    The introduction of advanced surveillance technologies in hospitals is consistent with Michel Foucault's observations about the spread of disciplinary systems and architectures throughout institutions. The panopticon is a compelling metaphor for how "docile bodies" are produced by technologies and techniques, discourses and practices (Foucault, *Discipline and Punish*). Margarete Sandelowski further observes that the various technologies of surveillance and screening of hospital patients in the twentieth century represents a "shift in the orientation of medicine from treatment and diagnosis to monitoring and recording." Sandelowski, *Devices & Desires: Gender, Technology, and American Nursing* (Chapel Hill: University of North Carolina Press, 2000), 136–137. I would call this one of the "techno-logics" of surveillance systems, of which monitoring patients' illnesses is part; the technologies themselves embody certain rationalities or privileged ways of seeing the world, which are then exerted upon social spaces and practices. This is not a deterministic argument: it neither denies the active mediation of techno-logics by social context nor does it rule out the selective adaptation and appropriation of technologies by social actors. That said, the power of complex technological systems to shape knowledge and practice is usually significantly stronger than the capabilities of actors to challenge the dominant logics of these systems in any serious way.

39. Fisher, "Indoor Positioning," 87.

40. Ibid, 82.

41. The term "prickly space" is adopted from Steven Flusty's provoking typology of interdictory spaces (Flusty, "Building Paranoia").

42. Fisher, "Indoor Positioning."

43. Ibid.

44. RFID systems are now commonly used to track commercial and other products (by retailers, libraries, shipping distributors, the military, and others), to regulate access (to buildings, parking structures, computer systems. and so on), and to tabulate charges (for example, for toll roads and public transportation).

45. Fisher, "Indoor Positioning," 86.

46. Monahan and T. Wall, "Somatic Surveillance."

47. Associated Press, "ID Chips Not Just for Pets Anymore," *CNN.com*, February 13, 2006, http://www.cnn.com/2006/TECH/02/13/security.chips.ap/index.html (accessed July 14, 2007); Jan Libbenga, "Video Surveillance Outfit Chips Workers," *The Register*, February 10, 2006, http://www.theregister.co.uk/2006/02/10/employees_chipped/ (accessed July 14, 2007).

48. Duncan Graham-Rowe, "Clubbers Choose Chip Implants to Jump Queues," *New-Scientist.com*, May 2004, http://www.newscientist.com/article.ns?id=dn5022 (accessed July 14, 2007).

49. Donna Haraway, *Primate Visions: Gender, Race, and Nature in the World of Modern Science* (New York: Routledge, 1989); Donna Haraway, *Simians, Cyborgs, and Women: The Reinvention of Nature* (New York: Routledge, 1991); Haraway, *Modest_Witness*.

50. Cameron, "Using Intelligent Transport Systems"; Patton, "Transportation Worlds."

51. Patton, "Transportation Worlds."

52. Graham and Marvin, *Splintering Urbanism*; Press, "Spatial Mismatch."

53. Cameron, "Using Intelligent Transport Systems"; Patton, "Transportation Worlds."

54. Barbara Hooper, "The Poem of Male Desires: Female Bodies, Modernity, and 'Paris, Capital of the Nineteenth Century,'" in *Making the Invisible Visible: A Multicultural Planning History*, ed. L. Sandercock (Berkeley: University of California Press, 1998), cited in Graham and Marvin, *Splintering Urbanism*, 124–125.

55. Dolores Hayden, *The Grand Domestic Revolution: A History of Feminist Designs for American Homes, Neighborhoods, and Cities* (Cambridge, MA: MIT Press, 1981); Gill Kirkup and Laurie S. Keller, *Inventing Women: Science, Technology, and Gender* (Cambridge, UK: Polity Press, 1992); Weisman, *Discrimination by Design*.

56. Winner, *The Whale and the Reactor*.

57. Haraway, *Simians, Cyborgs, and Women*.

58. David Hess, *Science Studies: An Advanced Introduction* (New York: New York University Press, 1997), 46.

59. Eubanks, "Technologies of Citizenship."

60. Fisher, "Indoor Positioning."

61. Glancy, "Whereabouts Privacy."

62. Kathryn Milun, *Pathologies of Modern Space: Empty Space, Urban Anxiety, and the Recovery of the Public Self* (New York: Routledge, 2007).

CHAPTER 9   COUNTERSURVEILLANCE

1. Michel Foucault, *The History of Sexuality: An Introduction* (New York: Vintage, 1978), 1:95.

2. For example, Laura Huey, Kevin Walby, and Aaron Doyle document the use of video cameras by the Cop Watch organization in Vancouver, which is a group dedicated to preventing police abuse of vulnerable populations. Huey, Walby, and Doyle, "Cop Watching in the Downtown Eastside: Exploring the Use of (Counter) Surveillance as a Tool of Resistance," in *Surveillance and Security: Technological Politics and Power in Everyday Life*, ed. T. Monahan (New York: Routledge, 2006).

3. See Castells, *The Rise of the Network Society*; Harvey, *The Condition of Postmodernity*.

4. Jennifer Gonnerman, "Slammed," *Mother Jones* 33, no. 4 (2008): 44–46.

5. Caldeira, *City of Walls*; Davis, *City of Quartz*; Low, *Behind the Gates*.

6. Sharon Zukin, *The Cultures of Cities* (Cambridge, MA: Blackwell, 1995).

7. Graham and Marvin, *Splintering Urbanism*; Monahan, *Globalization*; Reiman, "Driving to the Panopticon."

8. Stanley, "The Surveillance-Industrial Complex"; Gandy, "Data Mining and Surveillance"; Monahan, "The Surveillance Curriculum"; O'Harrow, *No Place to Hide*.

9. See Wiebe E. Bijker, Thomas Hughes, and Trevor Pinch, ed., *The Social Construction of Technological Systems: New Directions in the Sociology and History of Technology* (Cambridge, MA: MIT Press, 1987); Wiebe E. Bijker and John Law, *Shaping Technology / Building Society: Studies in Sociotechnical Change* (Cambridge, MA: MIT Press, 1992).

10. Erich W. Schienke and Institute for Applied Autonomy, "On the Outside Looking Out: An Interview with the Institute for Applied Autonomy (IAA)," *Surveillance & Society* 1, no. 1 (2002): 102–119.

11. Institute for Applied Autonomy, 2003, http://www.appliedautonomy.com/ (accessed October 20, 2006).
12. Bowker and Star, *Sorting Things Out.*
13. Winner, *The Whale and the Reactor.*
14. Mark Dery, "Hacking Barbie's Voice Box: 'Vengeance Is Mine!'" *New Media*, May 1994, http://www.levity.com/markdery/barbie.html (accessed February 18, 2005); Brigitte Greenberg, "The BLO—Barbie Liberation Organization—Strikes," Associated Press, 1994, http://www.etext.org/Zines/UnitCircle/uc3/page10.html (accessed February 18, 2005); RTMark, "The Barbie Liberation Organization," 2000, http://www.rtmark.com/blo.html (accessed February 18, 2005).
15. Democracy Now!, "Yes Men Hoax on BBC Reminds World of Dow Chemical's Refusal to Take Responsibility for Bhopal Disaster," December 6, 2004, http://67.15.90.110/article.pl?sid=04/12/06/1453248 (accessed February 18, 2005); DowEthics, "Dow 'Help' Announcement Is Elaborate Hoax" (Dow Company, 2004), http://www.dowethics.com/r/about/corp/bbc.htm (accessed February 18, 2005); Yes Men, "The Yes Men Hijinks: Dow," 2004, http://theyesmen.org/hijinks/dow/ (accessed February 20, 2005).
16. RTMark, "Guide to Closed Circuit Television (CCTV) Destruction," 2001, http://www.rtmark.com/cctv/ (accessed February 18, 2005).
17. RTMark, "Guide to Closed Circuit Television (CCTV) Destruction."
18. In contrast, RTMark's "The Yes Men" clearly do agitate for change on an institutional level. The group's Web site explains this mission: "Identity theft: Small-time criminals impersonate honest people in order to steal their money. Targets are ordinary folks whose ID numbers fell into the wrong hands. Identity correction: Honest people impersonate big-time criminals in order to publicly humiliate them. Targets are leaders and big corporations who put profits ahead of everything else." Yes Men, "The Yes Men" (2005), http://theyesmen.org/ (accessed February 20, 2005).
19. Koskela, "'The Gaze without Eyes'"; Norris and Armstrong, *The Unforgiving Eye*; Jeffrey Rosen, "A Cautionary Tale for a New Age of Surveillance," *New York Times Magazine*, October 7, 2001, http://www.schizophonia.com/archives/cctv.htm (accessed October 20, 2006); Lyon, *Surveillance Society.*
20. wearcam.org/shootingback.html (accessed February 18, 2005).
21. Steve Mann, "'Reflectionism' and 'Diffusionism,'" in *CTRL [Space]: Rhetorics of Surveillance from Bentham to Big Brother*, ed. T. Y. Levin, U. Frohne, and P. Weibel (Cambridge, MA: MIT Press, 2002).
22. Ibid., 541.
23. William G. Staples, *Everyday Surveillance: Vigilance and Visibility in Postmodern Life* (Lanham, MD: Rowman & Littlefield, 2000).
24. Surveillance Camera Players, *We Know You are Watching* (Factory School: Southpaw Culture, 2006).
25. Alex Burns, "Surveillance Camera Players," *Disinformation*, January 17, 2001, http://www.disinfo.com/archive/pages/dossier/id323/pg1/ (accessed October 20, 2006).
26. Greil Marcus, "Real Life Rock Top 10," *Salon.com*, April 3, 2000, http://archive.salon.com/media/col/marc/2000/04/03/marcus17/index1.html (accessed October 20, 2006).
27. Surveillance Camera Players, "Founding Documents of the Surveillance Camera Players" (2005), http://www.notbored.org/scp-founding.html (accessed February 17, 2005).
28. Surveillance Camera Players, "Why Legal Action Should Be Taken Against the City of New York for Its Installation of Surveillance Cameras in Public Places" (2001), http://www.notbored.org/to-the-lawyers.html (accessed February 17, 2005).
29. Foucault, *Discipline and Punish.*

30. Gilles Deleuze, *Foucault*, trans. S. Hand (Minneapolis: University of Minnesota Press, 1988), 27.

31. Gilles Deleuze, "Postscript on the Societies of Control," *October* 59 (1992): 3–7; Michel Foucault, *Power/Knowledge: Selected Interviews and Other Writings, 1972–1977* (Brighton, Sussex, UK: Harvester Press, 1980).

32. Michel de Certeau, *The Practice of Everyday Life*, trans. S. Rendall (Berkeley: University of California Press, 1984).

33. Heather Cameron likens this type of movement to "Spy vs. Spy" behavior, noting, "Choosing to address the problems of surveillance through technological fixes opens up some strategic options and shuts down others," perhaps deepening our "subjection" (143). Heather Cameron, "CCTV and (In)dividuation," *Surveillance & Society* 2, no. 2/3 (2004): 136–144.

34. Norman M. Klein, *The History of Forgetting* (New York: Verso, 1997); Monahan, "Los Angeles Studies."

35. Judson L. Jeffries, "Police Use of Excessive Force against Black Males: Aberrations or Everyday Occurrences," *Journal of Mundane Behavior* 3, no. 3 (2002), http://www.mundanebehavior.org/issues/v3n3/jeffries.htm (accessed October 20, 2006); Fred Mazelis, "What the Torture of Abner Louima Shows: Capitalism and Police Brutality," *International Workers Bulletin*, 1997, http://www.wsws.org/public_html/iwb9–22/louima.htm (accessed October 20, 2006).

36. Fernandez, *Policing Dissent*.

37. Steve Breyman, "Moyens de Communication, Mobilisation Rapide et Actions Préventives Contre le Guerre," *EcoRev: Revue Critique D'Écologie Politique* 12 (Printemps 2003): 37–44.

38. Independent Media Center Network (IMC), "IMC Statement on Genoa Police Raid 2001," http://italy.indymedia.org/news/2001/07/7092.php (accessed October 1, 2003); Jeffrey S. Juris, "The New Digital Media and Activist Networking within Anti–Corporate Globalization Movements," *Annals of the American Academy of Political and Social Science* 597, no. 1 (2005): 189–208.

39. *CNN.com*, "World Leaders Prepare for G8 Summit" (2002), http://archives.cnn.com/2002/WORLD/americas/06/25/g8.summit/ (accessed October 1, 2003); Robin Rowland, "Security at G-8; Watching on Three Fronts," CBC News Online, June 24, 2002, http://www.cbc.ca/news/features/g8/security.html (accessed October 1, 2003); David E. Sanger, "In Canada, World's Most Exclusive Summer Camp," *New York Times*, June 27, 2002, 15.

40. Hardt and Negri, *Empire*.

41. Ibid., 276.

42. Colin J. Bennett, *The Privacy Advocates: Resisting the Spread of Surveillance* (Cambridge, MA: MIT Press, 2008).

43. Gilliom, *Overseers of the Poor*.

44. Luis A. Fernandez and Laura Huey, "Editorial: Is Resistance Futile? Thoughts on Resisting Surveillance," *Surveillance & Society* 6, no. 3 (2009): 198–202.

45. Steve Breyman, *Why Movements Matter: The West German Peace Movement and U.S. Arms Control Policy* (Albany: State University of New York Press, 2001); David J. Hess, "Technology- and Product-Oriented Movements: Approximating Social Movement Studies and Science and Technology Studies," *Science, Technology, and Human Values* 30, no. 4 (2005): 515–535; Juris, *Networking Futures*.

CONCLUSION

1. Alyssa Katz, "Prime Suspect," *Mother Jones* 31, n0.5 (2006): 90–95, 112.

2. David M. Herszenhorn, "Bailout Plan Wins Approval; Democrats Vow Tighter Rules," *New York Times*, October 4, 2008, A1; Katrina vanden Heuvel, "Give Main

Street a Fair Shake," *The Nation*, September 22, 2008, http://www.thenation.com/blogs/edcut/363206/give_main_street_a_fair_shake (accessed July 3, 2009).
3. Karen A. Cerulo, *Never Saw It Coming: Cultural Challenges to Envisioning the Worst* (Chicago: University of Chicago Press, 2006), 6.
4. John Gilliom, "Lying, Cheating and Teaching to the Test: The Politics of Surveillance Under No Child Left Behind," in *Schools under Surveillance: Cultures of Control in Public Education*, ed. T. Monahan and R. D. Torres (New Brunswick, NJ: Rutgers University Press, 2010).
5. Joe Doherty et al., "Homelessness and Exclusion: Regulating Public Space in European Cities," *Surveillance & Society* 5, no. 3 (2008): 290–314.
6. Mona Lynch, "Selling 'Securityware': Transformations in Prison Commodities Advertising, 1949–99," *Punishment & Society* 4, no. 3 (2002): 305–319.
7. David Engwicht, *Reclaiming Our Cities and Towns: Better Living with Less Traffic* (Philadelphia: New Society Publishing, 1993); Kevin Lynch, *Good City Form* (Cambridge, MA: MIT Press, 1984); Mitchell, *The Right to the City*.
8. Julian Borger, "US Military in Torture Scandal," *The Guardian*, April 30, 2004, http://www.guardian.co.uk/media/2004/apr/30/television.internationalnews (accessed July 3, 2009); Joanne Mariner, "Private Contractors Who Torture," *CNN.com*, June 17, 2004, http://www.cnn.com/2004/LAW/06/17/mariner.contractors/index.html (accessed July 3, 2009).
9. Doherty et al., "Homelessness and Exclusion"; Surveillance Camera Players, *We Know You are Watching*; Zukin, *The Cultures of Cities*.
10. See David Murakami Wood, "I'm Back but Things Are Much the Same"; Robert Scheer, "Taxpayers Lose, Halliburton Gains," *The Nation*, June 27, 2007, http://www.thenation.com/doc/20070709/truthdig (accessed July 3, 2009).
11. Notable exceptions include academic research being done by members of an international project called "The New Transparency: Surveillance and Social Sorting," directed by David Lyon; reports generated by the ACLU on DHS fusion centers; and the work of journalist Robert O'Harrow. See Mike German and Jay Stanley, "ACLU Fusion Center Update" (July 2008), http://www.aclu.org/pdfs/privacy/fusion_update_20080729.pdf (accessed July 3, 2009); Torin Monahan, "The Murky World of 'Fusion Centres,'" *Criminal Justice Matters* 75, no. 1 (2009): 20–21; Robert O'Harrow, "Centers Tap into Personal Databases; State Groups Were Formed after 9/11," *Washington Post*, April 2, 2008, A01.
12. Appadurai, *Fear of Small Numbers*, 43.
13. Adey, "Divided We Move"; Pallitto and Heyman, "Theorizing Cross-Border Mobility."
14. Ticktin, "Policing and Humanitarianism in France."

Bibliography

Accent Marketing and Research. "Town Centres Survey 2003–4: Summary Report." London, 2004.

Adey, Peter. "'Divided We Move': The Dromologics of Airport Security and Surveillance." In *Surveillance and Security: Technological Politics and Power in Everyday Life*, edited by Torin Monahan, 195–208. New York: Routledge, 2006.

Adler, Patricia A., and Peter Adler. "The Deviance Society." *Deviant Behavior* 27 (2006): 129–148.

Agamben, Giorgio. *Homo Sacer: Sovereign Power and Bare Life*. Stanford, CA: Stanford University Press, 1998.

———. *State of Exception*. Chicago: University of Chicago Press, 2005.

Agnew, John. "Religion and Geopolitics." *Geopolitics* 11 (2006): 183–191.

Agre, Philip E. "Surveillance and Capture: Two Models of Privacy." *The Information Society* 10 (1994): 101–127.

Akrich, Madeleine. "The De-Scription of Technological Objects." In *Shaping Technology / Building Society: Studies in Sociotechnical Change*, edited by Wiebe E. Bijker and John Law. Cambridge, MA: MIT Press, 1992.

———. "User Representations: Practices, Methods and Sociology." In *Managing Technology in Society: The Approach of Constructive Technology Assessment*, edited by A. Rip, T. J. Misa, and J. Schot, 167–184. London: Pinter, 1995.

Allison, Stuart F. H., Amie M. Schuck, and Kim Michelle Lersch. "Exploring the Crime of Identity Theft: Prevalence, Clearance Rates, and Victim/Offender Characteristics." *Journal of Criminal Justice* 33 (2005): 19–29.

Altheide, David L. *Creating Fear: News and the Construction of Crisis*. New York: Aldine de Gruyter, 2002.

———. *Terrorism and the Politics of Fear*. Lanham, MD: Altamira Press, 2006.

Andreas, Peter. "Redrawing the Line: Borders and Security in the Twenty-first Century." *International Security* 28, no. 2 (2003): 78–111.

Andrejevic, Mark. *iSpy: Surveillance and Power in the Interactive Era*. Lawrence: University Press of Kansas, 2007.

Anthony, Jerry. "Family Self-sufficiency Programs: An Evaluation of Program Benefits and Factors Affecting Participants' Success." *Urban Affairs Review* 41, no. 1 (2005): 65–92.

Appadurai, Arjun. *Fear of Small Numbers: An Essay on the Geography of Anger*. Durham, NC: Duke University Press, 2006.

Associated Press. "ID Chips Not Just for Pets Anymore." *CNN.com*, February 13, 2006. http://www.cnn.com/2006/TECH/02/13/security.chips.ap/index.html (accessed July 14, 2007).

Austrin, Terry, and Jackie West. "Skills and Surveillance in Casino Gaming: Work, Consumption and Regulation." *Work, Employment & Society* 19, no. 2 (2005): 305–326.

Bajc,Vida. "Introduction: Debating Surveillance in the Age of Security." *American Behavioral Scientist* 50, no. 12 (2007): 1567–1591.

Ball, Kirstie S. "Exposure: Exploring the Subject of Surveillance Information." *Communication and Society* 12, no. 5 (2009): 639–657.

Ball, Kirstie, and Frank Webster, eds. *The Intensification of Surveillance: Crime, Terrorism and Warfare in the Information Age*. Sterling,VA: Pluto Press, 2003.

Balsamo, Anne. *Technologies of the Gendered Body*. Durham, NC: Duke University Press, 1996.

Barrett, David B. "A Century of Growth." *Christianity Today*, November 1998, 50–51.

Barstow, David. "A.T.M. Cards Fail to Live Up to Promises to Poor." *New York Times*, August 16, 1999. http://www.nytimes.com/library/politics/081699ny-welfare-atm.html (accessed July 3, 2009).

Bartholomew, Richard. "Religious Mission and Business Reality:Trends in the Contemporary British Christian Book Industry." *Journal of Contemporary Religion* 20, no. 1 (2005): 41–54.

Bauman, Zygmunt. *Community: Seeking Safety in an Insecure World*. Cambridge, UK: Polity Press, 2001.

———. *Globalization: The Human Consequences*. New York: Columbia University Press, 1998.

Bayard de Volo, Lorraine. "Service and Surveillance: Infrapolitics at Work among Casino Cocktail Waitresses." *Social Politics* 10, no. 3 (2003): 347–376.

BBC News. "Obama Orders Guantanamo Closure." BBC News, January 22, 2009. http://news.bbc.co.uk/2/hi/americas/7845585.stm (accessed March 3, 2009).

———. "Oyster Data Is 'New Police Tool.'" BBC News, March 13, 2006. http://news.bbc.co.uk/1/hi/england/london/4800490.stm (accessed July 3, 2009).

Beck, Ulrich. "From Industrial Society to the Risk Society: Questions of Survival, Social Structure and Ecological Enlightenment." *Theory, Culture & Society* 9 (1992): 97–123.

———. "The Terrorist Threat:World Risk Society Revisited." *Theory, Culture & Society* 19, no. 4 (2002): 39–55.

Bennett, Colin, Charles Raab, and Priscilla Regan. "People and Place: Patterns of Individual Identification within Intelligent Transportation Systems." In *Surveillance as Social Sorting: Privacy, Risk, and Digital Discrimination*, edited by David Lyon, 153–175. New York: Routledge, 2003.

Bennett, Colin J. *The Privacy Advocates: Resisting the Spread of Surveillance*. Cambridge, MA: MIT Press, 2008.

Bible: King James Version. http://www.hti.umich.edu/k/kjv/ (accessed December 16, 2006).

Bijker,Wiebe E.,Thomas Hughes, and Trevor Pinch, ed. *The Social Construction of Technological Systems: New Directions in the Sociology and History of Technology*. Cambridge, MA: MIT Press, 1987.

Bijker,Wiebe E., and John Law. *Shaping Technology / Building Society: Studies in Sociotechnical Change*. Cambridge, MA: MIT Press, 1992.

Blakely, Edward James, and Mary Gail Snyder. *Fortress America: Gated Communities in the United States*.Washington, DC: Brookings Institution Press, 1997.

Blanchette, Jean-François, and Deborah G. Johnson. "Data Retention and the Panoptic Society: The Social Benefits of Forgetfulness." *The Information Society* 18 (2002): 33–45.

Blomley, Nicholas. "Un-real Estate: Proprietary Space and Public Gardening." *Antipode* 36, no. 4 (2004): 614–641.

Bonné, Jon. "Lab-busting in the Northwest: Stalking an Elusive Foe." MSNBC, February 2001. http://www.msnbc.msn.com/id/3071775 (accessed June 5, 2006).

————. "Scourge of the Heartland: Meth Takes Root in Surprising Places." MSNBC, February 2001. http://www.msnbc.msn.com/id/3071773 (accessed June 5, 2006).

Borchard, Kurt. "Las Vegas Mon Amour." *Cultural Studies* <=> *Critical Methodologies* 7, no. 1 (2007): 74–96.

Borger, Julian. "US Military in Torture Scandal." *The Guardian*, April 30, 2004. http://www.guardian.co.uk/media/2004/apr/30/television.internationalnews (accessed July 3, 2009).

Bourdieu, Pierre. "The Essence of Neoliberalism." *Le Monde Diplomatique*, December 1998. http://mondediplo.com/1998/12/08bourdieu (accessed July 3, 2009).

————. *Outline of a Theory of Practice.* Translated by Richard Nice. Cambridge, UK: Cambridge University Press, 1977.

Bowker, Geoffrey C., and Susan Leigh Star. *Sorting Things Out: Classification and Its Consequences.* Cambridge, MA: MIT Press, 1999.

Boyer, Paul S. *When Time Shall be No More: Prophecy Belief in Modern American Culture.* Cambridge, MA: Belknap Press of Harvard University Press, 1992.

Bradley, Benjamin Sylvester, and John R. Morss. "Social Construction in a World at Risk." *Theory & Psychology* 12, no. 4 (2002): 509–531.

Bray, Francesca. *Technology and Gender: Fabrics of Power in Late Imperial China.* Berkeley: University of California Press, 1997.

Breyman, Steve. "Moyens de Communication, Mobilisation Rapide et Actions Préventives Contre le Guerre." *EcoRev: Revue Critique D'Écologie Politique* 12 (Printemps 2003): 37–44.

————. *Why Movements Matter: The West German Peace Movement and U.S. Arms Control Policy.* Albany: State University of New York Press, 2001.

Brown, Sheila. "The Criminology of Hybrids: Rethinking Crime and Law in Technosocial Networks." *Theoretical Criminology* 10, no. 2 (2006): 223–244.

Brown, Wendy. "American Nightmare: Neoliberalism, Neoconservatism, and De-Democratization." *Political Theory* 34, no. 6 (2006): 690–714.

Bullard, Robert D., Glenn S. Johnson, and Angel O. Torres. *Highway Robbery: Transportation Racism & New Routes to Equity.* Cambridge, MA: South End Press, 2004.

Burke, Anthony. *Beyond Security, Ethics and Violence: War against the Other.* New York: Routledge, 2007.

Burns, Alex. "Surveillance Camera Players." *Disinformation*, January 17, 2001, http://www.disinfo.com/archive/pages/dossier/id323/pg1/ (accessed October 20, 2006).

Bush, Corlann Gee. "Women and the Assessment of Technology." In *Technology and the Future*, edited by Albert H. Teich, 157–179. New York: St. Martin's Press, 1997.

Bush, George W. "Executive Order 13335." (2004). http://www.whitehouse.gov/news/releases/2004/04/20040427–4.html (accessed May 20, 2005).

————. "President Bush Delivers Remarks at West Point." *CNN.com*, June 1, 2002. http://transcripts.cnn.com/TRANSCRIPTS/0206/01/se.01.html (accessed July 3, 2009).

Caldeira, Teresa P. R. *City of Walls: Crime, Segregation, and Citizenship in São Paulo.* Berkeley: University of California Press, 2000.

Cameron, Heather. "CCTV and (In)dividuation." *Surveillance & Society* 2, no. 2/3 (2004): 136–144.

————. "Using Intelligent Transport Systems to Track Buses and Passengers." In *Surveillance and Security: Technological Politics and Power in Everyday Life*, edited by Torin Monahan, 225–241. New York: Routledge, 2006.

Campbell, Nancy D. "Everyday Insecurities: The Micro-behavioral Politics of Intrusive Surveillance." In *Surveillance and Security: Technological Politics and Power in Everyday Life*, edited by Torin Monahan, 57–75. New York: Routledge, 2006.

Campbell, Nancy D. "Suspect Technologies: Scrutinizing the Intersection of Science, Technology, and Policy." *Science, Technology, and Human Values* 30, no. 3 (2005): 374–402.

———. *Using Women: Gender, Drug Policy, and Social Justice*. New York: Routledge, 2000.

Carey, James W. *Communication as Culture: Essays on Media and Society*. New York: Routledge, 1992.

Castells, Manuel. *The Rise of the Network Society*. Cambridge, MA: Blackwell, 1996.

Castles, Stephen. "Towards a Sociology of Forced Migration and Social Transformation." *Sociology* 37, no. 1 (2003): 13–34.

CATA Alliance. "The Game Changer." http://www.cata.ca/Media_and_Events/Press _Releases/cata_pr10070802.html (accessed October 22, 2008).

Cavender, Gray. "Media and Crime Policy: A Reconsideration of David Garland's *The Culture of Control*." *Punishment & Society* 6, no. 3 (2004): 335–348.

Cerulo, Karen A. *Never Saw It Coming: Cultural Challenges to Envisioning the Worst*. Chicago: University of Chicago Press, 2006.

Chertoff, Michael. "DHS Homepage." Washington, DC: Department of Homeland Security. http://www.dhs.gov/dhspublic (accessed May 25, 2006).

Chih-Feng Shu, Simon. "Housing Layout and Crime Vulnerability." *Urban Design International* 5, no. 3/4 (2000): 177–188.

Clark, Lynn Schofield. *From Angels to Aliens: Teenagers, the Media, and the Supernatural*. New York: Oxford University Press, 2003.

CNN.com. "World Leaders Prepare for G8 Summit." 2002. http://archives.cnn.com/ 2002/WORLD/americas/06/25/g8.summit/ (accessed October 1, 2003).

Cockburn, Cynthia, and Susan Ormrod. *Gender and Technology in the Making*. Thousand Oaks, CA: Sage, 1993.

Cohen, Jay M. "DHS (Video) Welcome." Video at 9th Annual Technologies for Critical Incident Preparedness Conference and Exposition, San Francisco, 2007.

Cohen, Stanley. *States of Denial: Knowing about Atrocities and Suffering*. Cambridge, UK: Polity Press, 2001.

Cole, David. "Intolerable Cruelty." *The Nation*, November 21, 2005, 5–6.

Cole, David, and Jules Lobel. *Less Safe, Less Free: Why America Is Losing the War on Terror*. New York: New Press, 2007.

Cole, Simon A., and Henry N. Pontell. "'Don't Be Low Hanging Fruit': Identity Theft as Moral Panic." In *Surveillance and Security: Technological Politics and Power in Everyday Life*, edited by Torin Monahan, 125–147. New York: Routledge, 2006.

Coleman, Alice. *Utopia on Trial: Vision and Reality in Planned Housing*. London: H. Shipman, 1985.

Collier, Stephen J., and Andrew Lakoff. "Vital Systems Security." Manuscript, 2006. http://anthropos-lab.net/wp/publications/2007/01/collier_vital-systems.pdf (accessed June 13, 2007).

Comaroff, Jean, and John L. Comaroff. "Millennial Capitalism: First Thoughts on a Second Coming." *Public Culture* 12, no. 2 (2000): 291–343.

Congressional Record. "Conference Report on H.R. 1, Implementing Recommendations of the 9/11 Commission Act of 2007." Washington, DC: U.S. House of Representatives, 2007. http://www.fas.org/irp/congress/2007_cr/hr1-info.html (accessed August 20, 2008).

Cooper, Marc. "Lockdown in Greeley: How Immigration Raids Terrorized a Colorado Town." *The Nation*, February 26, 2007, 11–16.

Costanzo, Mark, Ellen Gerrity, and M. Brinton Lykes. "Psychologists and the Use of Torture in Interrogations." *Analyses of Social Issues and Public Policy* 7, no. 1 (2007): 7–20.

Council on Foreign Relations. "Republican Debate Transcript, South Carolina" May 15, 2007. http://www.cfr.org/publication/13338/ (accessed October 11, 2008).

Cowan, Richard. "Congress Passes New Iraq War Funds." Reuters, June 27, 2008. http://www.reuters.com/article/topNews/idUSN2648734820080627 (accessed July 3, 2009).

Cowan, Ruth Schwartz. *More Work for Mother: The Ironies of Household Technology from the Open Hearth to the Microwave*. New York: Basic Books, 1983.

Cozens, Paul, David Hillier, and Gwyn Prescott. "The Sustainable and the Criminogenic: The Case of New-Build Housing Projects in Britain." *Property Management* 17, no. 3 (1999): 252–261.

Davidson, Carl, and Jerry Harris. "Globalisation, Theocracy and the New Fascism: The US Right's Rise to Power." *Race & Class* 47, no. 3 (2006): 47–67.

Davis, Mike. *City of Quartz: Excavating the Future in Los Angeles*. New York: Vintage Books, 1990.

———. "Who Is Killing New Orleans?" *The Nation*, April 10, 2006. http://www.thenation.com/doc/20060410/davis (accessed July 3, 2009).

de Certeau, Michel. *The Practice of Everyday Life*. Translated by Steven Rendall. Berkeley: University of California Press, 1984.

Dear, Michael. "Los Angeles and the Chicago School: Invitation to a Debate." *City & Community* 1, no. 1 (2002): 5–32.

———. *The Postmodern Urban Condition*. Oxford: Blackwell, 2000.

Defense Advanced Research Projects Agency. "DARPA Urban Challenge." http://www.darpa.mil/GRANDCHALLENGE/ (accessed October 22, 2008).

Deleuze, Gilles. *Foucault*. Translated by Seán Hand. Minneapolis: University of Minnesota Press, 1988.

———. "Postscript on the Societies of Control." *October* 59 (1992): 3–7.

Demerath, Loren, and David Levinger. "The Social Qualities of Being on Foot: A Theoretical Analysis of Pedestrian Activity, Community, and Culture." *City and Community* 2, no. 3 (2003): 217–237.

Democracy Now! "Yes Men Hoax on BBC Reminds World of Dow Chemical's Refusal to Take Responsibility for Bhopal Disaster." December 6, 2004. http://67.15.90.110/article.pl?sid=04/12/06/1453248 (accessed February 18, 2005).

Dery, Mark. "Hacking Barbie's Voice Box: 'Vengeance Is Mine!'" *New Media*, May 1994. http://www.levity.com/markdery/barbie.html (accessed February 18, 2005).

Diken, Bülent, and Carsten Bagge Laustsen. "Zones of Indistinction." *Space & Culture* 5, no. 3 (2002): 290–307.

Dodge, Martin, and Rob Kitchin. "Code, Vehicles and Governmentality: The Automatic Production of Driving Spaces." Maynooth, Ireland: NIRSA Working Papers Series, no. 29 (March), 2006.

Doherty, Joe, Volker Busch-Geertsema, Vita Karpuskiene, Jukka Korhonen, Eoin O'Sullivan, Ingrid Sahlin, Antonio Tosi, Agostino Petrillo, and Julia Wyganska. "Homelessness and Exclusion: Regulating Public Space in European Cities." *Surveillance & Society* 5, no. 3 (2008): 290–314.

DowEthics. "Dow 'Help' Announcement Is Elaborate Hoax." Dow Company. http://www.dowethics.com/r/about/corp/bbc.htm (accessed February 18, 2005).

Drane, John. *The McDonaldization of the Church*. London: Darton, Longman, and Todd, 2000.

Drehle, David Von. "World War, Cold War Won. Now, the Gray War." *Washington Post*, September 12, 2001, A09.

Druckrey, Timothy. "Secreted Agents, Security Leaks, Immune Systems, Spore Wars . . ." In *CTRL [Space]: Rhetorics of Surveillance from Bentham to Big Brother*, edited by

Thomas Y. Levin, Ursula Frohne and Peter Weibel, 150–157. Cambridge, MA: MIT Press, 2002.

Dubbeld, Lynsey. "Observing Bodies: Camera Surveillance and the Significance of the Body." *Ethics and Information Technology* 5 (2003): 151–162.

Duggan, Lisa. *The Twilight of Equality?: Neoliberalism, Cultural Politics, and the Attack on Democracy*. Boston: Beacon Press, 2003.

Dupont, Danica, and Frank Pearce. "Foucault Contra Foucault: Rereading the 'Governmentality' Papers." *Theoretical Criminology* 5, no. 2 (2001): 123–158.

Durfee, Alesha, and Karen Rosenberg. "Domestic Violence in the United States: Current Research, New Directions." In *Agenda for Social Justice, Solutions 2004*, edited by Robert Perrucci, Kathleen Ferraro, JoAnn Miller and Paula C. Rodríguez Rust, 72–80. Knoxville, TN: Society for the Study of Social Problems, 2004.

Edelman, Murray. *Constructing the Political Spectacle*. Chicago: University of Chicago Press, 1988.

Egan, R. Danielle. "Eyeing the Scene: The Uses and (RE)uses of Surveillance Cameras in an Exotic Dance Club." *Critical Sociology* 30, no. 2 (2004): 299–319.

Eglash, Ron, Jennifer L. Croissant, Giovanna Di Chiro, and Rayvon Fouché. *Appropriating Technology: Vernacular Science and Social Power*. Minneapolis: University of Minnesota Press, 2004.

Ehrenreich, Barbara. *Nickel and Dimed: On (Not) Getting by in America*. 1st ed. New York: Metropolitan Books, 2001.

Electronic Frontier Foundation. "EFF Sues AT&T to Stop Illegal Surveillance." Press release, Electronic Frontier Foundation. http://www.eff.org/news/archives/2006_01.php#004369 (accessed June 5, 2006).

Elliott, James R., Kevin Fox Gotham, and Melinda J. Milligan. "Framing the Urban: Struggles Over HOPE VI and New Urbanism in a Historic City." *City & Community* 3, no. 4 (2004): 373–394.

Ellis, James, David Fisher, Thomas Longstaff, Linda Pesante, and Richard Pethia. "Report to the President's Commission on Critical Infrastructure Protection." Pittsburgh: Carnegie Mellon University, 1997.

Engelhardt, Tom. "What 'Progress' in Iraq Really Means." *The Nation* (online), August 13, 2007. http://www.thenation.com/doc/20070827/engelhardt (accessed August 20, 2008).

Engwicht, David. *Reclaiming Our Cities and Towns: Better Living with Less Traffic*. Philadelphia: New Society, 1993.

Ericson, Richard V. *Crime in an Insecure World*. Cambridge, UK: Polity, 2007.

Eskridge, Larry. "And the Most Influential American Evangelical of the Last 25 Years Is. . . ." *Evangelical Studies Bulletin* 17 (2001): 1–4.

Eubanks, Virginia. "Popular Technology: Citizenship and Inequality in the Information Economy." Ph.D. diss., Rensselaer Polytechnic Institute, 2004.

———. "Technologies of Citizenship: Surveillance and Political Learning in the Welfare System." In *Surveillance and Security: Technological Politics and Power in Everyday Life*, edited by Torin Monahan, 89–107. New York: Routledge, 2006.

Fainstein, Susan S. "Cities and Diversity: Should We Want It? Can We Plan for It?" *Urban Affairs Review* 41, no. 1 (2005): 3–19.

Falzon, Mark-Anthony. "Paragons of Lifestyle: Gated Communities and the Politics of Space in Bombay." *City & Society* 16, no. 2 (2004): 145–167.

"The Fashion of the Christ." *BusinessWeek Online*, May 23, 2005. http://www.businessweek.com/magazine/content/05_21/b3934018_mz001.htm (accessed July 3, 2009).

Federal Bureau of Investigation. "Crime in the United States 2004." Washington, DC: U.S. Department of Justice, 2005. http://www.fbi.gov/ucr/cius_04/documents/CIUS2004.pdf (accessed July 3, 2009).

Federal Trade Commission. "About Identity Theft." Washington, DC: Federal Trade Commission. http://www.ftc.gov/bcp/edu/microsites/idtheft/consumers/about-identity-theft.html (accessed October 19, 2008).

———. "Federal Trade Commission: Your National Resource about ID Theft." Washington, DC: Federal Trade Commission. http://www.consumer.gov/idtheft (accessed June 5, 2006).

———. "FTC Releases Top 10 Consumer Fraud Complaint Categories." Washington, DC: Federal Trade Commission. http://www.ftc.gov/opa/2006/01/topten.htm (accessed June 5, 2006).

Feenberg, Andrew. *Questioning Technology*. New York: Routledge, 1999.

Feig, Bruce E. "Audit of Office of Temporary and Disability Assistance Electronic Benefit Transfer System." Albany, NY: Office of the State Comptroller, 2001. http://www.osc.state.ny.us/audits/allaudits/093001/99s51.pdf (accessed July 3, 2009).

Fernandez, Luis. *Policing Dissent: Social Control and the Anti-Globalization Movement*. New Brunswick, NJ: Rutgers University Press, 2008.

Fernandez, Luis A., and Laura Huey. "Editorial: Is Resistance Futile?: Thoughts on Resisting Surveillance." *Surveillance & Society* 6, no. 3 (2009): 198–202.

Ferrell, Jeff. "Notes from the Trash Heaps of America." Lecture, Arizona State University, Tempe, March 23, 2006.

Fisher, Allan. "Five Surprising Years for Evangelical-Christian Publishing: 1998 to 2002." *Publishing Research Quarterly* (Summer 2003): 20–36.

Fisher, Jill A. "Coming Soon to a Physician Near You: Medical Neoliberalism and Pharmaceutical Clinical Trials." *Harvard Health Policy Review* 8, no. 1 (2007): 61–70.

———. "Indoor Positioning and Digital Management: Emerging Surveillance Regimes in Hospitals." In *Surveillance and Security: Technological Politics and Power in Everyday Life*, edited by Torin Monahan, 77–88. New York: Routledge, 2006.

———. *Medical Research for Hire: The Political Economy of Pharmaceutical Clinical Trials*. New Brunswick, NJ: Rutgers University Press, 2009.

Fisher, Jill A., and Torin Monahan. "Tracking the Social Dimensions of RFID Systems in Hospitals." *International Journal of Medical Informatics* 77, no. 3 (2008): 176–183.

Flusty, Steven. *Building Paranoia: The Proliferation of Interdictory Spaces and the Erosion of Spatial Justice*. West Hollywood, CA: Los Angeles Forum for Architecture and Urban Design, 1994.

———. "Building Paranoia." In *Architecture of Fear*, edited by Nan Ellin, 47–59. New York: Princeton Architectural Press, 1997.

Foucault, Michel. *Discipline and Punish: The Birth of the Prison*. New York: Vintage Books, 1977.

———. "Governmentality." In *The Foucault Effect: Studies in Governmentality*, edited by Graham Burchell, Colin Gordon and Peter Miller, 87–104. Chicago: University of Chicago Press, 1991.

———. *The History of Sexuality*. Vo. 1. New York: Pantheon Books, 1978.

———. *Power/Knowledge: Selected Interviews and Other Writings, 1972–1977*. Brighton, Sussex, UK: Harvester Press, 1980.

———. *"Society Must Be Defended": Lectures at the College de France, 1975–76*. Translated by David Macey. New York: Picador, 2003.

———. "The Subject and Power." In *Michel Foucault: Beyond Structuralism and Hermeneutics*, edited by Hubert L. Dreyfus and Paul Rabinow, 208–228. Chicago: University of Chicago Press, 1983.

Frykholm, Amy Johnson. *Rapture Culture: Left Behind in Evangelical America.* New York: Oxford University Press, 2004.

Gandy, Oscar H. "Data Mining and Surveillance in the Post-9/11 Environment." In *The Intensification of Surveillance: Crime, Terrorism and Warfare in the Information Age,* edited by Kirstie Ball and Frank Webster, 26–41. Sterling, VA: Pluto Press, 2003.

———. "Data Mining, Surveillance, and Discrimination in the Post-9/11 Environment." In *The New Politics of Surveillance and Visibility,* edited by Kevin D. Haggerty and Richard V. Ericson, 363–384. Toronto: University of Toronto Press, 2006.

———. *The Panoptic Sort: A Political Economy of Personal Information.* Boulder, Colo.: Westview, 1993.

Garland, David. *The Culture of Control: Crime and Social Order in Contemporary Society.* Chicago: University of Chicago Press, 2001.

German, Mike, and Jay Stanley. "ACLU Fusion Center Update." July 2008. http://www.aclu.org/pdfs/privacy/fusion_update_20080729.pdf (accessed July 3, 2009).

Gieryn, Thomas F. "City as Truth-Spot: Laboratories and Field-Sites in Urban Studies." *Social Studies of Science* 36, no. 1 (2006): 5–38.

Gilliom, John. "Lying, Cheating and Teaching to the Test: The Politics of Surveillance Under No Child Left Behind." In *Schools under Surveillance: Cultures of Control in Public Education,* edited by Torin Monahan and Rodolfo D. Torres, 194–209. New Brunswick, NJ: Rutgers University Press, 2010.

———. *Overseers of the Poor: Surveillance, Resistance, and the Limits of Privacy.* Chicago: University of Chicago Press, 2001.

Giroux, Henry A. *The Terror of Neoliberalism: Authoritarianism and the Eclipse of Democracy.* Boulder, CO: Paradigm Publishers, 2004.

Glancy, Dorothy J. "Whereabouts Privacy." *STS Nexus* (Spring 2004). http://www.scu.edu/sts/nexus/spring2004/privacy.cfm (accessed July 3, 2009).

Glassner, Barry. *The Culture of Fear: Why Americans Are Afraid of the Wrong Things.* New York: Basic Books, 1999.

Glasze, Georg, and Abdallah Alkhayyal. "Gated Housing Estates in the Arab World: Case Studies in Lebanon and Riyadh, Saudi Arabia." *Environment and Planning B: Planning and Design* 29 (2002): 321–336.

Gober, Patricia. *Metropolitan Phoenix: Place Making and Community Building in the Desert.* Philadelphia: University of Pennsylvania Press, 2006.

Goldstein, Rebecca A. "Who Needs the Government to Police Us When We Can Do It Ourselves? The New Panopticon in Teaching." *Cultural Studies <=> Critical Methodologies* 4, no. 3 (2004): 320–328.

Gonnerman, Jennifer. "Slammed." *Mother Jones* 33, no. 4 (2008): 44–46.

Goode, Erich, and Nachman Ben-Yehuda. *Moral Panics: The Social Construction of Deviance.* Cambridge, MA: Blackwell, 1994.

Gotham, Kevin Fox, and Krista Brumley. "Using Space: Agency and Identity in a Public-Housing Development." *City & Community* 1, no. 3 (2002): 267–289.

Graham, Stephen, and Simon Marvin. *Splintering Urbanism: Networked Infrastructures, Technological Mobilities and the Urban Condition.* New York: Routledge, 2001.

Graham, Stephen, and David Wood. "Digitizing Surveillance: Categorization, Space, Inequality." *Critical Social Policy* 23, no. 2 (2003): 227–248.

Graham-Rowe, Duncan. "Clubbers Choose Chip Implants to Jump Queues." *NewScientist.com,* May 2004. http://www.newscientist.com/article.ns?id=dn5022 (accessed July 14, 2007).

Greenberg, Brigitte. "The BLO—Barbie Liberation Organization—Strikes." Associated Press, 1994. http://www.etext.org/Zines/UnitCircle/uc3/page10.html (accessed February 18, 2005).

Gribben, Crawford. "Rapture Fictions and the Changing Evangelical Condition." *Literature and Theology* 18, no. 1 (2004): 77–94.

Grosz, Elizabeth. *Volatile Bodies: Toward a Corporeal Feminism*. Bloomington: Indiana University Press, 1994.

Haggerty, Kevin D. "Displaced Expertise: Three Constraints on the Policy-Relevance of Criminological Thought." *Theoretical Criminology* 8, no. 2 (2004): 211–231.

———. "Technology and Crime Policy: Reply to Michael Jacobson." *Theoretical Criminology* 8, no. 4 (2004): 491–497.

Haggerty, Kevin D., and Richard V. Ericson. *The New Politics of Surveillance and Visibility*. Toronto: University of Toronto Press, 2006.

Hajjar, Lisa. "Torture and the Future." *Middle East Report Online*, May 2004. http://www.merip.org/mero/interventions/hajjar_interv.html (accessed October 11, 2008).

Haraway, Donna J. Modest_Witness@Second_Millennium.FemaleMan_Meets_Onco-Mouse: Feminism and Technoscience. New York: Routledge, 1997.

———. *Primate Visions: Gender, Race, and Nature in the World of Modern Science*. New York: Routledge, 1989.

———. *Simians, Cyborgs, and Women: The Reinvention of Nature*. New York: Routledge, 1991.

Harding, Susan. "Imagining the Last Days: The Politics of Apocalyptic Language." In *Accounting for Fundamentalisms: The Dynamic Character of Movements*, edited by M. E. Marty and R. S. Appleby, 57–78. Chicago: University of Chicago Press, 1994.

Hardt, Michael, and Antonio Negri. *Empire*. Cambridge, MA: Harvard University Press, 2000.

Harris, Richard. "U.S. Plan to Stockpile Bird-Flu Vaccine a Big Gamble." *All Things Considered*, National Public Radio, 2006. http://www.npr.org/templates/story/story.php?storyId=5133306 (accessed July 3, 2009).

Harvey, David. *The Condition of Postmodernity: An Enquiry into the Origins of Cultural Change*. Cambridge, MA: Blackwell, 1990.

Hay, James, and Mark Andrejevic. "Introduction: Toward an Analytic of Governmental Experiments in These Times: Homeland Security as the New Social Security." *Cultural Studies* 20, no. 4–5 (2006): 331–348.

Hay, James, and Jeremy Packer. "Crossing the Media(-n): Auto-mobility, the Transported Self and Technologies of Freedom." In *Mediaspace: Place, Scale and Culture in a Media Age*, edited by Nick Couldry and Anna McCarthy, 209–232. New York: Routledge, 2004.

Hayden, Dolores. *The Grand Domestic Revolution: A History of Feminist Designs for American Homes, Neighborhoods, and Cities*. Cambridge, MA: MIT Press, 1981.

Hendershot, Heather. *Shaking the World for Jesus: Media and Conservative Evangelical Culture*. Chicago: University of Chicago Press, 2004.

Herman, Didi. "The New Roman Empire: European Envisionings and American Premillennialists." *Journal of American Studies* 34, no. 1 (2000): 23–40.

Hernandez, Greg. "Proving the Market in Faith-Based Films." *San Diego Union-Tribune*, October 18, 2002, E-4.

Herszenhorn, David M. "Bailout Plan Wins Approval; Democrats Vow Tighter Rules." *New York Times*, October 4, 2008, A1.

Hess, David J. *Alternative Pathways in Science and Industry: Activism, Innovation, and the Environment in an Era of Globalization*. Cambridge, MA: MIT Press, 2007.

———. *Science Studies: An Advanced Introduction*. New York: New York University Press, 1997.

Hess, David J. "Technology- and Product-Oriented Movements: Approximating Social Movement Studies and Science and Technology Studies." *Science, Technology, and Human Values* 30, no. 4 (2005): 515–535.

Hettne, Björn. "The Fate of Citizenship in Post-Westphalia." *Citizenship Studies* 4, no. 1 (2000): 35–46.

Heymann, Philip B., and Juliette N. Kayyem. *Protecting Liberty in an Age of Terror.* Cambridge, MA: MIT Press, 2005.

Hillier, B. "Can Streets Be Made Safe?" *Urban Design International* 9, no. 1 (2004): 31–45.

———. "City of Alice's Dreams." *Architects Journal* 184, no. 28 (1986): 39–41.

Homeland Security Council. "National Strategy for Pandemic Influenza: Implementation Plan." Washington, DC: Department of Homeland Security, 2006.

Hommels, Anique. "Studying Obduracy in the City: Toward a Productive Fusion between Technology Studies and Urban Studies." *Science, Technology, and Human Values* 30, no. 3 (2005): 323–351.

Hooper, Barbara. "The Poem of Male Desires: Female Bodies, Modernity, and 'Paris, capital of the nineteenth century.'" In *Making the Invisible Visible: A Multicultural Planning History,* edited by Leonie Sandercock, 227–254. Berkeley: University of California Press, 1998.

Hoover, Stewart M. *Religion in the Media Age.* New York: Routledge, 2006.

Hope, T. "Crime Community and Environment." *Journal of Environmental Psychology* 6, (1986): 65–78.

Huey, Laura, Kevin Walby, and Aaron Doyle. "Cop Watching in the Downtown Eastside: Exploring the Use of (Counter)Surveillance as a Tool of Resistance." In *Surveillance and Security: Technological Politics and Power in Everyday Life,* edited by Torin Monahan, 149–165. New York: Routledge, 2006.

Hughes, Thomas P. "The Evolution of Large Technological Systems." In *The Social Construction of Technological Systems: New Directions in the Sociology and History of Technology,* edited by Wiebe E. Bijker, Thomas P. Hughes, and Trevor Pinch. Cambridge, MA: MIT Press, 1987.

Hulse, Carl. "Senate Approves Avian Flu Aid." *New York Times,* October 28, 2005. http://query.nytimes.com/gst/fullpage.html?sec=health&res=9A00E0DD1E3FF93 BA15753C1A9639C8B63 (accessed July 3, 2009).

Hunter, Michelle. "Deaths of Evacuees Push Toll to 1,577," *Times-Picayune,* May 19, 2006. http://www.nola.com/news/t-p/frontpage/index.ssf?/base/news-5/1148020620117480 .xml&coll=1 (accessed August 23, 2009).

Inda, Jonathan Xavier, and Renato Rosaldo. *The Anthropology of Globalization: A Reader.* Malden, MA: Blackwell, 2002.

Independent Media Center Network (IMC). "IMC Statement on Genoa Police Raid." http://italy.indymedia.org/news/2001/07/7092.php (accessed October 1, 2003).

Institute for Applied Autonomy (IAA). http://www.appliedautonomy.com/ (accessed October 20, 2006).

Jacobs, Jane. *The Death and Life of Great American Cities.* 2002 ed. New York: Random House, 1961.

Jain, Sarah S. "'Dangerous Instrumentality': The Bystander as Subject in Automobility." *Cultural Anthropology* 19, no. 1 (2004): 61–94.

———. "The Prosthetic Imagination: Enabling and Disabling the Prosthesis Trope." *Science, Technology, and Human Values* 24, no. 1 (1999): 31–54.

———. "Urban Violence: Luxury in Made Space." In *Mobile Technologies of the City,* edited by Mimi Sheller and John Urry, 61–76. New York: Routledge, 2006.

Jameson, Fredric. "Postmodernism, or the Cultural Logic of Late Capitalism." *New Left Review* 146 (1984): 53–92.

Janoff-Bulman, Ronnie. "Erroneous Assumptions: Popular Belief in the Effectiveness of Torture Interrogation." *Peace and Conflict: Journal of Peace Psychology* 13, no. 4 (2007): 429–435.

Jarymowicz, Maria, and Daniel Bar-Tal. "The Dominance of Fear over Hope in the Life of Individuals and Collectives." *European Journal of Social Psychology* 36, no. 3 (2006): 367–392.

Jeffries, Judson L. "Police Use of Excessive Force against Black Males: Aberrations or Everyday Occurrences." *Journal of Mundane Behavior* 3, no. 3 (2002). http://www.mundanebehavior.org/issues/v3n3/jeffries.htm (accessed October 20, 2006).

Joerges, Bernward. "Do Politics Have Artefacts?" *Social Studies of Science* 29, no. 3 (1999): 411–431.

Juris, Jeffrey S. *Networking Futures: The Movements Against Corporate Globalization.* Durham, NC: Duke University Press, 2008.

———. "The New Digital Media and Activist Networking within Anti–Corporate Globalization Movements." *Annals of the American Academy of Political and Social Science* 597, no. 1 (2005): 189–208.

Katz, Alyssa "Prime Suspect." *Mother Jones* 31, no. 5 (2006): 90–95, 112.

Katz, Cindi. "Banal Terrorism." In *Violent Geographies: Fear, Terror and Political Violence,* edited by Derek Gregory and Allan Pred, 349–361. New York: Routledge, 2007.

———. "The State Goes Home: Local Hypervigilance of Children and the Global Retreat from Social Reproduction." In *Surveillance and Security: Technological Politics and Power in Everyday Life,* edited by Torin Monahan, 27–36. New York: Routledge, 2006.

Kawamoto, Dawn. "ChoicePoint to Pay $15 Million Over Data Leak." CNET News, January 26 2006. http://news.cnet.com/ChoicePoint-to-pay-15-million-over-data-leak/2100-7350_3-6031629.html (accessed August 25, 2009).

Kerwin, Donald. "The Use and Misuse of 'National Security' Rationale in Crafting U.S. Refugee and Immigration Policies." *International Journal of Refugee Law* 17, no. 4 (2005): 749–763.

Kimmel, Paul R., and Chris E. Stout. *Collateral Damage: The Psychological Consequences of America's War on Terrorism.* Westport, CT: Praeger, 2006.

Kirkup, Gill, and Laurie S. Keller. *Inventing Women: Science, Technology, and Gender.* Cambridge, UK: Polity Press, 1992.

Klein, Naomi. "China Unveils Frightening Futuristic Police State at Olympics." *Huffington Post,* August 8, 2008. http://www.alternet.org/story/94278 (accessed August 20, 2008).

———. *The Shock Doctrine: The Rise of Disaster Capitalism.* New York: Metropolitan Books, 2007.

Klein, Norman M. *The History of Forgetting.* Edited by Mike Davis, and Michael Sprinker. Haymarket Series. New York: Verso, 1997.

Konrad, Rachel. "Gap Job Applicants' Data Stolen." Associated Press, September 28, 2007. http://www.foxnews.com/printer_friendly_wires/2007Sep28/0,4675,GapSecurityBreach,00.html (accessed August 25, 2009).

Koskela, Hille. "'The Gaze without Eyes': Video-Surveillance and the Changing Nature of Urban Space." *Progress in Human Geography* 24, no. 2 (2000): 243–265.

———. "Video Surveillance, Gender, and the Safety of Public Urban Space: "Peeping Tom" Goes High Tech?" *Urban Geography* 23, no. 3 (2002): 257–278.

Krim, Jonathan, and Michael Barbaro. "40 Million Credit Card Numbers Hacked: Data Breached at Processing Center." *Washington Post,* June 18, 2005, A01.

Kupchik, Aaron, and Nicole Bracy. "To Protect, Serve, and Mentor? Police Officers in Public Schools." In *Schools under Surveillance: Cultures of Control in Public Education,* edited by Torin Monahan and Rodolfo D. Torres, 21–37. New Brunswick, NJ: Rutgers University Press, 2010.

Kupchik, Aaron, and Torin Monahan. "The New American School: Preparation for Post-Industrial Discipline." *British Journal of Sociology of Education* 27, no. 5 (2006): 617–631.

Kuppinger, Petra. "Exclusive Greenery: New Gated Communities in Cairo." *City & Society* 16, no. 2 (2004): 35–61.

LaHaye, Tim F., and Jerry B. Jenkins. *Left Behind: A Novel of the Earth's Last Days.* Wheaton, IL: Tyndale House, 2000.

———. *The Mark: The Beast Rules the World.* Wheaton, IL: Tyndale House, 2000.

———. "Planned Television Arts Teleprint Conference: Interview with Tim LaHaye and Jerry Jenkins." JSOnline. http://www2.jsonline.com:80/lifestyle/religion/oct01/endtrans102301.asp?format=print (accessed December 14, 2006).

Lakoff, Andrew. "Techniques of Preparedness." In *Surveillance and Security: Technological Politics and Power in Everyday Life,* edited by Torin Monahan, 265–273. New York: Routledge, 2006.

Landau, Saul. *The Business of America: How Consumers Have Replaced Citizens and How We Can Reverse the Trend.* New York: Routledge, 2004.

Landman, Karina. "Gated Communities in South Africa: Building Bridges or Barriers." Paper presented at the International Conference on the Privatisation of Urban Governance, Mainz, Germany, June 6–9, 2002.

Latour, Bruno. "Where Are the Missing Masses? The Sociology of a Few Mundane Artifacts." In *Shaping Technology / Building Society: Studies in Sociotechnical Change,* edited by Wiebe E. Bijker, and John Law, 225–258. Cambridge, MA: MIT Press, 1992.

Law, John. "Technology and Heterogeneous Engineering: The Case of Portuguese Expansion." In *The Social Construction of Technological Systems: New Directions in the Sociology and History of Technology,* edited by Wiebe E. Bijker, Thomas P. Hughes, and Trevor Pinch. Cambridge, MA: MIT Press, 1987.

Lefebvre, Henri. *The Production of Space.* Translated by Donald Nicholson-Smith. Cambridge, MA: Blackwell, 1991.

LeftBehind.com. "The Facts" (accessed September 22, 2006).

———. "Frequently Asked Questions" (accessed September 22, 2006).

Leinwand, Donna. "Immigration Raid Linked to ID Theft, Chertoff Says." *USAToday.com,* December 13, 2006. http://www.usatoday.com/news/nation/2006–12–13–immigration_x.htm (accessed July 3, 2009).

Leland, John, and Tom Zeller Jr. "Technology and Easy Credit Give Identity Thieves an Edge." *New York Times,* May 30, 2006.

Lenoir, Timothy. "Programming Theaters of War: Gamemakers as Soldiers." In *Bombs and Bandwidth: The Emerging Relationship Between Information Technology and Security,* edited by Robert Latham, 175–198. New York: New Press, 2003.

Lessig, Lawrence. *Code: And Other Laws of Cyberspace.* New York: Basic Books, 1999.

Levi, Michael, and David S. Wall. "Technologies, Security, and Privacy in the Post-9/11 European Information Society." *Journal of Law and Society* 31, no. 2 (2004): 194–220.

Lewis, Tom. *Divided Highways: Building the Interstate Highways, Transforming American Life.* New York: Viking, 1997.

Lewis, Tyson. "Critical Surveillance Literacy." *Cultural Studies <=> Critical Methodologies* 6, no. 2 (2006): 263–281.

Lianos, M., and M. Douglas. "Dangerization and the End of Deviance." *British Journal of Criminology* 40, no. 2 (2000): 261–278.

Libbenga, Jan. "Video Surveillance Outfit Chips Workers." *The Register,* February 10, 2006. http://www.theregister.co.uk/2006/02/10/employees_chipped/ (accessed July 14, 2007).

Lipman, Pauline. "The Politics of Education Accountability in a Post-9/11 World." *Cultural Studies <=> Critical Methodologies* 6, no. 1 (2006): 52–72.

Lipsitz, George. "Learning from New Orleans: The Social Warrant of Hostile Privatism and Competitive Consumer Citizenship." *Cultural Anthropology* 21, no. 3 (2006): 451–468.

Low, Setha M. *Behind the Gates: Life, Security and the Pursuit of Happiness in Fortress America*. New York: Routledge, 2003.

Lue, Thomas. "Torture and Coercive Interrogations." In *Protecting Liberty in an Age of Terror*, edited by Philip B. Heymann and Juliette N. Kayyem, 149–177. Cambridge, MA: MIT Press, 2005.

Lutterbeck, Derek. "Between Police and Military: The New Security Agenda and the Rise of Gendarmeries." *Cooperation and Conflict* 39, no. 1 (2004): 45–68.

Lynch, Kevin. *Good City Form*. Cambridge, MA: MIT Press, 1984.

Lynch, Mona. "Selling 'Securityware': Transformations in Prison Commodities Advertising, 1949–99." *Punishment & Society* 4, no. 3 (2002): 305–319.

Lyon, David. *Surveillance after September 11*. Malden, MA: Polity Press, 2003.

———. *Surveillance Society: Monitoring Everyday Life*. Buckingham, UK: Open University Press, 2001.

———. *Surveillance Studies: An Overview*. Cambridge, UK: Polity Press, 2007.

———. "Why Where You Are Matters: Mundane Mobilities, Transparent Technologies, and Digital Discrimination." In *Surveillance and Security: Technological Politics and Power in Everyday Life*, edited by Torin Monahan, 209–224. New York: Routledge, 2006.

Lyon, David, ed. *Surveillance as Social Sorting: Privacy, Risk, and Digital Discrimination*. New York: Routledge, 2003.

Maher, Kristen Hill. "Workers and Strangers: The Household Service Economy and the Landscape of Suburban Fear." *Urban Affairs Review* 38, no. 6 (2003): 751–786.

Mann, Steve. "'Reflectionism' and 'Diffusionism.'" In *CTRL [Space]: Rhetorics of Surveillance from Bentham to Big Brother*, edited by Thomas Y. Levin, Ursula Frohne, and Peter Weibel, 530–543. Cambridge, MA: MIT Press, 2002.

Marcus, Greil. "Real Life Rock Top 10." *Salon.com*, April 3, 2000. http://archive .salon.com/media/col/marc/2000/04/03/marcus17/index1.html (accessed October 20, 2006).

Mariner, Joanne. "Private Contractors who Torture." *CNN.com*, June 17, 2004. http://www.cnn.com/2004/LAW/06/17/mariner.contractors/index.html (accessed July 3, 2009).

Markens, Susan, C. H. Browner, and H. Mabel Preloran. "'I'm Not the One They're Sticking the Needle Into': Latino Couples, Fetal Diagnosis, and the Discourse of Reproductive Rights." *Gender & Society* 17, no. 3 (2003): 462–481.

Martin, Emily. *Bipolar Expeditions: Mania and Depression in American Culture*. Princeton, NJ: Princeton University Press, 2007.

———. "Flexible Survivors." *Cultural Values* 4, no. 4 (2000): 512–517.

Marx, Gary T. *Undercover: Police Surveillance in America*. Berkeley: University of California Press, 1988.

———. "What's New About the "New Surveillance"? Classifying for Change and Continuity." *Surveillance & Society* 1, no. 1 (2002): 9–29.

Mawby, R. I. "Defensible Space: A Theoretical and Empirical Appraisal." *Urban Studies* 14 (1977): 169–179.

Mayer, Jane. "Whatever it Takes: The Politics of the Man Behind '24.'" *The New Yorker*, February 19, 2007. http://www.newyorker.com/reporting/2007/02/19/070219fa _fact_mayer (accessed October 11, 2008).

Mayer, Jeremy D. "Christian Fundamentalists and Public Opinion toward the Middle East: Israel's New Best Friends?" *Social Science Quarterly* 85, no. 3 (2004): 695–712.

Mazelis, Fred. "What the Torture of Abner Louima Shows: Capitalism and Police Brutality." *International Workers Bulletin* (1997). http://www.wsws.org/public_html/iwb9-22/louima.htm (accessed October 20, 2006).

McCabe, Barbara Coyle. "The Rules are Different Here: An Institutional Comparison of Cities and Homeowners Associations." *Administration & Society* 37, no. 4 (2005): 404–425.

McKinley, Jesse. "On the Fire Lines, a Shift to Private Contractors." *New York Times*, August 17, 2008. http://www.nytimes.com/2008/08/18/us/18firefighters.html?_r=1&th&emc=th&oref=slogin (accessed August 20, 2008).

McLean, Scott L. "The War on Terrorism and the New Patriotism." In *The Politics of Terror: The U.S. Responds to 9/11*, edited by William Crotty, 64–92. Boston: Northeastern University Press, 2004.

Mechanic, David. *The Truth about Health Care: Why Reform Is Not Working in America*. New Brunswick, NJ: Rutgers University Press, 2006.

Menjívar, Cecilia, and Néstor Rodriguez. "State Terror in the U.S.-Latin American Interstate Regime." In *When States Kill: Latin America, the U.S., and Technologies of Terror*, edited by Cecilia Menjívar and Néstor Rodriguez, 3–27. Austin: University of Texas Press, 2005.

Merchant, Carolyn. *The Death of Nature: Women, Ecology, and the Scientific Revolution*. New York: HarperCollins, 1980.

Michel-Kerjan, Erwann. "New Challenges in Critical Infrastructures: A US Perspective." *Journal of Contingencies and Crisis Management* 11, no. 3 (2003): 132–141.

Milun, Kathryn. *Pathologies of Modern Space: Empty Space, Urban Anxiety, and the Recovery of the Public Self*. New York: Routledge, 2007.

Mitchell, Don. *The Right to the City: Social Justice and the Fight for Public Space*. New York: Guilford Press, 2003.

Mleynek, Sherryll. "The Rhetoric of the 'Jewish Problem' in the Left Behind Novels." *Literature and Theology* 19, no. 4 (2005): 367–383.

Monahan, Torin. "Dreams of Control at a Distance: Gender, Surveillance, and Social Control." *Cultural Studies* <=> *Critical Methodologies* 9, no. 2 (2009): 286–305.

———. "Electronic Fortification in Phoenix: Surveillance Technologies and Social Regulation in Residential Communities." *Urban Affairs Review* 42, no. 2 (2006): 169–192.

———. *Globalization, Technological Change, and Public Education*. New York: Routledge, 2005.

———. "Los Angeles Studies: The Emergence of a Specialty Field." *City & Society* 14, no. 2 (2002): 155–184.

———. "Naked Security." Surveillance Studies Blog, July 1 2007. http://www.surveillance-studies.org/blog/2007/07/03/naked-security-by-torin-monahan (accessed August 20, 2008).

———. "Preface." In *Surveillance and Security: Technological Politics and Power in Everyday Life*, edited by Torin Monahan, ix–xi. New York: Routledge, 2006.

———. "Questioning Surveillance and Security." In *Surveillance and Security: Technological Politics and Power in Everyday Life*, edited by Torin Monahan, 1–23. New York: Routledge, 2006.

———. "Securing the Homeland: Torture, Preparedness, and the Right to Let Die." *Social Justice* 33, no. 1 (2006): 95–105.

———. "The Surveillance Curriculum: Risk Management and Social Control in the Neoliberal School." In *Surveillance and Security: Technological Politics and Power in Everyday Life*, edited by Torin Monahan, 109–24. New York: Routledge, 2006.

Monahan, Torin, ed. *Surveillance and Security: Technological Politics and Power in Everyday Life*. New York: Routledge, 2006.

Monahan, Torin, and Rodolfo D. Torres, eds. *Schools under Surveillance: Cultures of Control in Public Education.* New Brunswick, NJ: Rutgers University Press, 2010.

Monahan, Torin, and Tyler Wall. "Somatic Surveillance: Corporeal Control through Information Networks." *Surveillance & Society* 4, no. 3 (2007): 154–173.

Morgan, David. *Protestants and Pictures: Religion, Visual Culture and the Age of American Mass Production.* New York: Oxford University Press, 1999.

MSNBC. "The Democratic Presidential Debate on MSNBC." *New York Times,* September 26, 2007. http://www.nytimes.com/2007/09/26/us/politics/26DEBATE-TRANSCRIPT.html?_r=2&pagewanted=1&oref=slogin (accessed October 11, 2008).

Murakami Wood, David. "I'm Back but Things Are Much the Same." http://blogs.ncl.ac.uk/blogs/index.php/d.f.j.wood/2008/10/13/i_m_back_but_things_are_much_the_same (accessed October 19, 2008).

Murakami Wood, David, and Stephen Graham. "Permeable Boundaries in the Software-sorted Society: Surveillance and Differentiations of Mobility." In *Mobile Technologies of the City,* edited by Mimi Sheller and John Urry, 177–191. New York: Routledge, 2006.

Musheno, Michael C., James P. Levine, and Denis J. Palumbo. "Television Surveillance and Crime Prevention: Evaluating an Attempt to Create Defensible Space in Public Housing." *Social Science Quarterly* 58, no. 4 (1978): 647–656.

Mycoo, Michelle. "The Retreat of the Upper and Middle Classes to Gated Communities in the Poststructural Adjustment Era: The Case of Trinidad." *Environment and Planning A* 38, no. 1 (2006): 131–148.

Newman, Oscar. *Defensible Space.* New York: Macmillan, 1972.

Nieto, Marcus, Kimberly Johnston-Dodds, and Charlene Wear Simmons. "Public and Private Applications of Video Surveillance and Biometric Technologies." Report, Sacramento, California Research Bureau, 2002. http://www.library.ca.gov/crb/02/06/02–006.pdf (accessed July 3, 2009).

Noble, David F. *America by Design: Science, Technology, and the Rise of Corporate Capitalism.* New York: Oxford University Press, 1977.

Norris, Clive, and Gary Armstrong. "The Unforgiving Eye: CCTV Surveillance in Public Space." Report, Centre for Criminology and Criminal Justice, Hull University, 1997.

———. *The Maximum Surveillance Society: The Rise of CCTV.* Oxford: Berg, 1999.

Nye, David. *American Technological Sublime.* Cambridge, MA: MIT Press, 1996.

O'Harrow, Robert. *No Place to Hide.* New York: Free Press, 2005.

———. "Centers Tap into Personal Databases." *Washington Post,* April 2, 2008. http://www.washingtonpost.com/wp-dyn/content/article/2008/04/01/AR2008040103049.html (accessed August 20, 2008).

O'Malley, Pat. *Risk, Uncertainty, and Government.* London: GlassHouse, 2004.

Olson, Carl E. "Will Catholics Be 'Left Behind'?: The 'Rapture' and the Left Behind Books." *Catholic Scripture Study, International* 1 (2005): 1–12.

Ong, Aihwa. "The Gender and Labor Politics of Postmodernity." *Annual Review of Anthropology* 20 (1991): 279–309.

Osborne, David, and Ted Gaebler. *Reinventing Government: How the Entrepreneurial Spirit Is Transforming the Public Sector.* New York: Plume, 1992.

Oudshoorn, Nelly. "On Masculinities, Technologies, and Pain: The Testing of Male Contraceptives in the Clinic and the Media." *Science, Technology, and Human Values* 24, no. 2 (1999): 265–289.

Oudshoorn, Nelly, Els Rommes, and Marcelle Stienstra. "Configuring the User as Everybody: Gender and Design Cultures in Information and Communication Technologies." *Science, Technology, and Human Values* 29, no. 1 (2004): 30–63.

Packer, Jeremy. "Becoming Bombs: Mobilizing Mobility in the War of Terror." *Cultural Studies* 20, no. 4–5 (2006): 378–399.

————. "Rethinking Dependency: New Relations of Transportation and Communication." In *Thinking with James Carey: Essays on Communications, Transportation, History*, edited by Jeremy Packer and Craig Robertson. New York: Peter Lang, 2006.

Paik, Peter Yoonsuk. "Smart Bombs, Serial Killing, and the Rapture." *Postmodern Culture* 14, no. 1 (2003): 1–17.

Pallitto, Robert, and Josiah Heyman. "Theorizing Cross-Border Mobility: Surveillance, Security and Identity." *Surveillance & Society* 5, no. 3 (2008): 315–333.

Patton, Jason W. "Transportation Worlds: Designing Infrastructure and Forms of Urban Life." Ph.D. diss., Rensselaer Polytechnic Institute, 2004.

Pfaffenberger, Bryan. "Technological Dramas." *Science, Technology, and Human Values* 17, no. 3 (1992): 282–312.

Phillips, David J. "From Privacy to Visibility. Context, Identity, and Power in Ubiquitous Computing Environments." *Social Text* 23, no. 2 (2005): 95–108.

Phoenix Police Department. "Identity Theft: Learn to Protect Yourself." Phoenix Police Department, Phoenix, Arizona. http://www.ci.phoenix.az.us/POLICE/idthef1.html (accessed June 5, 2006).

Pinch, Trevor. "The Social Construction of Technology: A Review." In *Technological Change: Methods and Themes in the History of Technology*, edited by Robert Fox, 17–35. Amsterdam: Harwood Academic Publishers, 1996.

Poster, Mark. *Information Please: Culture and Politics in the Age of Digital Machines.* Durham, NC: Duke University Press, 2006.

Press, Julie E. "Spatial Mismatch or More of a Mishmash? Multiple Jeopardy and the Journey to Work." In *Prismatic Metropolis : Inequality in Los Angeles*, edited by Lawrence D. Bobo, Melvin L. Oliver, James H. Johnson Jr., and Abel Valenzuela, 453–488. New York: Russell Sage Foundation, 2000.

Preston, Julia. "270 Illegal Immigrants Sent to Prison in Federal Push." *New York Times*, May 24, 2008.

Quinby, Lee. *Anti-Apocalypse: Exercises in Genealogical Criticism.* Minneapolis: University of Minnesota Press, 1994.

Regan, Priscilla M. *Legislating Privacy: Technology, Social Values, and Public Policy.* Chapel Hill: University of North Carolina Press, 1995.

Reiman, Jeffrey H. "Driving to the Panopticon: Philosophical Exploration of the Risks to Privacy Posed by the Highway Technology of the Future." *Santa Clara Computer and High Technology Law Journal* 11, no. 1 (1995): 27–44.

Reuters. "Data on 26.5 Million Veterans Stolen from Home." *CNN.com*, May 22, 2006. http://www.cnn.com/2006/US/05/22/vets.data.reut/index.html (accessed June 30, 2006).

Richmond, Anthony H. "Globalization: Implications for Immigrants and Refugees." *Ethnic and Racial Studies* 25, no. 5 (2002): 707–727.

Ridge, Tom. "Secretary Ridge Addresses American Red Cross in St. Louis." May 27, 2004. http://www.dhs.gov/dhspublic/interapp/speech/speech_0175.xml (accessed June 16, 2008).

Romig, Kevin. "The New Urban "Anthem": Neoliberal Design and Political Fragmentation." *Critical Planning* 11 (2004): 3–16.

————. "The Upper Sonoran Lifestyle: Gated Communities in Scottsdale, Arizona." *City & Community* 4, no. 1 (2005): 67–86.

Ronell, Avital. *The Telephone Book: Technology—Schizophrenia—Electric Speech.* Lincoln: University of Nebraska Press, 1989.

Rose, Nikolas S. *Powers of Freedom: Reframing Political Thought.* New York: Cambridge University Press, 1999.

Rosen, Jeffrey. "A Cautionary Tale for a New Age of Surveillance." *New York Times Magazine,* October 7, 2001. http://www.schizophonia.com/archives/cctv.htm (accessed October 20, 2006).

Rosenberg, Daniel, and Susan Harding. *Histories of the Future.* Durham, NC: Duke University Press, 2005.

Rothschild, Matthew. "FBI Deputizes Private Contractors with Extraordinary Powers, Including 'Shoot to Kill.'" *The Progressive,* February 8, 2008. http://www.alternet.org/story/76388/ (accessed August 20, 2008).

Rowland, Robin. "Security at G-8; Watching on Three Fronts." *CBC News Online,* June 24, 2002. http://www.cbc.ca/news/features/g8/security.html (accessed October 1, 2003).

RTMark. "The Barbie Liberation Organization." 2000. http://www.rtmark.com/blo.html (accessed February 18, 2005).

———. "Guide to Closed Circuit Television (CCTV) destruction." 2001. http://www.rtmark.com/cctv/ (accessed February 18, 2005).

Sallaz, Jeffrey J. "The House Rules: Autonomy and Interests among Service Workers in the Contemporary Casino Industry." *Work and Occupations* 29, no. 4 (2002): 394–427.

Salter, Mark B. *Barbarians and Civilization in International Relations.* London; Sterling, VA: Pluto Press, 2002.

———. *Politics at the Airport.* Minneapolis: University of Minnesota Press, 2008.

———. *Rights of Passage: The Passport in International Relations.* Boulder, CO: Lynne Rienner, 2003.

Samatas, Minas. *Surveillance in Greece: From Anticommunist to Consumer Surveillance.* New York: Pella, 2004.

Sandelowski, Margarete. *Devices & Desires: Gender, Technology, and American Nursing.* Chapel Hill: University of North Carolina Press, 2000.

Sanger, David E. "In Canada, World's Most Exclusive Summer Camp." *New York Times,* June 27, 2002, 15.

Sassen, Saskia. *The Global City: New York, London, Tokyo.* Princeton, NJ: Princeton University Press, 1991.

Saulny, Susan. "Hundreds Are Arrested in U.S. Sweep of Meat Plant." *New York Times,* May 13, 2008.

Scahill, Jeremy. *Blackwater: The Rise of the World's Most Powerful Mercenary Army.* New York: Nation Books, 2007.

———. "Blackwater's Private Spies." *The Nation,* June 5, 2008. http://www.thenation.com/doc/20080623/scahill (accessed August 20, 2008).

Scarry, Elaine. *The Body in Pain: The Making and Unmaking of the World.* New York: Oxford University Press, 1985.

Schaller, Mark, Jason Faulkner, H. Justin Park, L. Steven Neuberg, and T. Douglas Kenrick. "Impressions of Danger Influence Impressions of People: An Evolutionary Perspective on Individual and Collective Cognition." *Journal of Cultural and Evolutionary Psychology* 2, no. 3–4 (2004): 231–247.

Scheer, Robert. "Taxpayers Lose, Halliburton Gains." *The Nation,* June 27, 2007. http://www.thenation.com/doc/20070709/truthdig (accessed July 3, 2009).

Schiebinger, Londa. *The Mind Has No Sex?: Women in the Origins of the Scientific Revolution.* Cambridge, MA: Harvard University Press, 1989.

Schienke, Erich W., and Institute for Applied Autonomy (IAA). "On the Outside Looking Out: An Interview with the Institute for Applied Autonomy (IAA)." *Surveillance & Society* 1, no. 1 (2002): 102–119.

Schram, Sanford F. *Welfare Discipline: Discourse, Governance and Globalization.* Philadelphia: Temple University Press, 2006.

Schulman, Daniel, and James Ridgeway. "The Highwaymen." *Mother Jones* 32, no. 1 (2007): 48–55, 84.

Sclove, Richard E. *Democracy and Technology.* New York: Guilford Press, 1995.

Scott, W. Richard, Carol A. Caronna, Martin Ruef, and Peter J. Mendel. *Institutional Change and Healthcare Organizations: From Professional Dominance to Managed Care.* Chicago: University of Chicago Press, 2000.

Seghetti, Lisa M. "Immigration and Naturalization Service: Restructuring Proposals in the 107th Congress." Washington, DC: Congressional Research Service, 2002.

Sharrock, Justine. "Am I a Torturer?" *Mother Jones* 33, no. 2 (2008): 43–49.

Sheller, Mimi. "Bodies, Cybercars and the Mundane Incorporation of Automated Mobilities." *Social & Cultural Geography* 8, no. 2 (2007): 175–197.

Sheller, Mimi, and John Urry. *Mobile Technologies of the City.* New York: Routledge, 2006.

Shuck, Glenn W. "Marks of the Beast: The Left Behind Novels, Identity, and the Internationalization of Evil." *Nova Religio: The Journal of Alternative and Emergent Religions* 8, no. 2 (2004): 48–63.

Siegel, Marc. "The False Bird Flu Scare." *The Nation,* June 5, 2006, 5–6.

Simon, Jonathan. *Governing through Crime: How the War on Crime Transformed American Democracy and Created a Culture of Fear.* New York: Oxford University Press, 2006.

Singer, P. W. *Corporate Warriors: The Rise of the Privatized Military Industry.* Ithaca, NY: Cornell University Press, 2003.

Singh, Anne-Marie. "Private Security and Crime Control." *Theoretical Criminology* 9, no. 2 (2005): 153–174.

Slack, Jennifer Daryl, and J. Macgregor Wise. *Culture + Technology: A Primer.* New York: Peter Lang, 2005.

Solomon, John. "FBI Investigates Halliburton's No-Bid Contracts." Associated Press, October 28, 2004. http://www.globalpolicy.org/security/issues/iraq/contract/2004/1028greenhouse.htm (accessed March 3, 2009).

Stanley, Jay. "The Surveillance-Industrial Complex." New York: American Civil Liberties Union, 2004. http://www.aclu.org/FilesPDFs/surveillance_report.pdf (accessed July 3, 2009).

Staples, William G. *Everyday Surveillance: Vigilance and Visibility in Postmodern Life.* Lanham, MD: Rowman & Littlefield, 2000.

Stegman, Michael A., Jennifer S. Lobenhofer, and John Quinterno. "The State of Electronic Benefit Transfer (EBT)." Report, Center for Community Capitalism, University of North Carolina, Chapel Hill, 2003.

Steventon, Graham. "Defensible Space: A Critical Review of the Theory and Practice of a Crime Prevention Strategy." *Urban Design International* 1, no. 3 (1996): 235–245.

Stiglitz, Joseph E., and Linda Bilmes. *The Three Trillion Dollar War: The True Cost of the Iraq Conflict.* 1st ed. New York: W. W. Norton, 2008.

Stopijacking.com. "Stopijacking.com." Stopijacking.com (accessed June 30, 2006).

Strathern, Marilyn. *Audit Cultures: Anthropological Studies in Accountability, Ethics, and the Academy.* New York: Routledge, 2000.

Strauss, Marcy. "The Lessons of Abu Ghraib." *Ohio State Law Journal* 66 (2005): 1269–1310.

Strozier, Charles B. *Apocalypse: On the Psychology of Fundamentalism in America*. Boston: Beacon Press, 1994.

Sullivan, Bob. "The Meth Connection to Identity Theft: Drug Addiction Plays a Part in Many Crime Rings, Cops Say." MSNBC, March 10, 2004. http://www.msnbc.msn.com/id/4460349/ (accessed June 5, 2006).

Surveillance Camera Players. "Founding Documents of the Surveillance Camera Players." http://www.notbored.org/scp-founding.html (accessed February 17, 2005).

———. "New York Surveillance Camera Players." http://www.notbored.org/the-scp.html (accessed February 17, 2005).

———. *We Know You are Watching*. Factory School: Southpaw Culture, 2006.

———. "Why Legal Action Should Be Taken Against the City of New York for Its Installation of Surveillance Cameras in Public Places." http://www.notbored.org/to-the-lawyers.html (accessed February 17, 2005).

Synovate. "Federal Trade Commission—2006 Identity Theft Survey Report." McLean, VA: Federal Trade Commission, 2007. http://www.ftc.gov/os/2007/11/Synovate FinalReportIDTheft2006.pdf (accessed March 8, 2008).

Taussig, Michael T. *The Devil and Commodity Fetishism in South America*. Chapel Hill: University of North Carolina Press, 1980.

Terrall, Mary. "Gendered Spaces, Gendered Audiences: Inside and Outside the Paris Academy of Sciences." *Configurations* 2 (1995): 207–232.

Thrift, Nigel, and Shaun French. "The Automatic Production of Space." *Transactions of the Institute of British Geographers* 27, no. 4 (2002): 309–335.

Ticktin, Miriam. "Policing and Humanitarianism in France: Immigration and the Turn to Law as State of Exception." *Interventions* 7, no. 3 (2005): 347–368.

Timmons, Stephen. "A Failed Panopticon: Surveillance of Nursing Practice via New Technology." *New Technology, Work and Employment* 18, no. 2 (2003): 143–153.

Turow, Joseph. *Niche Envy: Marketing Discrimination in the Digital Age*. Cambridge, MA: MIT Press, 2006.

U.S. Department of Health and Human Services. "Pandemic Influenza Planning: A Guide for Individuals and Families." Washington, DC: U.S. Department of Health and Human Services, 2006. http://www.redcrossnrv.org/PandemicDocs/Guide%20for% 20Individuals%20and%20Families.pdf (accessed August 26, 2009).

U.S. Department of Homeland Security. "DHS Strengthens Intel Sharing at State and Local Fusion Centers." Washington, DC: U.S. Department of Homeland Security, 2006. http://www.dhs.gov/xnews/releases/press_release_0967.shtm (accessed August 20, 2008).

———. "Homeland Security: Science and Technology" (brochure). Washington, DC: U.S. Department of Homeland Security, 2007.

———. "Remarks by Secretary of Homeland Security Michael Chertoff, Immigration and Customs Enforcement Assistant Secretary Julie Myers, and Federal Trade Commission Chairman Deborah Platt Majoras at a Press Conference on Operation Wagon Train." December 13, 2006. http://www.dhs.gov/xnews/releases/pr _1166047951514.shtm (accessed July 3, 2009).

———. "State and Local Fusion Centers." Washington, D.C.: U.S. Department of Homeland Security, 2008. http://www.dhs.gov/xinfoshare/programs/gc_1156877184684 .shtm (accessed August 20, 2008).

U.S. Department of Transportation. "Developing Traffic Signal Control Systems Using the National ITS Architecture." Washington, DC: U.S. Department of Transportation, 1998.

U.S. Department of Transportation. "Frequently Asked Questions: Intelligent Transportation Systems." Washington, DC: U.S. Department of Transportation. http://www.its .dot.gov/faqs.htm (accessed January 9, 2007).

U.S. General Accounting Office. "Identity Theft: Greater Awareness and Use of Existing Data Are Needed." Washington, DC: U.S. General Accounting Office, 2002. http://www.gao.gov/new.items/d02766.pdf (accessed July 3, 2009).

United Nations Development Programme (UNDP). *Human Development Report 1994.* New York: Oxford University Press, 1994.

Urban, Hugh B. "America, Left Behind: Bush, the Neoconservatives, and Evangelical Christian Fiction." *Journal of Religion & Society* 8 (2006): 1–15.

Vahidi, A., and A. Eskandarian. "Research Advances in Intelligent Collision Avoidance and Adaptive Cruise Control." *IEEE Transactions on Intelligent Transportation Systems* 4, no. 3 (2003): 143–153.

Vamosi, Robert. "Of ID Theft, Paris Hilton, and Methamphetamines." *CNET Reviews,* May 27, 2005. http://reviews.cnet.com/4520–3513_7–6231353–1.html (accessed June 5, 2006).

vanden Heuvel, Katrina. "Give Main Street a Fair Shake." *The Nation,* September 22, 2008. http://www.thenation.com/blogs/edcut/363206/give_main_street_a_fair_shake (accessed July 3, 2009).

van der Ploeg, Irma. "Borderline Identities: The Enrollment of Bodies in the Technological Reconstruction of Borders." In *Surveillance and Security: Technological Politics and Power in Everyday Life,* edited by Torin Monahan, 177–193. New York: Routledge, 2006.

———. *The Machine-Readable Body: Essays on Biometrics and the Informatization of the Body.* Maastricht, Netherlands: Shaker, 2005.

Veith, Gene Edward. "When Truth Gets Left Behind." *Christian Research Journal* 24, no. 4 (2002): 11–19.

ViaMichelin. "Rescue, Assistance and Tracking with Volvo On Call." http://www .viamichelin.com/viamichelin/gbr/tpl/mag4/art20060115/htm/tech-volvo-on -call.htm (accessed October 22, 2008).

Virilio, Paul. *Negative Horizon: An Essay in Dromoscopy.* Translated by Michael Degener. New York: Continuum, 2005.

———. *Speed and Politics: An Essay on Dromology.* Cambridge, MA: Semiotext[e], 1986.

Virno, Paolo. *A Grammar of the Multitude: For an Analysis of Contemporary Forms of Life.* Cambridge, MA: Semiotext(e), 2004.

Wacquant, Loïc. "Deadly Symbiosis: When Ghetto and Prison Meet and Mesh." *Punishment & Society* 3, no. 1 (2001): 95–134.

———. *Punishing the Poor: The Neoliberal Government of Social Insecurity.* Durham, NC: Duke University Press, 2009.

Wajcman, Judy. *Feminism Confronts Technology.* Cambridge, UK: Polity Press, 1991.

Waldrop, Anne. "Gating and Class Relations: The Case of a New Delhi 'Colony.'" *City & Society* 16, no. 2 (2004): 93–116.

Walker, James M. Jr. "Virtual Alabama: Alabama Homeland Security's 3-D Visualization of State Geographic Data, Leveraging Existing State Asset Imagery and Infrastructure Data onto a State-wide Application." Presented at 9th Annual Technologies for Critical Incident Preparedness Conference and Exposition, San Francisco, 2007.

Wall, Tyler. "The Fronts of War: Military Geographies, Local Logics, and the Rural Hoosier Heartland." Ph.D. diss., Arizona State University, 2009.

———. "'School Ownership Is the Goal': Military Recruiting, Public Schools, and Fronts of War." In *Schools under Surveillance: Cultures of Control in Public Education,* edited by Torin Monahan and Rodolfo D. Torres, 104–119. New Brunswick, NJ: Rutgers University Press, 2010.

Weber, Max. *The Protestant Ethic and the Spirit of Capitalism*. New York: Routledge, 2000.

Webster, Chris. "Property Rights and the Public Realm: Gates, Green Belts, and Gemeinschaft." *Environment and Planning B: Planning and Design* 29 (2002): 397–412.

Weisman, Leslie Kanes. *Discrimination by Design: A Feminist Critique of the Man-Made Environment*. Chicago: University of Illinois Press, 1992.

Welch, Michael. *Scapegoats of September 11th: Hate Crimes & State Crimes in the War on Terror*. New Brunswick, NJ: Rutgers University Press, 2006.

Weldes, Jutta, Mark Laffey, Hugh Gusterson, and Raymond Duvall. *Cultures of Insecurity: States, Communities, and the Production of Danger*. Minneapolis: University of Minnesota Press, 1999.

Wesely, Jennifer, and Emily Gaardner. "The Gendered "Nature" of the Urban Outdoors: Women Negotiating Fear of Violence." *Gender & Society* 18, no. 5 (2004): 645–663.

White House. "National Strategy for the Physical Protection of Critical Infrastructures and Key Assets." Washington, DC, 2003. http://www.dhs.gov/xlibrary/assets/Physical _Strategy.pdf (accessed August 25, 2009).

Whitson, Jennifer, and Kevin D. Haggerty. "Stolen Identities." *Criminal Justice Matters* 68, (2007): 39–40.

Whitson, Jennifer Robin. "Assumed Identities: Responses to Identity Theft in an Era of Information Capitalism." M.S. thesis, University of Alberta, 2006.

Whitson, Jennifer R., and Kevin D. Haggerty. "Identity Theft and the Care of the Virtual Self." *Economy and Society* 37, no. 4 (2008): 572–594.

Wickham, Mark. "Weapons Technical Intelligence IED Lexicon and Information Sharing Using Metadata Standards." Presented at 9th Annual Technologies for Critical Incident Preparedness Conference and Exposition, San Francisco, 2007.

Winner, Langdon. *Autonomous Technology: Technics-Out-of-Control as a Theme in Political Thought*. Cambridge, MA: MIT Press, 1977.

———. *The Whale and the Reactor: A Search for Limits in an Age of High Technology*. Chicago: University of Chicago Press, 1986.

Wood, David, Eli Konvitz, and Kirstie Ball. "The Constant State of Emergency?: Surveillance after 9/11." In *The Intensification of Surveillance: Crime, Terrorism and Warfare in the Information Age*, edited by Kirstie Ball and Frank Webster, 137–150. London: Pluto Press, 2003.

Woodward, Wayne D. "Technologized Communications as Artifact/Discourse/Relation: The Case of the Technological City." *Cultural Studies* <=> *Critical Methodologies* 3, no. 3 (2003): 330–354.

Woolgar, Steve. "The Turn to Technology in Social Studies of Science." *Science, Technology, & Human Values* 16, no. 1 (1991): 20–50.

Yes Men. "The Yes Men." http://theyesmen.org/ (accessed February 20, 2005).

———. "The Yes Men Hijinks: Dow." http://theyesmen.org/hijinks/dow/ (accessed February 20, 2005).

Zimmer, Michael. "The Quest for the Perfect Search Engine: Values, Technical Design, and the Flow of Personal Information in Spheres of Mobility." Ph.D. diss., New York University, 2007.

Zukin, Sharon. *The Cultures of Cities*. Cambridge, MA: Blackwell, 1995.

Zureik, Elia, and Mark B. Salter. *Global Surveillance and Policing: Borders, Security, Identity*. Cullompton; Portland, OR: Willan, 2005.

Index

Abu Ghraib prison (Iraq), 16, 18
abuse. *See* torture
Afghanistan: military spending in, 22; private security companies in, 149
Agamben, Giorgio, 28
airports, 6, 8, 43, 150, 166*n*2
Albrecht, Katherine, 143
Altheide, David, 3
American Civil Liberties Union (ACLU), 128, 143
American Library Association, 21
Antichrist, 70, 74; alignment with, 65; imminent coming of, 65
anti-Semitism, 67, 76, 162*n*12
antiterrorism, 20. *See also* counterterriorism
apocalypse: industry, 71, 77, 78; literature, 67; necessity of war and, 76; prophecies of, 64; as rationalization for exclusion of others, 64; selling, 68
Appadurai, Arjun, 7, 150
Armageddon, 67
Armstrong, Gary, 134

Bagram Theater Internment Facility (Afghanistan), 16
"The Barbie Liberation Organization," 132
Beck, Ulrich, 6
Beers, Rand, 17
Bennett, Colin, 143
Bentham, Jeremy, 117
biopower, 24
black site detention centers, 153*n*22
Blackwater USA, 47

borders and boundaries: artificial, 94; for capital, 8; fortification of, 8; hyperregulation of, 81, 98; militarization of, 8, 20; security industry at, 37; social, 82; suspension of law beyond, 16
Boston Dynamics, Inc., 43, 44
Bourdieu, Pierre, 17
BreakAway, Ltd., 44
Brian, Bill, 40
Burke, Anthony, 153*n*32
Bush, George W., 5, 6, 8, 16, 19, 23, 32, 33, 34, 36, 40, 121, 155*n*20
Bybee, Jay, 17

Campbell, Nancy, 58
capital: accumulation, 51, 59, 84, 129; borders to, 8; deterritorialized, 7
capitalism: cultural responses to instabilities of, 60; disaster, 40; global, 129, 142; growth of, 142; measures of status and, 9; millennial, 65; neoliberal forms of, 65
CardSystems Solutions, Inc., 60
Caspian organization, 143
Central Intelligence Agency (CIA), 16, 45
Cerulo, Karen, 146
Cheney, Dick, 36, 153*n*20
Cheney, Lynn, 36
Cheney, Mary, 36
Chertoff, Michael, 17, 23, 55, 160*n*22
ChoicePoint data company, 60, 62
Citicorp Services Inc., 120
citizenship, proofs of, 8
civil defense, 4, 5, 6, 20, 152*n*32

data, 52; marginal, 90; molding, 3; national, 65; restoration of, 52; selective blurring of, 8; social, 114; vulnerable, 50–63
identity theft, 6, 50–63, 147; absorption of fraud category by, 53; conditional on heterogeneity of identity, 52; creating, 51–53; criminal, 51; data vulnerability and, 60–63; decrease in number of arrests for, 51, 52; due to lack of serious data-protection protocols, 61; dumpster diving, 51, 161*n51*; economic instability and, 59; fear of, 52; financial, 51; illegal immigration and, 55, 56; illustrative of transformation in social control toward individual responsibility, 63; integration with dominant security cultures, 50; loss of credit card information and, 60–63; methamphetamines and, 57–60; as moral panic, 51; "myth" of, 51; as national security concern, 56; pharming information, 51; phishing scams, 51; political/economic context for, 50; poorly managed information systems and, 61; privatized solutions to, 63; self-protection/self-policing, 53–57; "skimming" credit cards, 51; social construction of, 51, 55; social polarization and, 59; through stolen laptops, 51; victim-centered response to, 50
Identity Theft and Assumption Deterrence Act (1998), 52
immigration, illegal: conflation with terrorism, 6, 153; identity theft and, 55, 56; undocumented workers, 3, 20, 55, 56, 93, 146
Immigration and Customs Enforcement Agency, 20, 55
Immigration and Naturalization Service (INS), 20
imperialism, 141, 142
Independent Media Centers (IMC), 141
individual(s): asked to spy on other citizens, 20, 21; blamed for failures in

social infrastructure, 24; blamed for own victimization, 61; choices, 29; control of, 62; flu pandemic preparedness and, 23; identification of, 71; mandatory personal sacrifice, 29; metaphoric accusation of aiding criminals by not consuming technology, 53; need for proper identification, 72; responsibility for crime deterrence, 63; responsibility for security functions, 15, 19–24, 128, 155*n20*; risk, 56; sacrifice by, 28; self-protection, 53–57; vulnerability of, 31
industrialization, Second Coming and, 67
infrastructure: critical, 40, 41, 43, 46, 107, 108; database, 59; digital technologies embedded in, 111; division of populations by, 83; exclusionary material, 146; exclusion of marginalized groups through, 129; information, 62; material, 83; monitoring, 107, 108; preparedness, 22, 23, 24; protection of, 4, 5; public, 4, 22, 83, 116; rebuilding, 5; social, 24, 155*n20*; surveillance, 4, 8–11, 147; technological, 83; telecommunication, 59; uneven access to, 129; urban, 9
insecurity: absolute, 27–31; constructing, 1–12; contemporary, 77; crime and, 1; cultivated by politicians and media, 145; cultural/ideological barriers to recognition of, 146; cultural processes of cultivation of, 4; discourses of, 2; dominant perceptions of, 27; economic, 7, 77, 151*n1*; of electronic data, 50; expansion of, 15; fear and paranoia over, 3, 33; individual responsibility for remediating, 145; job, 6–7; as justification for harsh treatment of others, 64; meaning of, 1; media role in, 1; national, 3, 56; perceptions of degrees of, 2; permanent, 30; persistence of conditions of, 25; psychological manifestations of, 3; shaping mechanisms, 1; social construction, 1, 2, 3, 77

Phoenix (AZ) (continued)
gated communities in, 82, 165*n19*;
identity theft in, 53, 58, 59; public
housing in, 165*n19*, 166*n20*
Phoenix Crime Free Multi-Housing
Program, 86
Pictometry Company, 42
political: culture, 78; discourse, 1, 37;
economy, 59; instability, 34; mobilization of "war on terror," 15, 16
Pontell, Henry, 52
population security, 4, 5, 6, 153*n32*
Poster, Mark, 52, 159*n8*
postindustrialization, 59; cultural logic
and, 59
postmillennialism, 75, 76
Potratz, Steve, 69–70
power: biopolitical, 24; of consumption,
23; disciplinary, 6, 94; executive, 17, 34;
exercise of, 3, 29; gendered, 113; lack of
essence in, 140; over people, 3; productive capacity to generate social
relations, 139–140; of regularization,
24; relations, 10, 114, 130, 140; subjection of humans to fundamental operations of, 29; unequal relations of, 33,
90, 114, 116
premillennialism, dispensational, 67, 68,
74, 75, 77
preparedness: for avian flu, 21, 22, 23;
citizen responsibility in, 23; citizen-
soldiers and, 25; discourse of, 24;
enlistment of public in, 22, 23, 24;
instructions for flexibility in individual
work, education, and consumption patterns, 23; localization of responsibility
for, 22, 23, 24; purchase checklists and,
23; risk assessment and, 24; sublimation
of fear by engaging in activities of, 23;
voluntarism in community projects
and, 23
prisons, 56, 147; mass incarceration in,
129
privacy: limitations of concept of, 119,
143, 148; responses to threats to, 105,

126; at risk from public-private data
sharing, 49, 62, 102, 107, 138; voluntary sacrifice of, 2, 10
Privacy International, 143
privatization: of communities, 82; of
education, 33; of health care, 33; in
housing security, 81; of national
security, 37, 38–49; neoliberalism and,
26; of public goods and services, 120;
of public institutions, 2; of public
programs, 59; of public spaces, 82, 94,
129; of security services, 5, 6, 129; of
social programs, 33
production: capitalist, 36; flexible, 129; of
governmentalities, 95; just-in-time, 27,
59, 129; mass, 129; media, 56; religious,
68; religious perspectives on technologies of, 65; technologies of, 66
profiling, racial, 21, 64
Protecting Liberty in an Age of Terror
(Harvard University), 17
publishing: religious, 69–71; transformations in, 69; Tyndale House, 69

racism, 7, 131; institutional, 24; pathogens
of, 24; profiling in, 21, 40, 64, 84, 134
the Rapture, 65, 67, 71; fiction, 66–68;
reification of social relations by, 77
refugees, 7, 20, 72, 150
Reich, Wilhelm, 137
religious: ambiguity, 69; bookstores, 69;
conservatism, 70, 78; contemporary
ideology, 70; fiction, 65, 66–68;
homogenization, 70; media, 67, 68;
pluralism, 162*n12*; products, 65;
publishing, 69–71; right, 68
resistance: antiglobalization protests, 140,
141; demonization of antiglobalist
protesters and, 162*n56*; Institute for
Applied Autonomy and, 130–135; iSee
application, 130–132; limits to public
participation and, 141; possibilities for,
128; RTMark, 132–135; Shooting
Back project, 135–137; social interventions, 135–139; to surveillance, 128,

security industry (continued)
accountability, 37; partnerships with
U.S. government, 37, 44–48, 148, 149;
and privatization of national security,
37; profits from consumer information,
62; purchases from result in cutbacks in
other areas, 42; realigning of national
interests for profit motives by, 37, 38;
shared government data and, 46, 47,
48; situational awareness of, 37–49
segregation: economic, 83; enforced by
trends toward privatized gated living,
82; social-spatial, 8, 50, 82, 83, 98
Shooting Back project, 135–137
Shuck, Glenn, 73, 75
situated knowledges, 125, 126
Skonovd, Matthew, 40, 45, 159*n21*
Snow, Tony, 36
social: action, 128; address, 83; analysis,
114; boundaries, 82; conflict, 129; conformity, 91; control, 63, 73, 84, 93, 95,
114, 118, 120, 129, 142; crises, 31–32;
devolution, 31; exclusion, 2; exclusion
based on poverty, 3; fragmentation,
142; identity, 114; imaginary, 3;
inequalities, 2, 9, 21, 25, 102, 118, 129,
145, 151*n1*; infrastructure, 24, 155*n20*;
insecurity, 77; integration, 82; intervention, 32, 75; justice, 75; movements,
143, 144; needs, 63, 155*n20*; norms, 81,
82; order, 16, 26, 51, 82, 111; polarization, 59, 83; policy, 59; programs, 26,
33, 50; regulation, 93, 98; reproduction,
145; resistance, 128; security, 3; segregation, 83; services, 2, 3, 8, 24; space,
124; stability, 50, 60, 81, 97, 98; structures, 4; surveillance, 96; truth, 145;
welfare, 4, 24, 27, 145, 153*n32*
social sorting, 9, 10, 83, 103, 112, 117,
146
space: control of, 124, 142; control of availability for political opposition, 142; erosion of, 138; masculinization of, 115, 118;
postindustrial colonization of, 142; privatization of public, 82, 94; programming,

84; public, 148; social, 124; technology
and, 83–84; transformation of public, 129;
urban, 83
splintering urbanism, 83
spying: accountability for, 19; backlash
from public, 21; by citizens, 20; on citizens, 25; illegal, 6, 19; on library users,
21; Terrorism Information and Prevention System, 21
state: abdication of responsibility by, 145;
centralization of power structures by, 3;
collective well-being and, 3; delegation
of data-security responsibilities to its
citizens, 53–57; demands on citizens
for meeting needs of society, 56; diversion of funding in, 24; of exception, 6,
28, 29, 30; failure to provide social
welfare, 145; inability to provide for
social needs, 63; manipulation of population by, 27; mechanisms of control by,
56; minimization of social programs,
56; neglect of citizens' social needs,
113; new relationship with public, 56;
policing/security function, 83;
preparedness strategy of outsourcing
disaster management, 21; responsibilities for security, 2; security, 6; transfer
of responsibility to individuals by, 2,
19–24; transformation of functions, 57;
welfare, 27, 83
Statewatch, 143
statism, 156*n1*
Surnow, Joel, 36
surveillance: abuses, 60; automated, 2, 9,
10, 85, 99, 103, 110, 118, 119,
123–125; awareness of, 95; biometric,
150; burdens of, 82; "care and watching," 168*n20*; CCTV, 84, 104, 105;
control of people by, 8; data vulnerability and, 60–63; definition of, 8; digital,
85; electronic, 60, 81; to eliminate the
poor who are "cheating the system,"
97; embedded in infrastructure, 103;
everyday, 117–118; evolution of
through social conflict, 129; facilitation

of control of people by, 114; gender implications of, 114; global systems, 139–143; as hidden form of sexual harassment, 115; high-tech, 42; hospital, 120–123; individual, 82; infrastructures, 4, 8–11, 147, 148; intrusive, 60, 90; marginalizing, 10, 90, 146, 147; masculinized, 113; mediation of interactions among people and, 8; population's unawareness of, 8; post 9/11 intensification, 154*n42*; preferential treatment and, 9, 10; problems, 130–144; proliferation of, 9; in public housing, 84–98; remote management of, 103; residential, 84–98; resistance to, 128–144; role in maintaining social inequalities, 9, 10, 11; by school resource officers, 44; sightlines in public housing for, 82; "smart," 43; social, 96; social dangers of conformity and, 95; social sorting with, 9; spatial exclusion and, 81; surge, 152*n13*; as symbol of national security, 8; systems, 8; technological, 1, 37, 81, 84; telecommunications companies and, 19; in traditionally feminine spaces, 115; of transportation systems, 99–112; uninvited scrutiny of women and, 113, 114; used to police the poor, 97, 118–120; video, 37, 38, 85; visual, 42; voyeuristic uses of, 113, 114; and welfare systems, 97, 118–120

Surveillance Camera Players, 137–139
Sutherland, Kiefer, 26

Tancredo, Tom, 34–35
Taussig, Michael, 77
Taylor, Kenneth, 69
Technologies for Critical Incident Preparedness Conference (2007), 38–49
technology: "backscatter" body scans, 37; of the beast, 71–74; biblical prophesies and, 72; biometric identification systems, 37; body discrimination and, 114–117; Christian, 65; communication,

33; consumption of, 38–49; dependencies and, 9; determination of social relations by, 84; digital, 111; discrimination by abstraction, 114–117; domestic, 116; facilitation of monitoring by, 83, 84; for first responders, 43, 44; gender and, 114–117; geographic information systems, 42, 43, 47; global positioning systems, 99; government, 39; government support for, 48; information, 71, 83–84; information and communication, 8; issues of power and, 114; license-plate recognition systems, 99; masculine, 113–127; media, 68, 74; motion sensors, 37, 38; parks, 41; philosophy of, 84; political aspects of, 9; political production by, 84; of production, 65, 66; profusion of, 10; of regulation, 24; regulation of access to services by, 83, 84; regulation of human activity by, 72; religious warnings against, 65; residue detectors, 37; security applications used to protect assets of private companies, 47–48; to serve social and human needs, 130; space and, 83–84; surveillance, 37, 134; as tool of societal differentiation, 9, 10; unmanned aerial vehicles, 37; urban, 83; use discrimination of, 114–117; x-ray, 37
television. *See* entertainment
Terrall, Mary, 116
terrorism: asymmetrical threat of, 5; conflation with illegal immigration, 6; defining, 6; deterrence and, 5; fear of potential attacks of, 37, 160*n22*; as focus of security conferences selling new technologies, 39; media role in reshaping public perceptions of, 26–36; 9/11 attacks, 2, 5; surge of sale in religious goods, 69; threats of, 6
Terrorism Information and Prevention System (TIPS), 21
theft: of business data, 50; credit card, 50; identity, 50–63
Thomas, Clarence, 36

political mobilization of, 15, 16; security state and, 6; violations of policies on, 19
Watching Me (video), 119
Watson, Sydney, 67
Weber, Max, 76
Weisman, Leslie, 116
Welfare Reform Act (1996), 119

Wickham, Mark, 40
World Trade Organization, 141

xenophobia, 7, 64
Xe Services, 47

"The Yes Men" (RTMark), 132
Yoo, John, 17

About the Author

Torin Monahan is an associate professor of human and organizational development and an associate professor of medicine at Vanderbilt University. He is author of *Globalization, Technological Change, and Public Education* (Routledge, 2005), editor of *Surveillance and Security: Technological Politics and Power in Everyday Life* (Routledge, 2006), and coeditor of *Schools under Surveillance: Cultures of Control in Public Education* (Rutgers, 2010). His main theoretical interests are in social control and institutional transformations with new technologies. He is a member of the international Surveillance Studies Network, is an elected council member of the Sociology of Science and Technology division of the International Sociological Association, and is on the editorial board for the primary academic journal on surveillance, *Surveillance & Society*.

Available titles in the Critical Issues in Crime and Society series:

Breinigsville, PA USA
08 March 2010

233802BV00002B/1/P